D0813218

Creating Augmented and Virtual Realities

Theory and Practice for Next-Generation Spatial Computing

Edited by Erin Pangilinan, Steve Lukas, and Vasanth Mohan

Beijing · Boston · Farnham · Sebastopol · Tokyo

Table of Contents

Part I.   Design and Art Across Digital Realities

Part II.   How eXtended Reality Is Changing Digital Art

Part III.   Hardware, SLAM, Tracking

Part IV. Creating Cross-Platform Augmented Reality and Virtual Reality

Part V. Enhancing Data Representation: Data Visualization and Artificial Intelligence in Spatial Computing

Part VI. Use Cases in Embodied Reality

Foreword

In the 2016 Design in Tech Report, I referred to a November 1993 *Wired* article penned by my former boss MIT Media Lab Founder Nicholas Negroponte on the topic of virtual realities (VR). In his inimitable fashion, Nicholas writes:

> Neophytes have a mistaken sense that VR is very new because the press just learned about it. It is not. Almost 25 years ago, Ivan Sutherland developed, with support from ARPA, the first surprisingly advanced VR system. This may not be astonishing to old-timers, because Ivan seems to have had half the good ideas in computer science. However, Ivan's idea is now very affordable. One company, whose name I am obliged to omit, will soon introduce a VR display system with a parts cost of less than US $25.

If you stop for a second and think about how this was written back in 1993, and then consider how that was just over 25 years ago, it should give you a bit of pause. Furthermore, consider how as a good thought leader (and investor), Negroponte teases a startup that he personally seed-funded and that was most certainly set to reshape the future. Does that sound familiar to you at all here in the 21st century from similar movers and shakers today in the Valley?

But different from the latest and greatest technology pundit out there, I've found most of Negroponte's predictions to have come true—even his most outlandish and audacious ones. For example, is there really a VR system out there right now today that costs less than $25? Certainly—but only when you consider how that requires having a smartphone as table stakes, and then attached to a cardboard rig that easily runs under $25. Negroponte definitely got it right, eventually.

Regarding technologies that exceed a $25 budget, you're in luck! This comprehensive book on augmented, virtual, mixed, and eXtended realities (AR, VR, MR, and XR) covers the entire range of professional and consumer ways that one can, in William Gibson's parlance, "jack in" to cyberspace. Fortunately for us frugal types, many of these new technologies are absolutely free because they are open source and readily available in the commons. So there's never been a better time to get involved with this new form of reality that's finally been realized.

As you dig into this book, you'll notice that each successive chapter's authors baton touch to the next chapter's authors. You immediately detect a world-spanning community of experts who are making the next reality into a truly shared reality, together. Their enthusiastic commitment to sharing their knowledge outside the AR, VR, MR, XR communities reminds us that great technology for humans happens because great humans choose to collaborate with everyone when inventing the future.

It is rare to find in one volume such a wide range of topics ranging from women in AI, to the latest computer vision tracking systems, to how to bake optimized 3D forms without *n*-gons, to the dream of the "AR cloud," to autonomous behaviors in virtual characters, to applications in the sports and healthcare industry, and to realizing vastly improved ways to take employee training to a new level for the enterprise. Both the breadth and the depth of the work shared by the technologists and artists of this movement indicate that the remaining runway for XR is just as vast as the expansive realities that they've only just started to unlock for humankind.

Inspired by the work presented in this book, I spent some time thinking about my own first encounter with VR. It was in the 1980s—back when I was an undergraduate at MIT and I had the chance to try out the VPL Technology Data Glove. It was a skin-tight velour glove with fiber optic cables that were painted black such that light could escape at the joints of your fingers, and so a signal could be read that let you detect grasping movements. I was amazed at being able to stare at my virtual hand on the screen waving hello to my real hand waving back at it.

When I looked up the history of the Data Glove, I came across the head-mounted display that VPL developed and designed to accompany it. This display was called the "Eye Phone." Reading that name made me chuckle a bit because a few decades later the "Eye Phone" vision was totally spot on, but with a different spelling: the iPhone. And although we know that the iPhone isn't necessarily head-mounted, it certainly spends a lot of time near our eyes and face.

Is this a coincidence? Most likely, but as the astoundingly long list of references for each chapter will attest to—all work is often somehow related to other work. That's the reason why keeping an open, community-minded perspective is the fastest way to get the hardest things done. Gathering diverse points of view around the most difficult challenges is the most reliable means to spark unexpected innovations. For the vision of spatial computing to truly happen, an even wider set of artistic, scientific, and business-minded communities than represented in this compendium need to get involved. But what you have here before you is more than a solid foundation upon which to get us moving faster into the future.

I'm certain that a few decades from now technically difficult but not-impossible-to-one-day-build concepts like the AR cloud will be commonplace ideas albeit perhaps with a different name. The reason that one of these concepts may finally see their way to getting built could be because of you. So I strongly suggest reaching out to any of the authors of this book to ask how you might get involved in advancing their work with whatever skills that you can bring to the table. Get started!

— John Maeda
Head of Design and Inclusion, Automattic
Lexington, Massachusetts

Preface

A Note on Terminology

As a result of the emerging nature of our field and to respect personal opinions, you will see some of the latest terms (such as XR, eXtended Reality, and X) being used almost interchangeably throughout the book based on author preference and the topic at hand in each chapter. Debate over terminology continues as standards are developed. Each author uses terminology that accords to their own perspectives and beliefs. You can find definitions in each chapter.

Why We Wrote This Book

This book was conceptualized during a time shortly after Clay Bavor, VP of Virtual Reality (VR) at Google, noted in his keynote at Google I/O in 2017 that the future creators and consumers of technology will imagine in new world humans experience technology where the eye can enable anyone to *go anywhere* or *bring anything* to the end user with an instant gesture or voice command. We are at the forefront of spatial computing. Spatial computing here is used interchangeablly to describe various modes of the virtuality continuum to include terms in this book that switch between virtual reality (VR), augmented reality (AR), mixed reality, and eXtended reality (XR), as referenced by Paul Milgram and Fumio Kishino's 1994 book *A Taxonomy of Mixed Reality Visual Displays*.

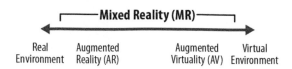

Virtuality Continuum (VC)

Figure P-1. Paul Milgram and Fumio Kishino conceived of the reality continuum concept in the mid-1990s to describe the spectrum across various realities from the virtual, physical, and so on

In 2019, we recognize that the future of spatial computing depends on open source knowledge that must be shared and built upon constantly in order for the field to succeed. The future is in the hands of seasoned veterans as well as young, up-and-coming professionals working in these spaces across various disciplines. Because of this, developing standards and innovating from every part of the technology stack to make spatial computing thrive becomes challenging. New terminologies and sets of technology paradigms are evolving every day; filtering through the noise requires education and clear, informative communication. By sharing our collective understandings of development, function/use of spatial computing, we hope to push the medium forward and avoid the past failings to bring VR to the mainstream market.

It becomes urgent to have more sufficient knowledge production disseminated to technology professionals across all roles: technical, creative storytellers and artists, and business/marketing-oriented professionals, including (but not limited to) hardware engineers, full stack software application engineers/developers, designers (whether their focus is industrial, computational, traditional graphic, product, or user experience/user interface, data scientists/machine learning engineers, 2D and 3D artists and graphic designers (modelers, painters, architects, product managers, directors and thespians, and more).

It is in our observed and combined experiences—in education, software engineering and design, and investment—that we identified a gap in literature for those entering into the field of spatial computing. It is at times, overwhelming for new software engineers, artists, designers, and business and marketing professionals entering into this space of technology. We have had many shortcomings of technical and creative education in a variety of areas in the past. This book seeks to change that, by enabling our readers to gain an understanding of how spatial computing was developed, how it functions, and how to create new experiences and applications for this medium. It is challenging for anyone to absorb a plethora of knowledge in the advanced areas of hardware and software, particularly in optics, tracking, design, and development best practices, especially cross-platform development on a variety of head-mounted displays (HMDs) and devices, given that standards are still being developed for many areas of spatial computing. It is easy to feel overwhelmed given the amount of intellectual knowledge, that is a massive undertaking for a single part of the software or hardware development stack to succeed in. Because there exists no literary or academic scholarship bridging the gap between theoretical frameworks to shape industry applications or even a single text to serve as a practical guide, we decided to put together an anthology of leading contributors across a variety of disciplines so that this information is more accessible in understanding, rich with condensed theoretical material, and practical to get started in this new space.

As an effect of lacking education in the field, professionals without a more solid foundation in the fundamentals of how some of the hardware, computer vision algorithms, or even design principles function, we as an industry subsequently create lower quality experiences and applications, which ultimately hurt everyone overall. Users trying out these experiences for the first time may ultimately be turned off by the idea of spatial computing because of "bad application design and experience" (sometimes with regard to accessibility, comfort that are a direct result of technological limitations or poor design understanding of the technology itself). While we recognize that technical standards or even design best practices evolve over time (as many of the professionals featured in this book have indicated, conducting technical and design research and experimentation is an ongoing cycle), it is our hope to start sharing some initial intermediate knowledge that can help other professionals entering into the industry with some base fundamentals (outside of "how to install Unity 101") that will ultimately help the industry as a whole create more enjoyable and successful applications and experiences in spatial computing.

To master this field, it is not uncommon for new professionals to read a great deal of literature in an effort to gain a theoretical and practical foundation to develop their knowledge, skills, and abilities. We have found, however, that in this search they are still left daunted and hungry for more in order to grasp the knowledge required to create successful applications and experiences in spatial computing. It also appears that most academic theory on this subject tends to be dense and inaccessible. We believe given our unique backgrounds in education, venture capital, and independent software development, that we can help bridge this gap along with a list of contributing industry and academic leaders in the field.

We hope our audience can gain a foundational understanding of augmented and virtual reality functions. Our contributing writers have provided software engineers with solid concrete tutorials on how to build practical applications and experiences grounded in theory and industry use cases as a starting point. New creators in spatial computing will be able to learn the full software development pipeline, where our contributors have provided informative material on foundations needed to have a more comprehensive understanding of spatial computing from various leading academic and industry experts from both technical and creative perspectives as well as get hands-on practice in order to continue honing their skills to work in the realities industry.

Spatial computing technology is the promise of the future, yet very few are well-versed in how it works today and where it is headed. It is the next evolution of human computing as replication of reality allows for deeper engagement and learning retention. We are currently on the ground floor of this technology, and those who board it now will be the leaders when this industry fully matures. The combined research from the contributors of this book are able to provide grounded industry use cases that validate the promise of spatial computing. This new market alone has warranted billions of dollars in investment, particularly AR (Magic Leap, raising nearly $3B) and VR (Acquisition of Oculus Rift for $3B by Facebook) in the last few years.

We hope to inspire professionals in a variety of areas where spatial computing is beginning to have an impact. We acknowledge that a lack of understanding of some of these foundational principles is a barrier to entry for many, and that with this text, we can make knowledge more accessible to the masses without having to read stacks of books that could be condensed and summarized by seasoned and rising professionals in spatial computing.

Our book covers native development and content creation on various HMDs and platforms, including: Magic Leap, Oculus Rift, Microsoft Hololens, and mobileAR (Apple's ARKit and Google's ARCore). The book is primarily featuring examples in Unity and C# and has a handful of Unreal Engine in C++/Blueprints.

To minimize the barrier to entry, we expect developers to have access to (a) a target device running mobile AR (ARKit, ARCore), and (b) a development machine such as a PC or Mac. We recognize the rapidly changing landscape of the industry and that a number of HMDs and new SDKs from major companies are released every quarter. As a result, we focus on theory and high-level concepts so that these learnings have the ability to scale as new platforms and paradigms are introduced over the next foundational years of spatial computing.

We understand that not everyone can afford to dispose of thousands of dollars for higher-end HMDs. Thus, we encourage groups to also learn more about mobile spatial computing, as several concepts apply and are adaptable to both. Outside of the paid Udacity's VR Developer Nanodegree or other Massive Open Online Courses (MOOCs) on Coursera and Udemy, additional technical and creative open source tutorials for our evolving space can be found with materials by several leaders in the space. Since 2015, ARVR Academy (a diversity and inclusion organization to which proceeds from this book will be donated), has published ongoing material (*http://bit.ly/2F7MVjT*) by co-founder Liv Erickson (a lead engineer at social VR startup, High Fidelity) that scaled in popularity with Google Cardboard curriculum.

Vasanth, our co-editor, as founder of FusedVR also had a plethora of videos on YouTube with detailed tutorials deconstructing spatial computing applications over the years which can be found at FusedVR's YouTube channel.

We have many more resources that can be found in our supplementary GitHub repository (*https://github.com/CreatingARVR*) and the website for our book (*https://www.creatingarvr.com*), recommended for our readers to refer to as they continue their learning beyond the confines of these pages.

What We Didn't Cover in This Book

There is such a vast array of important topics in this field that for space considerations, some technologies are beyond the scope of this book. These include but are not limited to: 360 degree, video, cryptocurrency, blockchain, virtual goods, AR museums, tourism, travel and teleportation, and education. More in-depth material can be found on audio/sound and WebXR through additional resources we can provide, as in themselves these topics can warrant their own books (a whole sense and also another part of the developer stack). Given the capacity of this book, the topics covered are those that we felt that would allow new and existing developers the ability to create experiences and applications not already present in the industry successfully given the use cases section that validate the market demand for this technology.

How This Book Is Organized

As standards are still being developed, we wanted to provide our readers with a comprehensive overview of three different areas: art and design; technical; and practical use cases that demonstrate the technology's historic development, the state of spatial computing today, and possibilities for the future.

Art and Design

Spatial computing starts with understanding how to optimize and work in 3D space that makes it distinct from any other prior computing mediums and is "all about user experience." Thus a focus on design, art, and foundations on actual content creation tools were essential to begin with in our book anthology. We begin first with an extensively detailed history of spatial computing and design interactions by Timoni West (Head of Research at Unity) and thoughts on Silka Miesnieks (Head of Emerging Design at Adobe) who discusses human-centered interaction and sensory design in this new technology paradigm. Then, technical 3D artist, entrepreneur turned venture capitalist, Tipatat Chennavasin gives an overview of content creation tools alongside technical 3D artist and marketing lead, Jazmin Cano, who provides an understanding for artists desiring to optimize art assets across various platforms.

Technical Development

We then transition to the second part of the book, which is focused on technical foundations to understand the development of hardware, software layers in dawn of the era of AR cloud beginning with computer vision pioneers, 6D.ai cofounders, Professor Victor Prisacariu (Oxford Vision Lab) and Matt Miesnieks discussing these topics in detail.

They cover an in-depth understanding of foundational principles describing how hardware, computer vision (SLAM) algorithms function, what new creators in the space must consider as technical benchmarks and business decisions (how to pick which HMD to develop for) as a framework for creating successful applications and experiences utilizing AR cloud. They go into great detail in comparing ARKit and ARCore.

Our esteemed collective writing about cross-platform open source development includes our co-editors, Steve Lukas of Magic Leap, Across XR and Vasanth Mohan, and VRTK, open source software library developed by Harvey Ball in conversation with VRTK developer evangelist, Clorama Dorvilias.

Developers who are getting started on building their game, or other mobile developers including those working on iOS and Android applications leveraging ARKit and ARCloud can learn much from these chapters.

Use Cases in Embodied Reality

Use cases across various verticals involve applications ranging from the use of simulations, new B2B experiences only optimized in 3D, particularly in spatial computing: data representation ranging from an understanding of data engineering pipelines, visualization, artificial intelligence (AI), education and training, sports, and a range of computational life sciences (healthtech, biotech, medtech).

Together, USF Diversity Fellow in Deep Learning and lead book co-editor, Erin Pangilinan along with Unity Director of AI Research, Nicolas Meuleau and Senior Software Engineer Arthur Juliani give those who may not be already seasoned in the areas of data engineering, artificial intelligence, machine learning, and computer vision various methods, models, and best practices to consider to incorporate data-driven techniques in spatial computing. Erin focuses on having creators distinguish 2D versus 3D data visualization design paradigms from giving them a more solid understanding on how to better visualize and understand data for an improved user experience. Meuleau and Juliani demonstrate how creators can utilize existing, generated, or loaded data for changing character behaviors in embodied reality. Showing software engineers how to incorporate data-driven design and human-centered AI for independent game developers looking to start developing in spatial computing.

Dilan Shah, founder of YUR Inc, Rosstin Murphy (software engineer at leading training company, STRIVR), and Marc Rowley (five-time Emmy winner, sports tech leader, formerly of ESPN) demonstrate how spatial computing optimizes applications involving the physical body ranging from the topics of healthtech, training, and sportstech.

Ultimately, any new students entering from a variety of disciplines will be able to learn technical and creative approaches to making successful applications and experiences.

Conventions Used in This Book

The following typographical conventions are used in this book:

Italic
> Indicates new terms, URLs, email addresses, filenames, and file extensions.

`Constant width`
> Used for program listings, as well as within paragraphs to refer to program elements such as variable or function names, databases, data types, environment variables, statements, and keywords.

`Constant width bold`
> Shows commands or other text that should be typed literally by the user.

`Constant width italic`
> Shows text that should be replaced with user-supplied values or by values determined by context.

 This element signifies a general note.

 This element indicates a warning or caution.

Using Code Examples

Supplemental material (code examples, exercises, etc.) is available for download at *https://github.com/CreatingARVR*.

This book is here to help you get your job done. In general, if example code is offered with this book, you may use it in your programs and documentation. You do not need to contact us for permission unless you're reproducing a significant portion of the code. For example, writing a program that uses several chunks of code from this book does not require permission. Selling or distributing a CD-ROM of examples from O'Reilly books does require permission. Answering a question by citing this book and quoting example code does not require permission. Incorporating a significant amount of example code from this book into your product's documentation does require permission.

We appreciate, but do not require, attribution. An attribution usually includes the title, author, publisher, and ISBN. For example: "*Creating Augmented and Virtual Realities* by Erin Pangilinan, Steve Lukas, and Vasanth Mohan (O'Reilly). Copyright 2019, 978-1-492-04419-2."

If you feel your use of code examples falls outside fair use or the permission given above, feel free to contact us at *permissions@oreilly.com*.

O'Reilly Online Learning

 For almost 40 years, O'Reilly has provided technology and business training, knowledge, and insight to help companies succeed.

Our unique network of experts and innovators share their knowledge and expertise through books, articles, conferences, and our online learning platform. O'Reilly's online learning platform gives you on-demand access to live training courses, in-depth learning paths, interactive coding environments, and a vast collection of text and video from O'Reilly and 200+ other publishers. For more information, please visit *http://oreilly.com*.

How to Contact Us

Please address comments and questions concerning this book to the publisher:

O'Reilly Media, Inc.
1005 Gravenstein Highway North
Sebastopol, CA 95472
800-998-9938 (in the United States or Canada)
707-829-0515 (international or local)
707-829-0104 (fax)

We have a web page for this book, where we list errata, examples, and any additional information. You can access this page at *http://bit.ly/creating-ar-vr*.

To comment or ask technical questions about this book, send email to *bookquestions@oreilly.com*.

For more information about our books, courses, conferences, and news, see our website at *http://www.oreilly.com*.

Find us on Facebook: *http://facebook.com/oreilly*

Follow us on Twitter: *http://twitter.com/oreillymedia*

Watch us on YouTube: *http://www.youtube.com/oreillymedia*

Acknowledgments

We would like to thank the following people for their dedication to this project.

First, we want to thank the creators of spatial computing for helping shape what it has become today.

We would like to express our gratitude toward the dedicated O'Reilly staff including VP Content, Mike Loukides, Content Development Editor, Angela Rufino, Brian Foster, and Josh Garstka who spent many hours with us in conference calls, tracking our progress, and handling content with utmost of care, and giving us the creative freedom to be able to make this project happen.

We want to thank our families, friends, and community members for their moral support of this book project.

We want to give a special thanks to one of our contributors, Rosstin Murphy, software engineer at STRIVR for going up and above and beyond for continued assistance with the book. We are grateful for our esteemed technical and creative reviewers who poured over several rewrites and drafts to make sure this book was up to speed with our ever-changing technology: Spandana Govindgari (Hype AR, Co-Foundee), Alexandria Heston (Magic Leap, UX & Interaction Designer), Dave Johnston (BBC R&D, Senior Product Manager), Katherine Mimnaugh (University of Oulu, Doctoral Researcher), Troy Norcross (GameHearts, Founder), Jon Oakes (SJSU), Micah Stubbs (LinkedIn, Data Visualization Infrastructure), Sunbin Song (National Institute of Health, Fellow), Diego Segura (A-Frame and Supermedium Founder).

We also want to recognize O'Reilly three-time published author and VR leader Tony Parisi for his tremendous support of this project.

We are privileged to open and close our anthology with remarks by design and engineering leaders who provide sharp insights into the future of spatial computing technology. The book begins with opening remarks from design engineer leader, Head of

Design and Inclusion at Automattic, John Maeda, and is concluded by VR legend, head of strategy at Unity 3D Technologies, Tony Parisi.

Thanks also to Kent Bye (Developer and Host Voices of VR Podcast) and Mary Clarke Miller (Professor, Berkeley City College) for their additional support.

Thank you for your time and attention in reading this book. We wish you well as you embark on your journey experiencing spatial computing!

PART I

Design and Art Across Digital Realities

We live in curious times. Of the nearly eight billion humans who live on Earth, for the first time in history, the majority are literate—that is, able to communicate with other humans asynchronously, with reasonably accurate mutual understanding.

But human expression goes beyond language. Design and art reflect that which might not be so succinctly defined. The unspoken behavioral patterns of the world, writ large, are reflected in excellent design. The emotions and social patterns that direct our unconscious brains are laid bare in art: sculpture, dance, paintings, and music. But until the digital era, these areas of human expression have been, in the end, always tied to physical constraints: physics, real materials, and time.

Computers are, in essence, our attempt to express ourselves with pure energy—light and sound beaming into eyes and ears, haptics buzzing, inputs manipulated any way we please. But, to date, much like design and art, computers themselves have been restricted to very real-world limitations; they are physics-bound glass windows beyond which we can see digital worlds, but to which worlds we cannot go. Instead, we take computers with us, making them lighter, faster, brighter.

In 2019, we find ourselves in another curious position: because we have made computers more mobile, we are finally able to move our digital worlds into the real world. At first glance, this seems a relatively easy move. It's pleasant to think that we can simply interact with our computers in a way that feels real and natural and mimics what we already know.

On second glance, we realize that much of how we interact with the real world is tedious and inconvenient. And on third glance, we realize that although humans have a shared understanding of the world, computers know nothing about it. Even though human literacy rates have increased, we find ourselves with a new set of objects to teach all over again.

In this part, we review several of the puzzle involved in moving computers out of two dimensions into real spatial computing. In Chapter 1, Timoni West covers the history of human–computer interaction and how we got to where we are today. She then talks about exactly *where* we are today, both for human input and computer understanding of the world.

In Chapter 2, Silka Miesnieks, Adobe's Head of Emerging Design, talks about the contexts in which we view design for various realities: how to bridge the gap between how we think we should interact with computers and real shared sensory design. She delves into human variables that we need to take into account and how machine learning will play into improving spatial computing.

There is much we don't cover in these chapters: specific best practices for standards like world-scale, or button mappings, or design systems. Frankly, it's because we expect them to be outdated by the time this book is published. We don't want to canonize that which might be tied to a set of buttons or inputs that might not even exist in five years. Although there might be historical merit to recording it, that is not the point of these chapters.

The writers here reflect on the larger design task of moving human expression from the purely physical realm to the digital. We acknowledge all the fallibilities, errors, and misunderstandings that might come along the way. We believe the effort is worth it and that, in the end, our goal is better human communication—a command of our own consciousnesses that becomes yet another, more visceral and potent form of literacy.

CHAPTER 1

How Humans Interact with Computers

Timoni West

In this chapter, we explore the following:

- Background on the history of human–computer modalities
- A description of common modalities and their pros and cons
- The cycles of feedback between humans and computers
- Mapping modalities to current industry inputs
- A holistic view of the feedback cycle of good immersive design

Common Term Definition

I use the following terms in these specific ways that assume a human-perceivable element:

Modality
    A channel of sensory input and output between a computer and a human

Affordances
    Attributes or characteristics of an object that define that object's potential uses

Inputs
    How you do those things; the data sent to the computer

Outputs
    A perceivable reaction to an event; the data sent from the computer

Feedback
> A type of output; a confirmation that what you did was noticed and acted on by the other party

Introduction

In the game Twenty Questions, your goal is to guess what object another person is thinking of. You can ask anything you want, and the other person must answer truthfully; the catch is that they answer questions using only one of two options: yes or no.

Through a series of happenstance and interpolation, the way we communicate with conventional computers is very similar to Twenty Questions. Computers speak in binary, ones and zeroes, but humans do not. Computers have no inherent sense of the world or, indeed, anything outside of either the binary—or, in the case of quantum computers, probabilities.

Because of this, we communicate everything to computers, from concepts to inputs, through increasing levels of human-friendly abstraction that cover up the basic communication layer: ones and zeroes, or yes and no.

Thus, much of the work of computing today is determining how to get humans to easily and simply explain increasingly complex ideas to computers. In turn, humans are also working toward having computers process those ideas more quickly by building those abstraction layers on top of the ones and zeroes. It is a cycle of input and output, affordances and feedback, across modalities. The abstraction layers can take many forms: the metaphors of a graphical user interface, the spoken words of natural language processing (NLP), the object recognition of computer vision, and, most simply and commonly, the everyday inputs of keyboard and pointer, which most humans use to interact with computers on a daily basis.

Modalities Through the Ages: Pre-Twentieth Century

To begin, let's briefly discuss how humans have traditionally given instructions to machines. The earliest proto-computing machines, programmable weaving looms, famously "read" punch cards. Joseph Jacquard created what was, in effect, one of the first pieces of true mechanical art, a portrait of himself, using punch cards in 1839 (Figure 1-1). Around the same time in Russia, Semyon Korsakov had realized that punch cards could be used to store and compare datasets.

Figure 1-1. Woven silk portrait of Joseph Jacquard, 1839, who used more than 24,000 punched cards to create the portrait

Punch cards can hold significant amounts of data, as long as the data is consistent enough to be read by a machine. And although pens and similar handheld tools are fantastic for specific tasks, allowing humans to quickly express information, the average human forearm and finger tendons lack the ability to consistently produce near identical forms *all* the time.

This has long been a known problem. In fact, from the seventeenth century—that is, as soon as the technology was available—people began to make keyboards. People invented and reinvented keyboards for all sorts of reasons; for example, to work against counterfeiting, helping a blind sister, and better books. Having a supportive plane against which to rest the hands and wrists allowed for inconsistent movement to yield consistent results that are impossible to achieve with the pen.

As mentioned earlier, proto-computers had an equally compelling motivation: computers need very consistent physical data, and it's uncomfortable for humans to make consistent data. So, even though it might seem surprising in retrospect, by the early 1800s, punch-card machines, not yet the calculation monsters they would become, already had keyboards attached to them, as depicted in Figure 1-2.

Figure 1-2. A Masson Mills WTM 10 Jacquard Card Cutter, 1783, which were used to create the punched cards read by a Jacquard loom

Keyboards have been attached to computational devices since the beginning, but, of course, they expanded out to typewriters before looping back again as the two technologies merged. The impetuous was similarly tied to consistency and human fatigue. From Wikipedia:

> By the mid-19th century, the increasing pace of business communication had created a need for mechanization of the writing process. Stenographers and telegraphers could take down information at rates up to 130 words per minute.

Writing with a pen, in contrast, gets you only about 30 words per minute: button presses were undeniably the better alphanumeric solution.

The next century was spent trying to perfect the basic concept. Later features, like the addition of the shift key, substantially improved and streamlined the design and size of early typewriters.

I want to pause for a moment here to point out the broader problem everyone was trying to solve by using typewriters, and specifically with the keyboard as input: at the highest level, people wanted to capture their ideas more *quickly* and more *accurately*. Remember this; it is a consistent theme across all modality improvements.

Modalities Through the Ages: Through World War II

So much for keyboards, which, as I just pointed out, have been with us since the beginning of humans attempting to communicate with their machines. From the early twentieth century on—that is, again, as soon as metalwork and manufacturing techniques supported it—we gave machines a way to communicate back, to have a dialogue with their operators *before* the expensive physical output stage: monitors and displays, a field that benefited from significant research and resources through the wartime eras via military budgets.

The first computer displays didn't show words: early computer panels had small light bulbs that would switch on and off to reflect specific states, allowing engineers to monitor the computer's status—and leading to the use of the word "monitor." During WWII, military agencies used cathode-ray tube (CRT) screens for radar scopes, and soon after the war, CRTs began their life as vector, and later text, computing displays for groups like SAGE and the Royal Navy.

Figure 1-3. An example of early computer interfaces for proprioceptive remapping; WAAF radar operator Denise Miley is plotting aircraft in the Receiver Room at Bawdsey "Chain Home" station in May 1945 (notice the large knob to her left, a goniometer control that allowed Miley to change the sensitivity of the radio direction finders)

As soon as computing and monitoring machines had displays, we had display-specific input to go alongside them. Joysticks were invented for aircraft, but their use for remote aircraft piloting was patented in the United States in 1926. This demonstrates a curious quirk of human physiology: we are able to instinctively remap *proprioception*—our sense of the orientation and placement of our bodies—to new volumes and plane angles (see Figure 1-3). If we weren't able to do so, it would be impossible to use a mouse on a desktop on the Z-plane to move the mouse anchor on the X. And yet, we can do it almost without thought—although some of us might need to invert the axis rotation to mimic our own internal mappings.

Modalities Through the Ages: Post-World War II

Joysticks quickly moved out of airplanes and alongside radar and sonar displays during WWII. Immediately after the war, in 1946, the first display-specific input was invented. Ralph Benjamin (*http://bit.ly/2UwqWII*), an engineer in the Royal Navy, conceived of the rollerball as an alternative to the existing joystick inputs: "The elegant ball-tracker stands by his aircraft direction display. He has one ball, which he holds in his hand, but his joystick has withered away." The indication seems to be that the rollerball could be held in the hand rather than set on a desk. However, the reality of manufacturing in 1946 meant that the original roller was a full-sized bowling ball. Unsurprisingly, the unwieldy, 10-pound rollerball did not replace the joystick.

This leads us to the five rules of computer input popularity. To take off, inputs must have the following characteristics:

- Cheap
- Reliable
- Comfortable
- Have software that makes use of it
- Have an acceptable user error rate

The last can be amortized by good software design that allows for nondestructive actions, but beware: after a certain point, even benign errors can be annoying. Autocorrect on touchscreens is a great example of user error often overtaking software capabilities.

Even though the rollerball mouse wouldn't reach ubiquity until 1984 with the rise of the personal computer, many other types of inputs that were used with computers moved out of the military through the mid-1950s and into the private sector: joysticks, buttons and toggles, and, of course, the keyboard.

It might be surprising to learn that styluses predated the mouse. The light pen, or gun, created by SAGE in 1955, was an optical stylus that was timed to CRT refresh cycles and could be used to interact directly on monitors. Another mouse-like option, Data Equipment Company's Grafacon, resembled a block on a pivot that could be swung around to move the cursor. There was even work done on voice commands as early as 1952 with Bell Labs' Audrey system, though it recognized only 10 words.

By 1963, the first graphics software existed that allowed users to draw on MIT Lincoln Laboratory's TX-2's monitor, Sketchpad, created by Ivan Sutherland at MIT. GM and IBM had a similar joint venture, the Design Augmented by Computer, or DAC-1, which used a capacitance screen with a metal pencil, instead—faster than the light pen, which required waiting for the CRT to refresh.

Unfortunately, in both the light pen and metal pencil case, the displays were upright and thus the user had to hold up their arm for input—what became known as the infamous "gorilla arm." Great workout, but bad ergonomics. The RAND corporation had noticed this problem and had been working on a tablet-and-stylus solution for years, but it wasn't cheap: in 1964, the RAND stylus—confusingly, later also marketed as the Grafacon—cost around $18,000 (roughly $150,000 in 2018 dollars). It was years before the tablet-and-stylus combination would take off, well after the mouse and graphical user interface (GUI) system had been popularized.

In 1965, Eric Johnson, of the Royal Radar Establishment, published a paper on capacitive touchscreen devices and spent the next few years writing more clear use cases on the topic. It was picked up by researchers at the European Organization for Nuclear Research (CERN), who created a working version by 1973.

By 1968, Doug Engelbart was ready to show the work that his lab, the Augmentation Research Center, had been doing at Stanford Research Institute since 1963. In a hall under San Francisco's Civic Center, he demonstrated his team's oNLine System (NLS) with a host of features now standard in modern computing: version control, networking, videoconferencing, multimedia emails, multiple windows, and working mouse integration, among many others. Although the NLS also required a chord keyboard and conventional keyboard for input, the mouse is now often mentioned as one of the key innovations. In fact, the NLS mouse ranked similarly useable to the light pen or ARC's proprietary knee input system in Engelbart's team's own research (*http://bit.ly/2XVHxYs*). Nor was it unique: German radio and TV manufacturer, Telefunken, released a mouse with its RKS 100-86, the *Rollkugel*, which was actually in commercial production the year Engelbart announced his prototype.

However, Engelbart certainly popularized the notion of the asymmetric freeform computer input. The actual designer of the mouse at ARC, Bill English, also pointed out one of the truths of digital modalities at the conclusion of his 1967 paper, "Display-Selection Techniques for Text Manipulation":

> [I]t seems unrealistic to expect a flat statement that one device is better than another. The details of the usage system in which the device is to be embedded make too much difference.

No matter how good the hardware is, the most important aspect is how the software interprets the hardware input and normalizes for user intent.

 For more on how software design can affect user perception of inputs, I highly recommend the book *Game Feel: A Game Designer's Guide to Virtual Sensation* by Steve Swink (Morgan Kaufmann Game Design Books, 2008). Because each game has its own world and own system, the "feel" of the inputs can be rethought. There is less wiggle room for innovation in standard computer operating systems, which must feel familiar by default to avoid cognitive overload.

Another aspect of technology advances worth noting from the 1960s was the rise of science fiction, and therefore computing, in popular culture. TV shows like *Star Trek* (1966–1969) portrayed the use of voice commands, telepresence, smart watches, and miniature computers. *2001: A Space Odyssey* (1968) showed a small personal computing device that looks remarkably similar to the iPads of today as well as voice commands, video calls, and, of course, a very famous artificial intelligence. The animated cartoon, *The Jetsons* (1962–1963), had smart watches, as well as driverless cars and robotic assistance. Although the technology wasn't common or even available, people were being acclimated to the idea that computers would be small, lightweight, versatile, and have uses far beyond text input or calculations.

The 1970s was the decade just before personal computing. Home game consoles began being commercially produced, and arcades took off. Computers were increasingly affordable; available at top universities, and more common in commercial spaces. Joysticks, buttons, and toggles easily made the jump to video game inputs and began their own, separate trajectory as game controllers. Xerox Corporation's famous Palo Alto Research Center, or PARC, began work on an integrated mouse and GUI computer work system called the Alto. The Alto and its successor, the Star, were highly influential for the first wave of personal computers manufactured by Apple, Microsoft, Commodore, Dell, Atari, and others in the early to mid-1980s. PARC also created a prototype of Alan Kay's 1968 KiddiComp/Dynabook, one of the precursors of the modern computer tablet.

Modalities Through the Ages: The Rise of Personal Computing

Often, people think of the mouse and GUI as a huge and independent addition to computer modalities. But even in the 1970s, Summagraphics was making both low- and high-end tablet-and-stylus combinations (*http://bit.ly/2F97Ovb*) for computers, one of which was white labeled for the Apple II as the Apple Graphics Tablet (*http://bit.ly/2O0HmGW*), released in 1979. It was relatively expensive and supported by only a few types of software; violating two of the five rules. By 1983, HP had released the HP-150, the first touchscreen computer. However, the tracking fidelity was quite low, violating the user error rule.

When the mouse was first bundled with personal computer packages (1984–1985), it was supported on the operating-system (OS) level, which in turn was designed to take mouse input. This was a key turning point for computers: the mouse was no longer an optional input, but an *essential* one. Rather than a curio or optional peripheral, computers were now required to come with tutorials teaching users how to use a mouse, as illustrated in Figure 1-4—similar to how video games include a tutorial that teaches players how the game's actions map to the controller buttons.

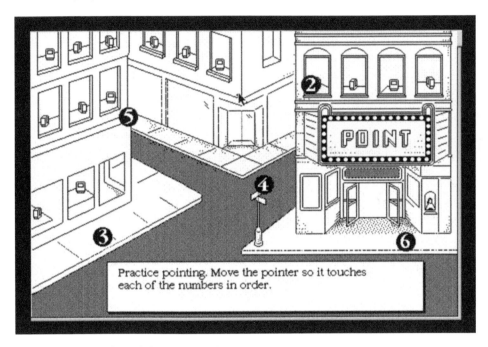

Figure 1-4. Screenshot of the Macintosh SE Tour, 1987

It's easy to look back on the 1980s and think the personal computer was a standalone innovation. But, in general, there are very few innovations in computing that single-handedly moved the field forward in less than a decade. Even the most famous innovations, such as FORTRAN, took years to popularize and commercialize. Much more often, the driving force behind adoption—of what feels like a new innovation—is simply the result of the technology finally fulfilling the aforementioned five rules: *cheap, reliable, comfortable, have software that makes use of the technolgy*, and *having an acceptable user error rate.*

It is very common to find that the first version of what appears to be recent technology was in fact invented decades or even centuries ago. If the technology is obvious enough that multiple people try to build it but it still doesn't work, it is likely failing in one of the five rules. It simply must wait until technology improves or manufacturing processes catch up.

This truism is of course exemplified in virtual reality (VR) and augmented reality (AR) history. Although the first stereoscopic head-mounted displays (HMDs) were pioneered by Ivan Sutherland in the 1960s and have been used at NASA routinely since the 1990s, it wasn't until the fields of mobile electronics and powerful graphics processing units (GPUs) improved enough that the technology became available at a commercially acceptable price, decades later. Even as of today, high-end standalone HMDs are either thousands of dollars or not commercially available. But much like smartphones in the early 2000s, we can see a clear path from current hardware to the future of spatial computing.

However, before we dive in to today's hardware, let's finish laying out the path from the PCs of the early 1980s to the most common types of computer today: the smartphone.

Modalities Through the Ages: Computer Miniaturization

Computers with miniaturized hardware emerged out of the calculator and computer industries as early as 1984 with the Psion Organizer. The first successful tablet computer was the GriDPad, released in 1989, whose VP of research, Jeff Hawkins, later went on to found the PalmPilot. Apple released the Newton in 1993, which had a handwritten character input system, but it never hit major sales goals. The project ended in 1998 as the Nokia 900 Communicator—a combination telephone and personal digital assistant (PDA)—and later the PalmPilot dominated the miniature computer landscape. Diamond Multimedia released its Rio PMP300 MP3 player in 1998, as well, which turned out to be a surprise hit during the holiday season. This led to the rise of other popular MP3 players by iRiver, Creative NOMAD, Apple, and others.

In general, PDAs tended to have stylus and keyboard inputs; more single-use devices like music players had simple button inputs. From almost the beginning of their manufacturing, the PalmPilots shipped with their handwriting recognition system, Graffiti, and by 1999 the Palm VII had network connectivity. The first Blackberry came out the same year with keyboard input, and by 2002 Blackberry had a more conventional phone and PDA combination device.

But these tiny computers didn't have the luxury of human-sized keyboards. This not only pushed the need for better handwriting recognition, but also real advances in speech input. Dragon Dictate came out in 1990 and was the first consumer option available—though for $9,000, it heavily violated the "cheap" rule. By 1992, AT&T rolled out voice recognition for its call centers. Lernout & Hauspie acquired several companies through the 1990s and was used in Windows XP. After an accounting scandal, the company was bought by SoftScan—later Nuance, which was licensed as the first version of Siri.

In 2003, Microsoft launched Voice Command for its Windows Mobile PDA. By 2007, Google had hired away some Nuance engineers and was well on its way with its own voice recognition technology. Today, voice technology is increasingly ubiquitous, with most platforms offering or developing their own technology, especially on mobile devices. It's worth noting that in 2018, there is no cross-platform or even cross-company standard for voice inputs: the modality is simply not mature enough yet.

PDAs, handhelds, and smartphones have almost always been interchangeable with some existing technology since their inception—calculator, phone, music player, pager, messages display, or clock. In the end, they are all simply different slices of computer functionality. You can therefore think of the release of the iPhone in 2007 as a turning point for the small-computer industry: by 2008, Apple had sold 10 million more than the next top-selling device, the Nokia 2330 classic, even though the Nokia held steady sales of 15 million from 2007 to 2008. The iPhone itself did not take over iPod sales until 2010, after Apple allowed users to fully access iTunes.

One very strong trend with all small computer devices, whatever the brand, is the move toward touch inputs. There are several reasons for this.

The first is simply that visuals are both inviting and useful, and the more we can see, the higher is the perceived quality of the device. With smaller devices, space is at a premium, and so removing physical controls from the device means a larger percentage of the device is available for a display.

The second and third reasons are practical and manufacturing focused. As long as the technology is cheap and reliable, fewer moving parts means less production cost and less mechanical breakage, both enormous wins for hardware companies.

The fourth reason is that using your hands as an input is perceived as natural. Although it doesn't allow for minute gestures, a well-designed, simplified GUI can work around many of the problems that come up around user error and occlusion. Much like the shift from keyboard to mouse-and-GUI, new interface guidelines for touch allow a reasonably consistent and error-free experience for users that would be almost impossible using touch with a mouse or stylus-based GUI.

The final reason for the move toward touch inputs is simply a matter of taste: current design trends are shifting toward minimalism in an era when computer technology can be overwhelming. Thus, a simplified device can be perceived as easier to use, even if the learning curve is much more difficult and features are removed.

One interesting connection point between hands and mice is the *trackpad*, which in recent years has the ability to mimic the multitouch gestures of touchpad while avoiding the occlusion problems of hand-to-display interactions. Because the tablet allows for relative input that can be a ratio of the overall screen size, it allows for more minute gestures, akin to a mouse or stylus. It still retains several of the same issues that plague hand input—fatigue and lack of the physical support that allows the human hand to do its most delicate work with tools—but it is useable for almost all conventional OS-level interactions.

Why Did We Just Go Over All of This?

So, what was the point of our brief history lesson? To set the proper stage going forward, where we will move from the realm of the known, computing today, to the unknown future of spatial inputs. At any given point in time it's easy to assume that we know everything that has led up to the present or that we're always on the right track. Reviewing where we've been and how the present came to be is an excellent way to make better decisions for the future.

Let's move on to exploring human–computer interaction (HCI) for spatial computing. We can begin with fundamentals that simply will not change in the short term: how humans can take in, process, and output information.

Types of Common HCI Modalities

There are three main ways by which we interact with computers:

Visual
    Poses, graphics, text, UI, screens, animations

Auditory
    Music, tones, sound effects, voice

Physical
    Hardware, buttons, haptics, real objects

Notice that in the background we've covered so far, physical inputs and audio/visual outputs dominate HCI, regardless of computer type. Should this change for spatial computing, in a world in which your digital objects surround you and interact with the real world? Perhaps. Let's begin by diving into the pros and cons of each modality.

Visual modalities

Pros:

- 250 to 300 words per minute (WPM) understood by humans
- Extremely customizable

- Instantly recognizable and understandable on the human side
- Very high fidelity compared to sound or haptics
- Time-independent; can just hang in space forever
- Easy to rearrange or remap without losing user understanding
- Good ambient modality; like ads or signs, can be noticed by the humans at their leisure

Cons:

- Easy to miss; location dependent
- As input, usually requires robust physical counterpart; gestures and poses very tiring
- Requires prefrontal cortex for processing and reacting to complicated information, which takes more cognitive load
- Occlusion and overlapping are the name of the game
- Most likely to "interrupt" if the user is in the flow
- Very precise visual (eye) tracking is processor intensive

Best uses in HMD-specific interactions:

- Good for limited camera view or other situations in which a user is forced to look somewhere
- Good for clear and obvious instructions
- Good for explaining a lot fast
- Great for tutorials and onboarding

Example use case—a smartphone:

- Designed to be visual-only
- Works even if the sound is off
- Works with physical feedback
- Physical affordances are minimal
- Lots of new animation languages to show feedback

Physical modalities

Pros:

- Braille: 125 WPM
- Can be very fast and precise
- Bypasses high-level thought processes, so is easy to move into a physiological and mental "flow"
- Training feeds into the primary motor cortex; eventually doesn't need the more intensive premotor cortex or basal ganglia processing
- Has strong animal brain "this is real" component; a strong reality cue
- Lightweight feedback is unconsciously acknowledged
- Least amount of delay between affordance and input
- Best single-modality input type, as is most precise

Cons:

- Can be tiring
- Physical hardware is more difficult to make, can be expensive, and breaks
- Much higher cognitive load during teaching phase
- Less flexible than visual: buttons can't really be moved
- Modes require more memorization for real flow
- Wide variations due to human sensitivity

Best uses in HMD-specific interactions:

- Flow states
- Situations in which the user shouldn't or can't look at UI all the time
- Situations in which the user shouldn't look at their hands all the time
- Where mastery is ideal or essential

Example use case—musical instruments:

- Comprehensive physical affordances
- No visuals needed after a certain mastery level; creator is in flow
- Will almost always have audio feedback component
- Allows movement to bypass parts of the brain—thought becomes action

Audio modalities

Pros:

- 150 to 160 WPM understood by humans
- Omnidirectional
- Easily diegetic to both give feedback and enhance world feel
- Can be extremely subtle and still work well
- Like physical inputs, can be used to trigger reactions that don't require high-level brain processing, both evaluative conditioning and more base brain stem reflex
- Even extremely short sounds can be recognized after being taught
- Great for affordances and confirmation feedback

Cons:

- Easy for users to opt out with current devices
- No ability to control output fidelity
- Time based: if user misses it, must repeat
- Can be physically off-putting (brain stem reflex)
- Slower across the board
- Vague, imprecise input due to language limitations
- Dependent on timing and implementation
- Not as customizable
- Potentially processor intensive

Best uses in HMD-specific interactions:

- Good for visceral reactions
- Great way to get users looking at a specific thing
- Great for user-controlled camera
- Great when users are constrained visually and physically
- Great for mode switching

Example use case—a surgery room:

- Surgeon is visually and physically captive; audio is often the only choice
- Continual voice updates for all information
- Voice commands for tools, requests, and confirmations

- Voice can provide most dense information about current state of affairs and mental states; very useful in high-risk situations

Now that we've written down the pros and cons of each type of modality, we can delve into the HCI process and properly map out the cycle. Figure 1-5 illustrates a typical flow, followed by a description of how it maps to a game scenario.

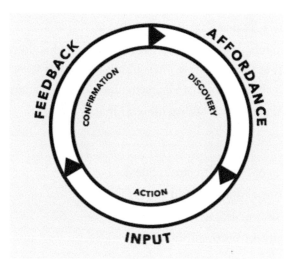

Figure 1-5. Cycle of a typical HCI modality loop

The cycle comprises three simple parts that loop repeatedly in almost all HCIs:

- The first is generally the affordance or discovery phase, in which the user finds out *what they can do*.
- The second is the input or action phase, in which the user *does the thing*.
- The third phase is the feedback or confirmation phase, in which the computer *confirms the input* by reacting in some way.

Figure 1-6 presents the same graphic, now filled out for a conventional console video game tutorial UX loop.

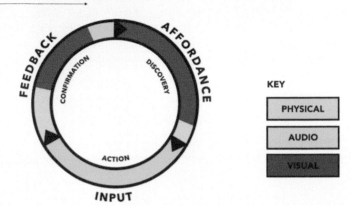

Getting to a good modality loop: typical game for console with controller

KEY

PHYSICAL

AUDIO

VISUAL

Figure 1-6. The cycle of a typical HCI modality loop, with examples

Let's walk through this. In many video game tutorials, the first affordance with which a user can do something is generally an unmissable UI overlay that tells the user the label of the button that they need to press. This sometimes manifests with a corresponding image or model of the button. There might be an associated sound like a change in music, a tone, or dialogue, but during the tutorial it is largely supporting and not teaching.

For conventional console video games, the input stage will be entirely physical; for example, a button press. There are exploratory video games that might take advantage of audio input like speech, or a combination of physical and visual inputs (e.g., hand pose), but those are rare. In almost all cases, the user will simply press a button to continue.

The feedback stage is often a combination of all three modalities: the controller might have haptic feedback, the visuals will almost certainly change, and there will be a confirmation sound.

It's worth noting that this particular loop is specifically describing the *tutorial* phase. As users familiarize themselves with and improve their gameplay, the visuals will diminish in favor of more visceral modalities. Often, later in the game, the sound affordance might become the primary affordance to avoid visual overload—remember that, similar to physical modalities, audio can also work to cause reactions that bypass higher-level brain functions. Visuals are the most information-dense modalities, but they are often the most distracting in a limited space; they also require the most time to understand and then react.

New Modalities

With the rise of better hardware and new sensors, we have new ways both to talk to computers and have them monitor and react to us. Here's a quick list of inputs that are either in the prototype or commercialization stage:

- Location
- Breath rate
- Voice tone, pitch, and frequency
- Eye movement
- Pupil dilation
- Heart rate
- Tracking unconscious limb movement

One curious property of these new inputs—as opposed to the three common modalities we've discussed—is that for the most part, the less the user thinks about them, the more useful they will be. Almost every one of these new modalities is difficult or impossible to control for long periods of time, especially as a conscious input mechanic. Likewise, if the goal is to collect data for machine learning training, any conscious attempt to alter the data will likely dirty the entire set. Therefore, they are best suited to be described as passive inputs.

One other property of these specific inputs is that they are one-way; the computer can react to the change in each, but it cannot respond in kind, at least not until computers significantly change. Even then, most of the list will lead to ambient feedback loops, not direct or instant feedback.

The Current State of Modalities for Spatial Computing Devices

As of this writing, AR and VR devices have the following modality methods across most hardware offerings:

Physical

- For the user input: controllers
- For the computer output: haptics

Audio

- For the user input: speech recognition (rare)

- For the computer output: sounds and spatialize audio

Visual

- For the user input: hand tracking, hand pose recognition, and eye tracking
- For the computer output: HMD

One peculiarity arises from this list: immersive computing has, for the first time, led to the rise of *visual inputs* through computer vision tracking body parts like the hands and eyes. Although hand position and movement has often been incidentally important, insofar as it maps to pushing physical buttons, it has never before taken on an importance of its own. We talk more on this later, but let's begin with the most conventional input type: controllers and touchscreens.

Current Controllers for Immersive Computing Systems

The most common type of controllers for mixed, augmented, and virtual reality (XR) headsets, owes its roots to conventional game controllers. It is very easy to trace any given commercial XR HMD's packaged controllers back to the design of the joystick and D-pad. Early work around motion tracked gloves, such as NASA Ames' VIEWlab from 1989, has not yet been commoditized at scale. Interestingly, Ivan Sutherland had posited that VR controllers should be joysticks back in 1964; almost all have them, or thumbpad equivalents, in 2018.

Before the first consumer headsets, Sixsense was an early mover in the space with its magnetic, tracked controllers, which included buttons on both controllers familiar to any game console: A and B, home, as well as more genericized buttons, joysticks, bumpers, and triggers.

Current fully tracked, PC-bound systems have similar inputs. The Oculus Rift controllers, Vive controllers, and Windows MR controllers all have the following in common:

- A primary select button (almost always a trigger)
- A secondary select variant (trigger, grip, or bumper)
- A/B button equivalents
- A circular input (thumbpad, joystick, or both)
- Several system-level buttons, for consistent basic operations across all applications

Figure 1-7. The Sixsense Stem input system

Generally, these last two items are used to call up menus and settings, leaving the active app to return to the home screen.

Standalone headsets have some subset of the previous list in their controllers. From the untracked Hololens remote to the Google Daydream's three-degrees-of-freedom (3DOF) controller, you will always find the system-level buttons that can perform confirmations and then return to the home screen. Everything else depends on the capabilities of the HMD's tracking system and how the OS has been designed.

Although technically *raycasting* is a visually tracked input, most people will think of it as a physical input, so it does bear mentioning here. For example, the Magic Leap controller allows for selection both with raycast from the six-degrees-of-freedom (6DOF) controller and from using the thumbpad, as does the Rift in certain applications, such as its avatar creator. But, as of 2019, there is no standardization around raycast selection versus analog stick or thumbpad.

As tracking systems improve and standardize, we can expect this standard to solidify over time. Both are useful at different times, and much like the classic Y-axis inversion problem, it might be that different users have such strongly different preferences that we should always allow for both. Sometimes, you want to point at something to select it; sometimes you want to scroll over to select it. Why not both?

Body Tracking Technologies

Let's go through the three most commonly discussed types of body tracking today: *hand tracking*, *hand pose recognition*, and *eye tracking*.

Hand tracking

Hand tracking is when the entire movement of the hand is mapped to a digital skeleton, and input inferences are made based on the movement or pose of the hand. This allows for natural movements like picking up and dropping of digital objects and gesture recognition. Hand tracking can be entirely computer-vision based, include sensors attached to gloves, or use other types of tracking systems.

Hand pose recognition

This concept is often confused with hand tracking, but hand pose recognition is its own specific field of research. The computer has been trained to recognize specific hand poses, much like sign language. The intent is mapped when each hand pose is tied to specific events like grab, release, select, and other common actions.

On the plus side, pose recognition can be less processor intensive and need less individual calibration than robust hand tracking. But externally, it can be tiring and confusing to users who might not understand that the pose re-creation is more important than natural hand movement. It also requires a significant amount of user tutorials to teach hand poses.

Eye tracking

The eyes are constantly moving, but tracking their position makes it much easier to infer interest and intent—sometimes even more quickly than the user is aware of themselves, given that eye movements update before the brain visualization refreshes. Although it's quickly tiring as an input in and of itself, eye tracking is an excellent input to mix with other types of tracking. For example, it can be used to triangulate the position of the object a user is interested in, in combination with hand or controller tracking, even before the user has fully expressed an interest.

I'm not yet including body tracking or speech recognition on the list, largely because there are no technologies on the market today that are even beginning to implement either technology as a standard input technique. But companies like Leap Motion, Magic Leap, and Microsoft are paving the way for all of the nascent tracking types listed here.

A Note on Hand Tracking and Hand Pose Recognition

Hand tracking and hand pose recognition both must result in interesting, and somewhat counterintuitive, changes to how humans often think of interacting with computers. Outside of conversational gestures, in which hand movement largely plays a supporting role, humans do not generally ascribe a significance to the location and pose of their hands. We use hands every day as tools and can recognize a mimicked gesture for the action it relates to, like picking up an object. Yet in the history of HCI, hand location means very little. In fact, peripherals like the mouse and the game controller are specifically designed to be hand-location agnostic: you can use a mouse on the left or right side, you can hold a controller a foot up or down in front of you; it makes no difference to what you input.

The glaring exception to this rule is touch devices, for which hand location and input are necessarily tightly connected. Even then, touch "gestures" have little to do with hand movement outside of the fingertips touching the device; you can do a three-finger swipe with any three fingers you choose. The only really important thing is that you fulfill the minimum requirement to do what the computer is looking for to get the result you want.

Computer vision that can track hands, eyes, and bodies is potentially extremely powerful, but it can be misused.

Voice, Hands, and Hardware Inputs over the Next Generation

If you were to ask most people on the street, the common assumption is that we will ideally, and eventually, interact with our computers the way we interact with other humans: talking normally and using our hands to gesture and interact. Many, many well-funded teams across various companies are working on this problem today, and both of those input types will surely be perfected in the coming decades. However, they both have significant drawbacks that people don't often consider when they imagine the best-case scenario of instant, complete hand tracking and NLP.

Voice

In common vernacular, voice commands aren't precise, no matter how perfectly understood. People often misunderstand even plain-language sentences, and often others use a combination of inference, metaphor, and synonyms to get their real intent across. In other words, they use multiple modalities and modalities within modalities to make sure they are understood. Jargon is an interesting linguistic evolution of this: highly specialized words that mean a specific thing in a specific context to a group are a form of language hotkey, if you will.

Computers can react much more quickly than humans can—that is their biggest advantage. To reduce input to mere human vocalization means that we significantly slow down how we can communicate with computers from today. Typing, tapping, and pushing action-mapped buttons are all very fast and precise. For example, it is much faster to select a piece of text, press the hotkeys for "cut," move the cursor, and then press the hotkeys for "paste" than it is to describe those actions to a computer. This is true of almost all *actions*.

However, to describe a scenario, tell a story, or make a plan with another human, it's often faster to simply use words in conversations because any potential misunderstanding can be immediately questioned and course-corrected by the listener. This requires a level of working knowledge of the world that computers will likely not have until the dawn of true artificial intelligence.

There are other advantages to voice input: when you need hands-free input, when you are otherwise occupied, when you need transliteration dictation, or when you want a fast modality switch (e.g., "minimize! exit!") without other movement. Voice input will always work best when it is used in tandem with other modalities, but that's no reason it shouldn't be perfected. And, of course, voice recognition and speech-to-text transcription technology has uses beyond mere input.

Hands

Visual modalities such as hand tracking, gestures, and hand pose recognition are consistently useful as a secondary confirmation, exactly the same way they are useful as hand and posture poses in regular human conversation. They will be most useful for spatial computing when we have an easy way to train personalized datasets for individual users very quickly. This will require a couple of things:

- Individuals to maintain personalized biometric datasets across platforms
- A way for individuals to teach computers what they want those computers to notice or ignore

The reasons for these requirements are simple: humans vary wildly both in how much they move and gesture and what those gestures mean to them. One person might move their hands constantly, with no thought involved. Another might gesture only occasionally, but that gesture has enormous importance. We not only need to customize these types of movements broadly per user, but also allow the user themselves to instruct the computer what it should pay special attention to and what it should ignore.

The alternative to personalized, trained systems is largely what we have today: a series of predefined hand poses that are mapped specifically to certain actions. For Leap Motion, a "grab" pose indicates that the user wants to select and move an object. For the Hololens, the "pinch" gesture indicates selection and movement. The Magic Leap supports 10 hand poses, some of which map to different actions in different experiences. The same is true of Oculus Rift controllers, which support two hand poses (point, and thumbs up), both of which can be remapped to actions of the developer's choice.

This requires the user to memorize the poses and gestures required by the hardware instead of a natural hand movement, much like how tablet devices standardized swipe-to-move and pinch-to-zoom. Although these types of human–computer sign language do have the potential to standardize and become the norm, proponents should recognize that what they propose is an *alternative* to how humans use their hands today, not a remapping. This is especially exacerbated by the fact that human hands are imprecise on their own; they require physical support and tools to allow for real precision, as demonstrated in Figure 1-8.

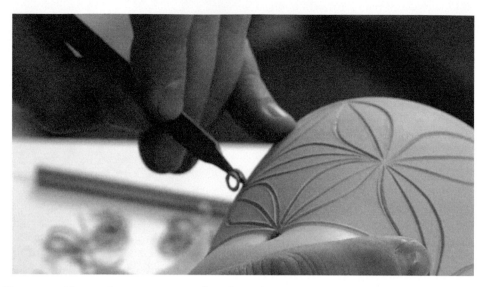

Figure 1-8. Triangulation to support hand weight is important—even if you have a digital sharp edge or knife, you need to have a way to support your hand for more minute gestures

Controllers and other physical peripherals

As we saw in the introduction, there has been a tremendous amount of time and effort put into creating different types of physical inputs for computers for almost an entire century. However, due to the five rules, peripherals have standardized. Of the five rules, two are most important here: it is cheaper to manufacture at scale, and inputs have standardized alongside the hardware that supports them.

However, we are now entering an interesting time for electronics. For the first time, it's possible for almost anyone to buy or make their own peripherals that can work with many types of applications. People make everything out of third-party parts: from keyboards and mice, to Frankenstein-ed Vive trackers on top of baseball bats or pets, and custom paint jobs for their Xbox controllers.

It's a big ask to assume that because spatial computing will allow for more user customization, that *consumers* would naturally begin to make their own inputs. But it is easy to assume that *manufacturers* will make more customized hardware to suit demand. Consider automobiles today: the Lexus 4 has more than 450 steering wheel options alone; when you include all options, this results in four million combinations of the same vehicle. When computing is personal and resides in your house alongside you, people will have strong opinions about how it looks, feels, and reacts, much as they do with their vehicles, their furniture, and their wallpaper.

This talk of intense customization, both on the platform side and on the user side, leads us to a new train of thought: spatial computing allows computers to be as personalized and varied as the average person's house and how they arrange the belongings in their house. The inputs therefore need to be equally varied. The same way someone might choose one pen versus another pen to write will apply to all aspects of computer interaction.

CHAPTER 2

Designing for Our Senses, Not Our Devices

Silka Miesnieks

Imagine a future in which our relationship with technology is as rich as reality. We don't often rave about how much time is spent in front of screens, and fortunately, most technology companies feel the same way. They have invested heavily in sensors and AI to create sensing machines. By utilizing speech, spatial, and, biometric data, fed into artificial intelligence they are developing technologies into more human-relatable forms. But not much is understood about how to design sensing machine driven technologies that are engaging, accessible, and responsible. Because of this, the technology industry needs to invest more in understanding humanly responsive design along with the engineering practices, policies, and tools needed.

We all want better solutions for a happier future, but how do we get it right in the today's technology evolution? In this chapter, we'll explore this topic and hopefully inspire further exploration.

As Head of Emerging Design at Adobe, I work with several teams across the company to bring emerging technologies into products and services to solve real human and societal challenges. Over 25 years of pushing design forward through three major technology shifts, I've seen the internet powering our knowledge economy, and mobile computing transforming how we communicate. In the future, spatial computing, powered by AI, will dramatically expand our means for collaborating with one another and using information. It will profoundly change the way we work, live, learn, and play. I believe its effect on society will be larger than the internet and mobile computing combined. As a designer, I'm super excited and sometimes a little scared to take part in this extraordinary period of human history.

Envisioning a Future

Tea Uglow, a creative director at Google, was the first design leader whose perspective on spatial computing deeply influenced me and my team. She helped us picture a better future toward which we can build. I'd like to take you on an imaginary journey that Tea shared in a Ted Talk:

> Close your eyes for just a minute. Imagine your happy place, we all have one. Even if it's a fantasy. For me, this place is on the beach in Australia with my friends around me, the sun shining, the feel of the salt water on my toes and the sound of a barbecue sizzling. This is a place that makes me feel happy because it's natural, it's simple and I'm connected to friends. When I sit in front of my computer or spend too much time looking at my mobile screen, I don't feel very happy. I don't feel connected. But after a day being in my happy place, I start to miss the information and other connections I get through my phone. But I don't miss my phone. My phone doesn't make me happy. So, as a designer I am interested in how we access information in a way that feels natural, is simple and can make us happy.

This mindset helps we as designers understand the value and importance of our work anytime we embark on a new product or design.

Sensory Technology Explained

Before we can explore the importance of design with spatial computing, we need to define the technologies involved. Spatial experiences are driven by sensor data fed into machine learning driven machines. Here is a quick summary of spatial computing and its sensory machines.

Spatial computing is not locked in rectangles but can flow freely in and through the world around us, unlike mobile computing and desktop computing before it. In other words, spatial computing uses the space around us as a canvas for digital experiences.

A dream of spatial computing is that technology will fade away and digital interaction will be humanized. For example, input devices like the mouse, keyboard, and even touchscreens intermediate our experiences. With spatial computing we can use our voice, sight, touch (in 3D), gestures, and other natural inputs to directly connect with information. We no longer need to think and behave like a computer for it to understand us, because it will relate humanly to us.

Presuming that computers understand us, then spatial computing could also understand our differences and support our human abilities and differences. For instance, we could provide verbal information about the world around a person with vision loss or translate cultural nuances, not just language, when communicating across cultures. In reverse, spatial computing could enhance our existing abilities, like giving someone who is a mathematical savant the ability to see and interact with more facts and data that others couldn't comprehend.

Sensory data is generated from our sensory machines powered by AI technologies. Computer vision, machine hearing, and machine touch can output data like your camera's exact location; dimensions of space around you; identify objects, people, and speech; biodata, and much more. Using AI technologies, we can interpret this data in a way that mimics human perception. As we perceive the world, so too can machines perceive the world.

As machine senses are increasingly being added into everything, and placed everywhere, more use cases are emerging. Here are some current uses of sensory machines and data:

- Augmented reality (AR)-enabled cameras will reach 2.7 billion phones by the end of 2019 (*http://bit.ly/2JbRmyf*). With the power of AI technology, AR cameras are rapidly able to understand what they "see." Google Lens (Google's AR system for Pixel Phone) can now identify one billion products, four times more than when it launched in 2017.

- Through your AR-enabled phone, AI technologies can detect basic human emotions like anger, contempt, disgust, fear, happiness, neutral, sadness, and surprise from your facial expression (*http://bit.ly/2TKa0Bf*). These emotions are understood to be cross-culturally and commonly used, but they are not always a true measure of how someone might be actually feels inside. Mark Billinghurst, AR pioneer, and Director of the Empathic Computer Laboratory at the University of South Australia said, "Face expressions alone can be a poor measure of emotion. For example, if a person is frowning, is it because they are unhappy, or maybe just concentrating on a complex task? For a better estimate of emotion, it is important to take into account other contextual cues, such as the task the person is doing, the environment they are in, what they are saying, and their body's physiological cues (e.g. heart rate), etc. People take all of these cues into account to understand how they are feeling, or the feelings of others. Machines should do the same."

- AR is accelerating training by tapping into our human sense of *proprioception*, the understanding of the space around us, for training and safety.

- Our microphones and speakers have become our virtual assistants and are increasingly entering our homes, phones, hearables and other devices.

- Clothes and watches embedded with sensors have the potential to measure our emotional intensity with perspiration (*galvanic skin response*) and monitor our health 24/7 through our heartbeat.

- Our cities are becoming "smart" with a massive number of sensors placed in our streets, cars, and public transport systems. Integrating their data lets municipalities get more detailed insights into how to solve interconnected problems. These sensors monitor things like weather, air quality, traffic, radiation, and water levels, and they can be used to automatically inform fundamental services like traffic and street lights, security systems, and emergency alerts.

Spatial computing has come about from the interplay of technology advances in machine sensors, rendering power, AI and machine learning, 3D capture, and displays. Voice-user interface (VUI), gesture, and XR displays provide new contexts for computing. Spatial computing happens everywhere we are, on our wrists, in our eyes and ears, on kitchen counters and conference room tables, and in our living rooms, offices and favorite means of transportation. Just ask a car's GPS how to reach your road trip destination.

While VUI has already reached our homes, phones, and cars, AR services have not yet reached mass consumer adoption. Some people believe this will come when consumer-grade AR glasses are here. I believe the tipping point will arrive only when devices, sensory dates, and AI systems together unlock our natural human creative superpower through spatial collaboration. I'll explain this more later on in this chapter.

Artificially intelligent machines think independently and find new ways of doing things—this is the goal, but no machine is yet intelligent on its own. But machine learning and its significantly smarter younger sibling, deep learning, provide a way for machines to interpret massive amounts of data in new and amazing ways. Our intelligent machines today can learn, but they do not completely understand.

For spatial computing, machine learning acts a bit like the human nervous system for our senses. As our cities' systems and building systems integrate an ever-growing number of sensors, they too reflect a nervous system. Data from sensors such as cameras (sight), microphones (hearing), and inertial measurement units (IMUs) is collected and interpreted by a complex machine learning (nervous) system. If you can't read Dutch, your camera can translate it for you; if you can't hear well, your speaker could amplify that voice or translate speech to text; if your car goes through a pothole, your vehicle could immediately notify the local public works department about repairing the hole; a toy could tell if it was being used or left in the toy box, leading to better toys and reduced landfills.

Machine learning and historical data remembers and understands the past. We are already seeing our sentences being finished for us in Gmail based on our historical writing style. One day, my kids might experience my life when they are my age; maybe we could "see" a predicted future of our inventions based on historical events.

As AI continues to advance, sensory design will continue to become more natural, giving our devices natural human senses. We envision a world in which our tools are more natural, and I believe this is the future people are craving. The more natural and intuitive tools are, the more accessible they will be, which is where sensory design plays a crucial role.

So, Who Are We Building This Future For?

We are building the future for people like the two boys in Figure 2-1. They'll be building the products and services based on ecosystems we construct today. Let's listen to them and be inspired by their needs for a better future. Here are some things they are saying.

Figure 2-1. Two generation Z'ers

The boys are GenZ'ers, a group who will "comprise 32% of the global population of 7.7 billion in 2019" (*https://bloom.bg/2TxYppN*). Today GenZ'ers are aged 9 to 24 years old or born after 2000. They have more devices than previous generations. In the United States, they have Amazon's Alexa in their homes, they're always carrying AI chips in their phones, and in 10 years they might have AR glasses on their noses.

Their identity is not drawn on race or gender but on meaningful identities that shift as they do. They fluidly and continuously express their personality. So, when asked, "Do you think you'll marry a girl or a boy?" the two young gentlemen in Figure 2-1 didn't think it was a strange question. One of them said "a girl" and the other said, "I'm working it out." Their answers were not awkward or uncomfortable, because they are not binary thinkers.

I'm seeing brands shift from creating self-creation-type experiences for YouTube or Instagram to brands that allow for fluid-identities by using AR facemasks in Snapchat and Facebook Messenger.

This is the kind of shift expected with spatial computing. We're moving from the place where information is held on screens to a world in which creative expression can flow freely into the environment around us with AR powered by AI. Future thinkers will need to be able to navigate through the chaos while building connections, which is why creativity is a core skill needed for future generations.

We all need to make creative expression simpler, more natural, and less tied to devices and more to our human senses. In many ways, spatial tools will be democratized. Tools like real-time animation is a core skill needed in spatial computing, but, today, the difficulty of animation causes it to be left to professionals with access to specific tools.

This is why my team at Adobe built a tool that lets you record the movement of a bird flying or friend dancing just by capturing the motion through your phone's camera and instantly transfer it to a 3D object or 2D design. It is incredible seeing the wonder on people's faces as they used the magic of sensing technologies (Figure 2-2).

Figure 2-2. One generation Z'er wearing a Microsoft HoloLens

Members of GenZ want to create collaboratively in real time. They also expect to create with anything, anywhere, just by looking at it or interacting with it (which we call playing).

Today, many kids learn by exploring the world around them from their classrooms using mobile AR. Or they ask Google to solve their math homework—yep, my kids do that. By the time GenZ reaches the workforce, they'll have AR-enabled interfaces projecting information on and around objects so that they can use both hands to learn the guitar. As Tea Uglow says, it will be a bit like a "wonderful mechanical You-Tube."

Creativity is being enhanced and extended into the world around us, giving everyone skills that only trained professionals have today. Skills like animation, 3D object creation, and the design of 3D spaces will be made easy and accessible in the same way that the internet made publishing available to everyone. AR, virtual reality (VR), and AI will shift us from sharing what's on our minds to also sharing what's in our hearts.

As AR, AI, and spatial computing expand into the world around us, creative expression will become as important as literacy. As a member of the broader tech industry, Adobe wants to make our creative tools available to everyone (XD is free!), inclusive of different abilities and cultures, and respectful of people's rights to privacy and transparency. It's an exciting time for creating tools that shape our relationship to spatial reality.

The Future Role of Designers and Teams

Sensory design put simply is the glue that joins spatial design disciplines (like architectural, interior, inductrial, systems, and UI designers) to sciences (like cognitive and neuroscience), artists, activists and policymakers, and AI engineers. Designing for the future with AI-powered spatial computing requires a great diversity of skills and a deep understanding of human behavior by everyone involved.

This is a growth area of design and requires a great diversity of roles to be created so that it will bring out the best in humanity.

In August 2018, I met an inspiring deaf performance artist, Rosa Lee Timm. She asked Adobe Design to (*https://adobe.ly/2T66soU*):

> [h]ave them [people with different abilities like herself] included in the design process and be a member of the team. And who knows, some of us may have some new inventions and ideas and creativity that you wouldn't think about, so then it becomes organic. And then when it's done, it's designed readily with easy distribution from the start.

Rosa went on to ask us if we could build a tool that translates spoken words into sign language so that we could "read" in her own language. She pointed out that many training videos don't even have text captions. This inspired me to think of how face and hand tracking and recognition technologies could be used to translate sign language to English and English back into sign language.

Another person that has deeply inspired our teams to think more globally, cross-culturally, and inclusively is Farai Madzima, Shopify's UX Lead. Last year, he visited us at Adobe Design and shared these thoughts (*https://adobe.ly/2T66soU/*):

> If you're under the impression that diversity is just about shades of brown, you're not paying attention. If you think diversity is just about gender or ability, then you're not paying attention. You need to work with people who don't walk, think, and talk like you. You need to have those people be a part of how you're working. This sounds like a difficult thing, on top of solving the problems of designing a product, but it is abso-

lutely critical. The challenges that we see in society are born of the fact that we have not seen what the world needs from our industry. We have not understood what our colleagues need from us and what we need for ourselves, which is this idea of being much more open-minded about what is different in the world.

The Role of Women in AI

My vision for the future of design begins with inclusiveness and diversity. As we create this new design language, we need diverse teams to set the foundation. This includes women. I believe that there are always multiple ways to solve a challenge, and seeking out different perspectives will be critical to the success of sensory design.

I believe that we need women and men leading the future of digital design for spatial computing and AI. In the past 30 years, we have seen men predominantly lead the design of our computer platforms, and, as a result, we now see a lack of women engineers in technology sectors. AI is personalizing our finances, entertainment, online news, and home systems. The people who design the spatial computing systems today will have a direct impact on the world around us tomorrow. It's going to require a variety of minds, bringing together different perspectives to solve real problems in a sustainable and empathic way. This is not just good for business, but for society as a whole.

Luckily, in the past two years, we've seen substantial industry backing and lofty goals set to change the way we approach AI. There are many programs being led by women. Women like Fei-Fei Li at Stanford; Kate Crawford, director of Microsoft's AI Now Institute; Terah Lyons, heading up Partnership for AI; and even Michelle Obama supporting Olga Russakovsky, cofounder of AI4ALL to educate women in AI during high school, just to name a few. I am personally excited for what's ahead and what we will accomplish when we embrace diversity in ideas.

Sensory Design

It is a diversity of ideas alongside a deep understanding of being human that will drive the longest lasting spatial designs. Historically our designs have been limited by medium and dimension. We can look to the world around us to see what designs have passed the test of time, such as familiar architecture or the layout of websites. Limitations of a designer's medium, be it physical or on-screen, have determined the resulting designs and over time the accepted norms.

In our future spatial computing–filled world, the number of limitations approaches zero. No longer limited by physical resources or a 2D screen, sensory design opens a world of possibilities far beyond any design medium currently in existence. In order to use sensory design, we first need to understand it, and that's why we're developing Sensory Design Language.

An Introduction

Sensory design is an adapted, humanity-inspired, industry-wide, design language for spatial computing. Just as material design language became the default guide for mobile interface design, we hope sensory design language will be the default design guide for interactions beyond the screen.

Sensory design flips existing design paradigms on their heads and so requires a new approach. For example, screen design focuses on the actions that users want users to perform, but sensory design instead focuses on the motivations users have by engaging the cognitive abilities of their senses. With this in mind, we at Adobe decided to go back to basics and focus on the universal first principles of human behavior. We also needed to understand the differences and layers between organized societies, cultures, and individuals. Lucky for us, there already has been an enormous amount of work done in this field. We just had to sift through hundreds of research papers to produce key starting points.

With this idea in mind, I gathered a group of designers, cognitive scientists, entrepreneurs, and engineers to help create a new design language for spatial computing that we can all understand and use. The first people to join our sensory design team were two cognitive scientists, Stefanie Hutka and Laura Herman and a machine learning coder/designer Lisa Jamhoury.

We began with the understanding that humans have excellent spatial memory. We use our sense of proprioception to understand and encode the space around us. I bet you could be blindfolded at home and still walk to and open the fridge. We've already seen virtual reality using proprioception as an effective tool for spatial training, but sensory design is more than spatial, it involves our senses.

Psychologists have proven that smiling makes you feel happier even on a chemical level. This connection between a brain, body, and senses is how we understand and perceive our world. By designing for human senses and cognitive abilities, we can hack our perceptions of reality. You could even say Sensory Design is the design of perceived realities.

Approaching sensory design

It's a fantastic opportunity to be able to design for human perception, but it's one that comes with great responsibility. The thought of changing someone's perception of reality via design, and the potential consequences, is daunting. So the sensory design team, wrote an approach to sensory design that holds us accountable:

- **Be human-centered** by building a language around intuitive human interactions. We can do this only by understanding fundamental human behavior, our bodies, and our cognitive abilities.
- **Be collaborative** by sharing our insights, listening to feedback, and learning from a wide range of people, from industry experts to our end users.
- **Be design leaders** through our work, sharing our insights openly and collectively.
- **Define the principles, methodologies, and patterns** we can use to work more effectively together and improve on the products we build.
- **Respect people** by respecting their physical and digital privacy; giving them control, or agency, over the tools we build; and thinking first of their well-being over a pat on the back.
- **Do good** human behavior by building systems to lead to greater empathy for our diversity of skills, cultures, and needs.

We see this list as a guide or inspiration and not a list of rules. We are all in this together adn the days of sensory design have just begun.

A sensory framework

Next, we drew up a framework, which you can see in Figure 2-3, to see opportunities and connections.

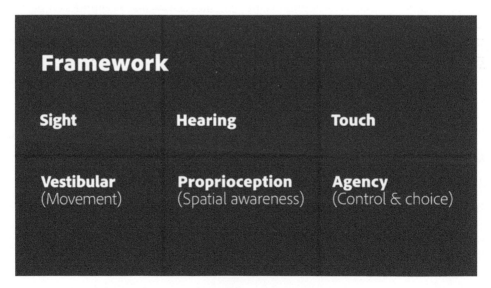

Figure 2-3. Breakdown of commonly used human senses

We broke up our human and machine senses so that we can put them together again in new ways to solve real-world problems. What are some of the problems that sensory design can solve that no other medium can? One example is using computer vision and AR to understand sign language, translate it to text, and then back again to sign language. Computer vision can understand facial expressions, and when combined with hand gestures and biometric data, a machine can get some idea of how you're feeling. Machine learning is very good at seeing patterns in massive amounts of sensory data. Organizations are already using this data to help organize the plan of cities and solve climate issues. My hope is that one day it will allow us to understand one another better.

How can a combination of senses and intelligence help us be more empathetic across different cultures and different ways of communicating? Can we give people new abilities, similar to how voice-to-text has let me express myself more easily despite my dyslexia? We have so many questions and so many opportunities.

Five Sensory Principles

Zach Lieberman and Molmol Kuo, previous artists-in-residence at Adobe, proposed using AR facial tracking as input to a musical instrument. Blinking eyes could trigger animations and mouth movements could generate music.

Artists break boundaries and create new ways of seeing the world with technology. We can look to artists to craft new experiences we never considered before. As more artists dive into spatial computing and sensory design, we will need a set of principles to help guide experiences in a direction users will understand. The first generation of Sensory Design users will have no clear preconception of what to expect. Design principles can ease adoption and improve the overall experience of spatial computing.

The following are five Sensory Design principles made to guide designers to create engaging and understandable spatial computing driven experiences.

1. Intuitive Experiences Are Multisensory

Our products will be intuitive when they are multisensory. By allowing our tools to take in and combine different senses, we will enable products to become more robust and able to better understand user intent.

We are multisensory beings, so adding more senses enhances the joy of an experience. Seeing a band in concert is more memorable than listening to a recording through headphones. Going skydiving is a more life-changing experience than watching a video of it. We love to hang out in person with friends rather than just Facebook or Snap. Oxytocin, a social bonding hormone, is released when we feel a real hug, not when we click a 'like' button.

Last month I went to see the band Massive Attack in concert, an event that engaged all of my senses. It brought me to tears, and the 90-minute experience gave me a deeper understanding of Massive Attack's message that I hadn't yet gleaned from more than 20 years of listening to their albums. I believe this was because all of my senses were engaged, allowing me to understand and feel the message in new and concrete ways, ways inexpressible through just sound or 2D screens.

2. 3D Will Be Normcore

In 5 to 10 years, 3D digital design will be as normal as 2D digital design is today. Like photography, desktop publishing, and the internet before it, we will need design tools, consumer-grade hardware, and cloud services that are readily available, easy to use, and quick to pick up for everyone.

Right now, we are having fun eperimenting with mobile AR, using it as the special effects filter of the real world, namely our faces. In the future, living with AR will be more normal than selfies are for millennials today.

Soon we will expect to be able to create throughout our 3D environment using our voice, hand gestures, and the environment itself. Our bodies will be the mouse of tomorrows spatial computing world, and the world around us will be clickable, editable, redesignable. Traditional inputs like a keyboard, mouse, and touch screen make software complicated by nature. Controlling software spatially with all our natural senses and the human body will change the way we express our human creativity.

In an AR world devoid of 2D technology, it might seem ridiculous to look at two-dimensional maps on our mobile devices, instead of looking through our AR glasses to see 3D directions laid over road or sidewalk in front of us. Watching a video in advance to set up your home audio system will seem archaic when AR instructions directly overlaid onto the equipment guide you immediately.

Everyone will be able to create when inspiration hits us in whatever space we are in, not just when we're at our desks. If it's a color, light, texture, motion, sound, or even an object, they can capture in 3D with their AR devices. We will expect to be able to create using our 3D environment and our voice and hand gestures as the input mechanism, not a mouse or a keyboard.

Traditional inputs like keyboards, mice, and touchscreens make software complicated by nature. Controlling software with all our senses in 3D, will unleash our creative superpowers.

For example, I'm dyslexic, so transferring my thoughts onto paper is incredibly frustrating. When physically writing out words, my creative flow is lost, and I become speechless. I wrote this piece using voice-to-text technology. It's not perfect, but it helps me get my words down and my voice on paper.

3. Designs Become Physical Nature

Our products need to be physical by nature. Designs placed in the world will only be accepted when they act naturally and humanely. We'll still be shouting at Alexa until the technology listens and responds as well as our friends do. There is a new UI standard when the design enters the world.

The new user interface standard for spatial design demands digital designs placed in the world act as if they are physically real. We expect a virtual mug will smash just like a physical one if we toss it on the ground.

Just as screen designs are triggered by a mouse click or a screen tap, designs in the world are triggered by our senses. The designs and their interactions should feel natural and in context to the world around them. We can at times break these rules, so long as the user doesn't think the app is broken too.

4. Design for the Uncontrollable

Design elements placed in the world cannot be controlled in the same way pixels on a screen have been. Digital experiences in 3D space must adapt to the lighting conditions, dimensions, and context of the surrounding environment. This means designers can no longer control the camera or the view. Users are free to prescribe their own viewpoint, location, and context.

When we showcased Project Aero at Apple WWDC 2018, I instantly understood what Stefano Corazza, the fearless product leader of Adobe's Project Aero, meant when he said, "AR is forcing creators to give some thought to the viewer's sense of agency (or self-directed choices), and this fosters more empathy toward the viewer." Giving the viewer control over the camera assigns them a role to play. They become part-creator. I saw a user assume the role of cinematographer the moment the person moved the AR-powered camera through a layered 2D artwork placed virtually on stage.

Another way we discover design for the uncontrollable is through the eyes of our artists that venture through Adobe's AR Residency program held over three months, three times per year. Two of these artists-in-residence were Zach Lieberman and Molmol Kuo. They collaborated to make *Weird Type*, an iOS AR app that lets you write and animate anything, anywhere in 3D space. After launching the app, we all got to sit back and watch how typography in space could be reimagined. People used *Weird Type* to guide someone through a building, tell a story about a location; build sculptures; and share a feeling by the wind by animating words, flying and scattering letters randomly into space, making text look more like snow (Figure 2-4). These new forms of communication were discovered by providing creative agency to the AR viewer, which itself opens a new medium of creativity.

Figure 2-4. An image made with the Weird Type app available on Apple's App Store

5. Unlock the Power of Spatial Collaboration

I believe the unique creative and economic power of that AR enables is *spatial collaboration*. When it feels like you're in the same room, communicating naturally with our whole body, magically designing digital–physical things with decisions amplified by AI alongside real human team members, then the power of remote emotional and physical connections becomes the driver for adoption of spatial computing. In other words, you could say, human connection is the killer-application for AR.

One of Adobe's artists-in-residence, Nadine Kolodzey, took the idea of AR collaboration one step further when she said, "I want people to not just look at my pictures, but to add something." We realized then she was giving the viewer agency, the ability to be an artist, too. At that moment Nadine became a toolmaker and the viewer became the artist. In this way, AR gives storytelling abilities to everyone, just like desktop publishing did for print and the internet did for knowledge.

Adobe's AR Story

AR guided by AI will profoundly change what designers create, how companies connect with their consumers, and expand the ways in which we collaborate in our daily lives. That is why Adobe recently announced Project Aero, a mobile AR design tool for designers and artists.

Project Aero's goal is to bring the new medium of AR into all of our products and establish a design discipline for spatial computing driven by AI. The following is a slice of the future of spatial computing as I see it today.

In 5 to 10 years, it will seem ridiculous to look at 2D maps on our screens instead of just looking out at our 3D directions drawn in the world around us. Wikipedia will seem archaic when you can learn about objects and places surrounding us just by looking at them and playing them a bit like experiencing a magical three-dimensional X-ray machine.

Designers will soon be able to create when the moment of inspiration hits them, wherever they may be. If it's a color, light, texture, motion, spatial sound, and even an object, they can capture it in 3D with their AR devices. Then, they can add the natural element to their existing work, create a new design or share the raw inspiration. Right now, designers are having fun with mobile AR using it as the special effects filter of the world.

We know that it's *our responsibility* at Adobe to build the interactive, animated, enriching tools that bridge this gap between today and the future for our designers and new emerging designers.

Recently, when our artist-in-residence Nadine Kolodziey said, "I want people to not just look at [my] pictures, but to add something," we realized that she was tapping into an emerging need for real-time collaborative design made possible with AR-enabled smartphones and the AR cloud. Adidas, the "creator's brand," thinks of its consumers as creators, too. So, when we asked Adidas to help build the "right" AR tool for creator collaborations, it jumped right in. But Adobe's AR story doesn't begin or end with Project Aero.

By deeply integrating Aero into our tools like After Effects; our 3D animation tool, Dimension CC; our 3D design tool, XD; our UI design tool, now with voice, Adobe Capture; our camera app, which lets you grab elements of the world, along with our cloud services; all driven by our AI platform, Sensei, we are creating an *ecosystem* to unlock the potential of AR.

Just like a machine ecosystem combines features, we combine our senses, voice, touch, sight, and proprioception (our sense of space around us) to understand the world. Machines that mimic human senses like our sense of sight with AR are only designed well when they act as expected: humanly. We'll still be shouting at Alexa if it doesn't understand what I'm saying as well as my friend. This new standard of good sensory design has led Adobe Design to rethink design principles, the role of a designer, and the core mechanics of our tools.

Conclusion

As we tackle this new world of spatial computing, I remind myself what Scott Belsky, Adobe's chief product officer said: "Creativity is the world's most human craft and, despite countless new devices and mediums, creative people remain at the center. The more the world changes, the more important creativity becomes." I see creativity exploding in all parts of our lives. Creativity is as important as literacy. So let's make our creative tools available to everyone, inclusive of different abilities, cultures, and respectful of people's right to privacy and transparency.

In 1970, industrial designer Dieter Rams famously wrote 10 principles for good design. Today, we live in a world in which design can push back, respond, or sense anything. Design was a one-time thing. Rams didn't have adaptive imaging technologies that understood intentions, remembered past actions, and provided personalization of your interface. Design has changed. It responds empathically to the API nervous system.

We are the people that are actually building the foundations for this period. It's us, the designers, engineers, cognitive scientists, entrepreneurs, and many others. If we challenge ourselves to look beyond technology and focus some energy toward building a good design foundation, we can actually create a future that is a little more empathic by nature. Let's challenge ourselves to develop tools that use sensing technologies that enable products to show empathy for a better future.

PART II

How eXtended Reality Is Changing Digital Art

Computers have forever changed how we think of art and animation, first with the pixel and then with the polygon. And now there is about to be another revolution thanks to virtual reality (VR) and augmented reality (AR). Because we now have spatially aware displays, we can finally see digital objects in true 3D. This means that art for VR and AR should be optimized in unique ways to take full advantage of these spatial displays. And with spatially aware input devices, we can interact with digital objects in true 3D, as well. Thus, we can actually use VR to create 3D art in new and intuitive ways.

In Chapter 3, digital-artist-turned-venture-capitalist Tipatat Chennavasin, whose self-portrait you can see in Figure II-1, explains how VR is improving the way 3D art and animation is created while democratizing 3D artistry. He discusses the pioneering tools that are at the forefront of the VR art and animation movement and why they are so important. Unfortunately, due to the restrictions of time and the space available within this book, he isn't able to cover all of the amazing VR art tools out there, like the low poly modeling of Google Blocks or the spline-based modeling of Gravity Sketch. However, by covering the concepts of VR painting and VR sculpting, you should have a good framework to understand the impact VR is having on 3D art. There are also new VR and AR tools for design prototyping, like Microsoft Maquette and Torch 3D, that provide WYSIWYG environments for spatial designers. These are both beyond the scope of this introductory chapter, but they are also worth exploring and just as transformative for their respective fields.

Figure II-1. VR self-portrait by Tipatat Chennavasin, made in Google Blocks and Tilt Brush

In Chapter 4, digital artist Jazmin Cano, whose self-portrait graces Figure II-2, talks about some of the challenges for creating art for use in VR and explains some best practice tips and techniques. She covers a variety of modeling and texturing techniques used in traditional 3D art creation to incorporate into your new pipeline to ensure that your art looks great while running smoothly. This will be your guide to creating the best VR experiences that you can offer to keep users comfortable.

Hopefully, these two chapters impart a good sense of how VR and AR are affecting the digital art world. The biggest takeaway is that the tools and techniques are in constant change; being a successful digital artist means to be forever a student, learning new tools and techniques and oftentimes pioneering these techniques yourself and sharing them with the community.

Figure II-2. VR self-portrait by Jazmin Cano, created in the Finger Paint app (by Mimicry), painted in High Fidelity

CHAPTER 3

Virtual Reality for Art

Tipatat Chennavasin

A More Natural Way of Making 3D Art

Traditionally, making digital 3D art was more like drafting than like painting or sculpting. A lot of the challenge was in understanding how to manipulate 3D space with a 2D interface. To view 3D objects on a 2D display, the artist often works from multiple views, like working on a technical drawing. These 3D objects are made from geometric shapes, which in turn are made of vertices or points in space. Moving these points in 3D space with a 2D mouse required much more abstract thinking instead of traditional art, which is more directly applied.

Looking at the interfaces for the most popular 3D programs like Autodesk Maya (Figure 3-1) and 3D Studio reflect these complexities. Because of these challenges, very few people could make 3D art. Then there was a new wave of 3D modeling programs, such as Pixologic's Z-Brush (Figure 3-2) that had a fundamentally different take. Such programs used a pen tablet as input and a sculpting-like interface that transformed the field of 3D modeling and allowed more artists to work in 3D. By using a pen and letting artists directly manipulate the geometry with gestures that were more natural, the creation of 3D art was further democratized. But even though the interface was more direct, it was still awkward to work on 3D objects through 2D displays and 2D interfaces. With the introduction of the consumer wave of virtual reality (VR), that all changed.

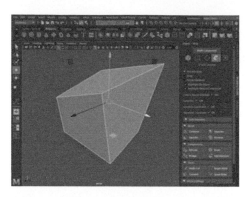

Figure 3-1. The interface for popular 3D modeling and animation software Autodesk Maya (source: CGSpectrum (http://bit.ly/2XQigPH))

Figure 3-2. A digital artist working with a Wacom Pen Tablet and Pixologic Z-Brush (source: Wacom (http://bit.ly/2u4khKs))

When most people think of VR, they think of the head-mounted display (HMD), with sensors and screens that take over the visual field and fully immerse a person into a digital world. But equally, if not more important, is the input device or controller that is equipped with similar sensors that let you interact and manipulate the digital world in a natural and intuitive way. The VR HMD became the ultimate 3D display, and the tracked hand controllers became the best 3D interface. There is no better example of the power of VR than in the applications that combine both the unique display and input to allow users to create and express themselves like never before. For the wave of modern VR, it all began with an app called Tilt Brush, which you can see in Figure 3-3.

Figure 3-3. Promotional image for Google Tilt Brush

Tilt Brush was developed by the two-person startup Skillman & Hackett and was one of the first art programs in modern VR. Because it was designed with the Oculus Development Kit 2, which had only an HMD but no spatial input device, the duo designed it for use with a Wacom pen tablet. Users drew on a 2D plane which they could tilt and move to paint in multiple planes to create in 3D. When Valve and HTC put out the Vive developer kit, Skillman & Hackett took advantage of the included fully tracked hand controllers and room-scale tracking to allow users to intuitively paint in 3D space. Now the entire room was the canvas and the digital paint flowed from the end of the hand controller and floated in space, creating a magical feel that went beyond reality but felt completely natural and easy to do. Google would later acquire Skillman & Hackett, and Tilt Brush would be bundled with the first HTC Vive consumer kits. This would become one of the most used VR applications to date. It was not only a true pioneer in art applications, it was also a shining example of excellent and intuitive user experience (UX) in VR.

Tilt Brush was always designed as a consumer application and, as such, has always been a very approachable tool with a simple and playful design. It features a wide variety of brushes that have visual effects like lighting and animation, which creates a very specific stylized look that sets it apart from other tools on the market and first-time users can quickly achieve stunning visual results. Even though the tools are flexible enough to accommodate many different styles by default, it is easy to recognize art created in Tilt Brush, as you can see in Figure 3-4.

Figure 3-4. Tilt Brush VR painting by VR artist Peter Chan (http://bit.ly/2Cix4x5/)

Even with its recognizable art, Tilt Brush has an outright unlimited potential. It has been used as a performance art tool (see Figure 3-5), for making music videos, featured in television commercials, in news reports for adding dynamic infographics, for production design, and even fashion design. There have even been games made for which all of the artwork was created in Tilt Brush. This product is constantly evolving, and with new features and functionality, it will continue to pave the way for a new type of digital art in a spatial world.

Figure 3-5. VR artist Danny Bittman giving a live Tilt Brush performance at VMWorld 2017 (photo by WMWare (http://bit.ly/2T0JXS3))

Because of its massive success within and outside of the VR industry, Google Tilt Brush was the first to popularize the idea of VR painting. It uses a paint stroke metaphor for creation that was very different from how 3D art had been previously made. However, it wasn't the only VR painting program in existence. Not far from where the now-Google team was working on Tilt Brush, there was in fact another team working on a quite different approach to VR painting as a part of Oculus, called the Oculus Story Studio.

Oculus Story Studio was the internal development group within Oculus to explore storytelling in VR. Its first two animated VR shorts, *Lost* and *Henry*, used fairly standard art production workflows for creating beautiful real-time animated shorts stories. However, for its third piece, *Dear Angelica*, it went for something radically different. *Dear Angelica* was a surreal dream using VR painting style that felt more like 2D animation than 3D animation, as demonstrated in Figure 3-6. To achieve this look, the Oculus Story Studio team created its own VR painting program named Quill. Although both use a painting stroke–like approach to creation, they achieve very different looking results and have widely dissimilar approaches to UX.

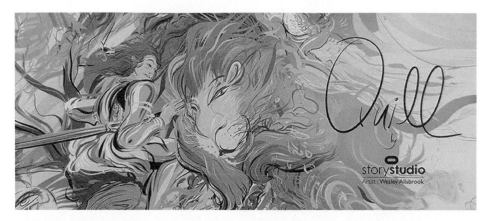

Figure 3-6. Promotional image of Quill from Facebook featuring artwork from Dear Angelica by artist Wesley Allsbrook

Quill was built as a professional tool and its UX reflects that both in visual layout and function, resembling other professional digital art tools like Adobe Photoshop. It also doesn't have a lot of the stylized effects that Tilt Brush has, like real-time lighting or animated brushes. This gives the artist much more control over the look. However, it also takes a lot more effort to get certain results. Quill also brings a lot of new ideas to what VR art can be, with interesting features such as nearly infinite scale, perspective-dependent viewing, and timeline-based animation. Oculus art director and artist-in-residence Goro Fujita has pioneered some truly unique creations that use these features, like his *Worlds in Worlds* piece, depicted in Figure 3-7, or the tree that changes seasons as you turn it in your hand. These examples showcase how original and compelling art can be when it's not only made but also viewed in VR.

Figure 3-7. Zooming in progression of VR artist Goro Fujita's Worlds in Worlds, painted in Quill from Facebook

The animation in particular is really where Quill shines and allows a generation of 2D artists and animators to work in 3D in a very familiar way with really magical results. In only three weeks, Fujita was able to make a beautiful six-minute animated short called *Beyond the Fence*. The visual look and feel of animations made in Quill have a very organic feel much closer to 2D animation but exist in 3D to create something original and special that will have long-term impact on visual storytelling that we have yet to fully comprehend. But virtual painting is just one approach to creating virtual art. Another approach, more based on sculpting, was also being worked on by another team at Oculus Story Studio, and it would become known as Medium (Figure 3-8).

Figure 3-8. Oculus Medium promotional art from Oculus

Oculus Medium was actually being worked on long before Quill. Whereas virtual painting was about allowing traditional 2D artists to work in 3D, virtual sculpting was more about allowing traditional 3D artists to work in 3D. With virtual sculpting, the artist is always working with 3D volume in a very organic way, shaping and forming virtual clay and then applying color and texture to it. As Figure 3-9 illustrates, this allows for the creation of 3D models that were closer to what is familiar to the existing 3D production pipelines and could more readily be converted to 3D polygon geometry for use in games and movies or even 3D printed into the real world. During its infancy the program still required some processing and refinement, but even in the early stages, it was very clear how much easier it would be for so many people to create 3D objects in this way over the traditional non-VR 3D applications. Now it's being used in concept art; prototyping; architectural, product, and toy design; and even final game and movie assets. Using Medium speeds up design iteration time, reducing preproduction on projects by as much as 80% according to the Oculus Medium team. But, again, where VR tools like Medium really make the difference is by empowering artists who traditionally wouldn't create 3D objects with non-VR tools to now make 3D intuitively.

Figure 3-9. VR artist working on a 3D sculpt in Oculus Medium (image from Oculus (http://bit.ly/2HuMIsB))

VR for Animation

VR isn't just great for making 3D art; VR is transformative for bringing that art to life, as well. Similar to traditional 3D art creation, traditional 3D animation relied on moving and manipulating 3D points in 3D space but with a 2D interface on a 2D display. With VR, there is now the opportunity to reimagine this workflow to be more natural and intuitive. One approach would be to treat the 3D objects like real physical objects in the real world and take an approach similar to stop motion animation in the real world. VR animation programs like Tvori take just such an approach. But for character animation, which is typically the most complex and time consuming to do, VR has an even better trick up its sleeve.

Motion capture is a technique of putting motion trackers on an actor and then using cameras to capture the motion performance of that actor and then applying that to a 3D model for lifelike character animation. This technique has been used for animation in games and movies for decades but requires expensive equipment and a lot of clean up. For VR to work, the computer must properly track the users' heads and hands. This makes VR by default a very rudimentary motion capture system that costs a tenth or less the cost of a full motion-capture setup.

The makers of VR animation program, Mindshow, recognized this and that anyone with a VR headset could potentially do some basic character animation and become a storyteller. Now, instead of drawing thousands of drawings or spending days moving points around on screen, an animator can just act out a scene like an actor would on set. Likewise, that same actor could then go in and act out another part, working with the recording. This shortcuts basic animation by transforming a process that would normally take a week to accomplish down to mere minutes, and allow even one person to be an animation studio. Although the quality is not at Hollywood levels yet, even at the early stage, the results are impressive and promising. This process is one of the main reasons why Mindshow, depicted in Figure 3-10, was nominated for an Emmy Award for Outstanding Innovation in Interactive Media in 2018.

Figure 3-10. An animator acting out a performance in VR translated onto a digital character in real-time with Mindshow

In the past three years, it has been amazing to watch how VR has transformed how art is both viewed and created. There is a language of spatial storytelling that we are just beginning to explore thanks to the developers making amazing tools like Tilt Brush, Quill, Medium, Mindshow, and others. This especially includes the important works and artists who have wielded these tools in order to create art. At first, a lot of the art seemed to mirror what we have seen before, but we are already getting glimpses of things unique for the medium, and I personally can't wait to see where we go from here.

VR has democratized 3D creation in the same manner as the desktop computer democratized 2D creation. Now, people who never considered themselves to be traditional artists can join in the conversation of shaping the future of the visual and spatial arts. With VR, anyone can create a warehouse-sized installation piece that would have costs tens of thousands in materials alone. But, even better, now they can create a planet-sized installation piece that wouldn't be possible in the real world. VR is truly the ultimate canvas, not just for empowering artists, but by igniting the artist in everyone to create works limited only by their imaginations.

CHAPTER 4

3D Art Optimization

Jazmin Cano

Introduction

In this chapter, I cover why optimization is an immense challenge when it comes to developing assets for virtual reality (VR) and augmented reality (AR), with a heavy focus on the side of VR. I share different approaches and thought processes to consider in various areas involved in creating 3D art. Instead of focusing on specific tools, techniques, and tutorials, you will see an overall view of what you can do to optimize your 3D art. I share why it is important to really keep optimization as a high priority in the entire design process.

Let's begin by talking about why optimization for VR is new to most artists who are beginning to work with VR content.

A typical 2D LCD monitor has a refresh rate of 60 Hz. When you look at a flat monitor running at this rate, you will have a fantastic visual experience. This has allowed for traditional asset development to be "heavy," with heavy in this circumstance meaning that assets have higher *poly counts* and larger *texture images*, along with the scene itself having a higher quantity of *models* to view.

Head-mounted displays (HMDs) run at 90 Hz. To have a comfortable and convincing experience, VR content needs to run at 90 frames per second (FPS). If your experiences run lower than 90 FPS, you risk causing your users discomfort. Discomfort can include headaches, nausea, and eye pain. This will result in a subpar experience that users will want to leave quickly. Because of this high level of discomfort, you should not force users into a low-frame-rate experience.

Soon, VR is going to enter other fields. Instead of simply making VR, you will be making tools, experiences, apps, and so on in a field, and VR is your medium. Some of these fields will already be familiar with creating 3D content, and optimization will be important to learn. There will be multiple individuals whose background experience might not have prepared them properly for this major change in asset development, and it will be a challenge to acclimate to these new processes. Here are some examples of industry-related positions that will need to learn to create with optimization in mind:

- High-resolution rendering (creating realistic models of real objects)
- High-end games for PCs
- In-VR art creation

These examples have benefits that will no longer be something that can be taken advantage of for VR and AR. Excluding high-end tethered headsets like the Oculus Rift or HTC Vive, most other devices out there will be lighter and more portable. You must keep in mind that the bigger your files are and the more content and draw calls there are, the closer you will get to risking the user having a poor performance.

Individuals creating content for film and rendering have the privilege to create 3D models with high poly counts. They aren't limited to the complexity their models could have or the amount of rendering data required for the computer to visualize them. Following is an example of what can occur when someone new to optimization attempts to develop for VR:

Create a 3D Model of a Camera

Delivered model
  High-poly camera model with high-resolution textures (4096 x 4096 texture)

Problem
  he model is taking most of the scene's poly count budget, so the rest of the content quality must be sacrificed. If the rest of the content needs to keep its current quality and size, you run into performance issues. The developer will need to balance which art has lower priority and make more room for the high-poly camera model.

But why is this such a large problem for the developer? If the person's background is creating models to be rendered for photos, they're most likely used to creating with high poly counts. It is not uncommon to see high numbers ranging from 50,000 triangles (called "tris" within the industry) to 1,000,000 triangles.

This however does not translate well over to real-time VR rendering. As stated earlier, the performance issues will prevent the end user from having a quality experience.

Options to Consider

Here are a couple of things to try to solve the problem:

- Running a decimation tool to autoreduce the poly count.

  You can find these in popular 3D modeling software. They usually do a good job of removing 50% of the triangle count without it affecting the shape and silhouette of the model.

- Take a look at the layout of the model's UVs (the axes of the 2D texture that's being projected onto a 3D).

  Is the UV texture laid out to take advantage of the entire square space? Are the UVs to scale and prioritizing the areas that need the most detail to be shown? We explore textures and materials in more detail later in the chapter.

Another good option to contemplate on is whether your model will enter a social VR place that permits user-generated content (UGC)? This will most likely continue to be a challenge for a long time. Keep in mind that the more avatars there are in a space, the less of a budget each person should have to respect everyone's frame rate, allowing for a good experience.

Ideal Solution

The best solution is to reduce the model's triangle count to the absolute minimum that it can have without affecting the shape. Reduce the texture size to the smallest size it can have without forcing the model to be blurry or having a lesser quality than preferred.

Make sure when the object is placed in its final environment that it allows enough leeway for the system's frame rate in order for the experience to feel natural.

Let's recap. Why is it important to optimize your 3D art?

Every model in your 3D environment is going to affect your experience's performance. The more you add, the more you will need to consider how close you are getting to your budget. Talk with your team to determine what your ideal budget is.

Another consideration for where your 3D models are going includes social VR platforms. There are some social VR platforms out there that are built with UGC. You'll most likely exist in these spaces as an avatar, and if you're able to customize your avatar, remember that everything you learn here applies there, as well. Like with the rest of what you'll learn here, try to keep everything about your avatar and what you're wearing low poly and with the smallest number of draw calls that you can create. You might run into filters that help lower how much you're making people download, but think ahead to what you're asking people's screens to render. Be mindful of their hardware and connection and keep yourself easy to render and download.

Let's continue with a comprehensive overview of what you will need to check for when making 3D models for VR and AR.

Poly count budget

Do you have a concrete number of polygons that you cannot pass in a scene? Do you have a limit of poly count per model?

Always look for the number of triangles. The count of faces won't always be accurate for gauging how many polys you have on your model. A face made up of four vertices, such as a square, is actually two triangles in one.

Delete any faces that will never be seen. If you are creating a street environment in which the interiors of the buildings will never be entered, the scene will need only building facades. The backs of the walls and interiors are not needed. If you are using content that has already been built, you can delete everything that won't be seen.

If you are working on 3D models that will stay far from you in the experience, they don't need all of the details you'd probably want were they closer. Doors and windows can be modeled and textured with less detail. The lower your poly count is, the better.

The following sections present some things to keep in mind when modeling.

Topology

Inspect the edge loops and spot any edge loops that do not contribute anything more to the shape. If an edge is running across a flat area, you would know that it's not needed if you delete the entire edge and spot no difference in the silhouette. If it still holds up the shape and has the desired curve, you're on your way to reducing poly count. There are even some areas where you can bring in edges to merge with others. Double-check that all of the removed edge loops did not leave any vertices behind, and delete those vertices that aren't connecting any edges.

Figures 4-1 through 4-4 show the process of creating a gaming console. In Figure 4-1, you can see, in wireframe mode, the start of its creation using edge loops to define where more geometry will be needed; there are two steps between reducing polygons and the final version in Figure 4-4, which results in fewer triangles than its first pass.

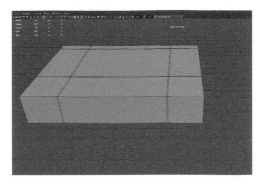

Figure 4-1. First pass on the game console: basic shapes established; triangle count: 140

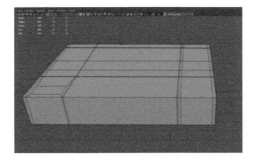

Figure 4-2. Second pass on the game console: defining where faces and edges will lift and curve; triangle count: 292

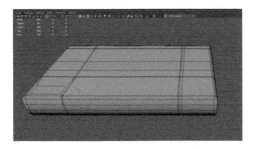

Figure 4-3. Third pass on the game console: softening edges and beginning to think about edge removal; triangle count: 530

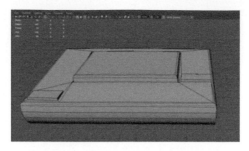

Figure 4-4. Fourth and final version: removed edges that didn't contribute to the model's shape; triangle count: 136

The process shown in Figures 4-1 through 4-4 is similar to the process taken to model a few more assets for this gaming console set. Figure 4-5 depicts the result of the set. It contains several models in one combined mesh that is ready to have the textures applied to them. Together, they will share one texture atlas. Later in this chapter, you will see how the texture atlas looks.

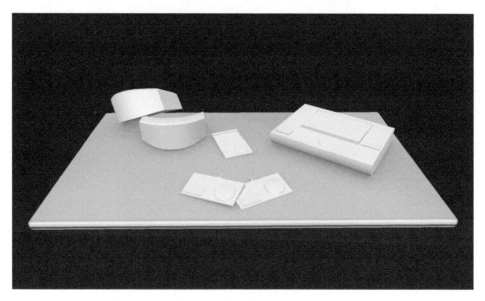

Figure 4-5. A look at the assets before they receive their materials

Here are a few more things to keep in mind when modeling:

- Avoid *n-gons*. An *n*-gon is a face that has more than four sides. Most engines have issues with *n*-gons. They can cause issues with collision, they might be rendered completely wrong, and they can also even be invisible. 3D modeling software such as Autodesk's Maya provides you with an option to clean up the scene and remove any *n*-gons that are found.

- Run a cleanup using your modeling software to find and remove all coplanar faces. You might often find sneaky faces hidden within a clone of itself, which will appear invisible to the naked eye and will increase your poly count. There is also the issue of *z-fighting*. Z-fighting is when there are two faces occupying the same 3D space.

- Turn on a viewer to ensure that the normals are facing in the direction that is intended. Normals will be rendered from one direction in your preferred engine, so don't let 3D modeling software fool you with two-sided rendering.

It's important to think about all of these considerations at the very beginning before you start working on a 3D model.

Figure 4-6 presents an example of an optimization project that I personally worked on. I was given a 3D model of glasses that comprised 69,868 triangles. This amount totaled more than my avatar itself, which is around 40,000, including the body, clothing, hair, and accessories. The glasses were purchased from an online store selling files of 3D models, and it was clear that the artist created this with the intention to show that they can model to match what the object is like in "real life." The artist hand-modeled each and every piece, including hinges for the temples.

Because I was going to create these glasses for people to wear in a social VR platform, I knew that most of the detail was neither going to be seen nor needed, so I deleted a lot of those pieces. I managed to preserve the look of the glasses while deleting and redirecting most edge loops. The finished result was just under 1,000 triangles.

Figure 4-6. A glasses model for use in a social VR space

Specifically, for AR use, getting it under 1,000 triangles would be an absolute must. On a Hololens, for example, you will want to aim for a maximum of about 60,000 triangles in an entire scene. Unless the application focuses heavily on inspecting a realistically detailed pair of sunglasses, you would want to reduce them all the way down like I did in this example. Figure 4-7 presents a close-up showing the hard edges you can see around the rounded parts of the frames, which are unnoticeable if looked at from a distance.

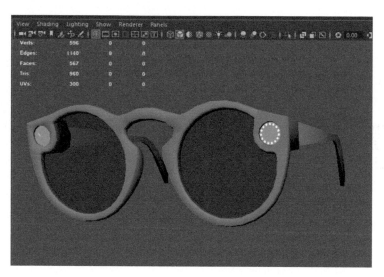

Figure 4-7. Example of hard edges around the rounded parts of the frames

Baking

Another trick you can do to help your poly count is by *baking* your high-poly model's details into a lower-poly model. By doing so, you can generate a normal map that will trick viewers into seeing height and depth that is not present on the geometry itself.

Now that we've covered a lot of what goes into a model, let's talk about UV unwrapping and texture painting.

UVs are used to describe a 3D model on a flat plane. Those UVs reference a texture that the model uses in order to have color and material information mapped accordingly. For optimization, let's go over the approach to texture creation that is created, with the goal being to keep the draw call count low. (More on draw calls later.)

A *texture atlas* is a texture image that contains data describing what the materials are made up of. It's always better to create a texture atlas because it drastically reduces the number of draw calls.

Figure 4-8 demonstrates a robot avatar that is made up of many pieces, has been merged into one mesh, and has its UVs shared within the one space, all unwrapped and ready to be textured.

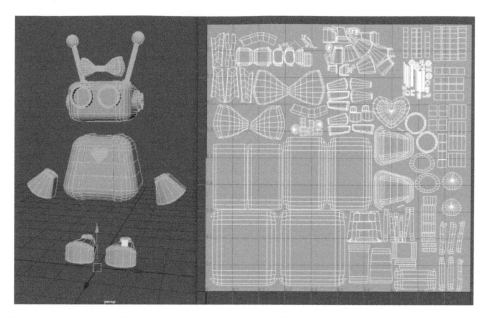

Figure 4-8. These are the pieces that comprise the robot and its accompanying textures

There is one area on this model that I wanted to keep higher resolution: the detail on the eyes. The model itself is flat; however, I gave it a texture map of one eye that was shared across both flat, circular meshes. The detail on the flat 2D image tricks the viewer into thinking that there could be more depth than there really is.

If I had included it in the texture atlas, I would have needed to increase the texture size and make the rest of the UVs much smaller because the detail on the pupil and the highlights on the eyes were more important, requiring more UV space.

Instead, the UVs of an eye mesh take up the entire UV space in the quadrant for the eye texture. The submesh shows all of the details that the eyes need. That same sub-mesh is then duplicated to the other socket because there is no neeed for unique details to differentiate between the eyes. Figure 4-9 shows the areas of the UVs that are shared on the small texture for the eyes.

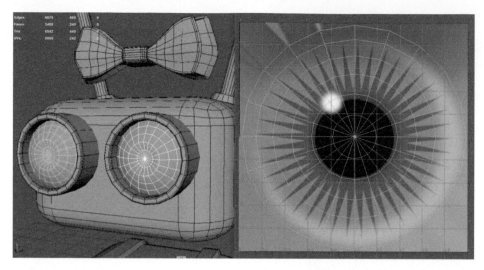

Figure 4-9. The robot model's eye shares the same UVs, duplicated before combining into a single mesh

For more realistic art styles, you will still need to keep the poly count on the lower side; however, you can keep the quality of the models high by using physically based shaders and rendering. This robot model uses physically based rendering (PBR) to have a realistic look, as illustrated in Figure 4-10. PBR uses realistic lighting models and surface values that represents real materials.

Figure 4-10. A look at the robot with all of its PBR materials

Let's go over some PBR textures that I used on the robot model as an example. Hopefully this helps you to understand how PBR will work on models for your VR experience.

Remember the gaming console models that we looked at earlier in this chapter? Figures 4-11 through 4-13 show the texture atlas used for that set; notice the individual textures used for its PBR material.

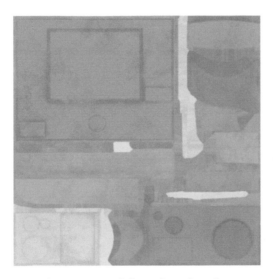

Figure 4-11. A color map where texture defines the colors that are represented on the model

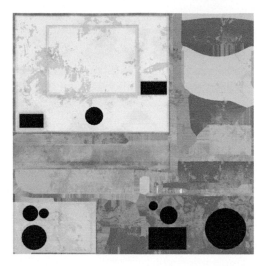

Figure 4-12. A roughness map where texture defines the surface of the model, ranging from smooth to rough

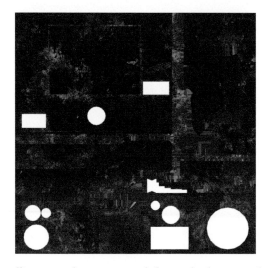

Figure 4-13. The metallic map where texture defines whether a surface is metallic

Figures 4-14 through 4-17 show a final look at the 3D models within the program they were painted in, Allegorithmic Substance Painter, and showing how they look in VR within the social VR application, High Fidelity.

Figure 4-14. A look at the gaming systems, combined into one mesh using one material that uses PBR textures to define the color and surface

Figure 4-15. These controllers show the high contrast that the texture uses to define metallic and nonmetallic surfaces

Figure 4-16. This gaming system has more roughness information on the nonmetallic parts, showing grime and dirt

Figure 4-17. Here is their final version located in a large-scale virtual art gallery where the models float in a sky

There are other types of texture maps such as *normal, bump,* and *ambient occlusion* maps. They each play a role in defining the look of the model whether it's faking depth or creating shadows. Spend some time experimenting with these texture maps and find what your models need.

Now that you've seen how you can create texture atlases, we next talk about why it's important to make them as we examine draw calls.

Draw Calls

A *draw call* is a function that results in rendering the objects on your screen. The CPU works with the graphics processing unit (GPU) to draw every object using information about the mesh, its textures, shaders, and so on. You should always work toward having the smallest number of draw calls possible because having too many will cause a reduction in frame rate.

To lower how many draw calls you have, follow these guidelines:

- Combine all of the submeshes of your model into one combined mesh.
- Create a texture atlas for all of the UVs in the model.
- Give your mesh the fewest number of materials possible that uses all of the textures the model or models need.

Think of any of your favorite VR experiences and picture all of the 3D models that make up those scenes. Each and every one of those contribute to draw call counts in one way or another. They always add up. If this context is experienced in social VR, also consider how many people will experience rendering everything in your scenes, as well.

As we get close to the end of this chapter, I want to restate that it is important to keep optimization a high priority in the entire design process—from the start of a model to the completed textures. Keep numbers and sizes small without having to sacrifice everything you wanted for your VR content.

Using VR Tools for Creating 3D Art

At this juncture, you might be wondering why thus far this chapter has been focused on 3D artwork created on a 2D screen if we are talking about VR here. Although we are seeing a lot of options for artwork creation arise with many tools available (such as Tiltbush, Medium, Unbound, Quill, and Google Blocks), traditional manipulation of 3D assets will be done on programs meant for 2D viewers.

It's not much different when it comes to having a model that needs optimizing. Currently, it is not surprising to export a considerable amount of content from these programs. The magical feeling of creating art in a 3D space around you comes from the content coming out as expected. This means that a lot of the geometry is created with enough edge loops to give you the expected curves. Several materials might also be used to make the piece extremely colorful and bright. What you make with these programs will most likely need to be optimized if being added to a space with more content that will need to be drawn on your screen.

No matter what program you use, even if you find tools that will help optimize the assets used for your immersive experience, it will most likely require creators and designers to make the choices to ensure sizes, counts, and quality are acceptable for the experience. An appropriate balance will always be required, no matter what medium is used to create this content.

Acquiring 3D Models Versus Making Them from Scratch

Be careful when purchasing models from online stores. Take into consideration how long ago the model was made. Do you think it was made with VR in mind? Will you need to clean up the model and optimize it for your use? Does the time you might need to spend on it cost less than your time creating one from scratch? Purchasing 3D models can be fast and easy, but it can affect your performance later on and take up a large amount of time to modify it so that it performs well.

Following is a list of what to look for in an item's listing and what questions you should ask when downloading a 3D model from places like Poly, Turbosquid, CGTrader, and so on (if you don't see any of the information listed, be very cautious and plan for inconvenience):

- Poly count
- Is this an appropriate number of triangles?

- If the model is good but high poly, how much time will you spend reducing the poly count and cleaning up the geometry to make the asset VR-ready?
- Texture maps.
- Is the model textured in an optimized way, using a texture atlas?
- If there are several separate texture maps, do you think the time it will take to optimize them is acceptable?
- Are the texture files in a format supported by the engine that will be rendering it?
- What are the texture file sizes? Beware of textures larger than 2,048, especially if a texture that large is for a model that will be small in scale. Also, look for small textures if what you want is higher resolution on some models.
- File format.
- Are you buying files you can work with?
- Do your programs support opening and editing of the models?

Always test the appearance of your model. Drop it into your engine of choice and see it in VR or AR for yourself. You will be surprised by how different scale feels when you are immersed by it.

Summary

In this chapter, you looked at different approaches and thought processes to consider in various areas involved in creating 3D art. It will take time and practice to learn how to optimize 3D art, so make sure optimization is always kept a high priority during the entire design process. You might be an artist new to creating for VR or AR. You might be a developer learning about areas other people work in. You might be a producer who is curious about the artists' pipeline. I'm glad you made it this far to learn about the importance of optimization because it is an immense challenge when it comes to developing assets for VR and AR. Everyone working on immersive experiences should know about the challenging work that goes into asset creation.

With technology changing rapidly, some of the techniques or programs you looked at in this chapter might be irrelevant in the near future, so it is important to remember the reasons behind these methods. As mentioned earlier, it is important to keep people comfortable in your experiences. Make sure to be mindful and keep that frame rate high with optimized art!

PART III

Hardware, SLAM, Tracking

The augmented reality (AR) user experience is compelling and often feels like magic. At its best, though, you shouldn't even notice it at all. The better AR system designers do their job, the less you notice their work, and you can focus on the content and interactions that help you to achieve what you wanted to do in AR in the first place. Solving the technical problems to achieve this is a very difficult problem; huge progress has been made, but many problems remain to be solved. This section aims to help explain how everything under the hood works, how we got here, and how to make choices as to where to invest your energy going forward. Hopefully, this chapter helps to clarify why, when the system seems to break on you, what's going on, and give you some clues on how to design around that. For the next few years, building AR apps is going to heavily depend on how AR developers build products that work within the constraints of the systems while the system builders work to eliminate those constraints.

We cover the core technology underpinning all AR systems, *simultaneous localization and mapping* (SLAM), and why that's a broad term that doesn't really help explain anything! We address the components that go into a SLAM system and the limitations of these, plus we look at how some of these limitations (e.g., SLAM maps that are bigger than one device can handle) are being solved via the AR cloud to enable experiences like shared content, persistent content, and semantic understanding of the world while virtual content can physically interact with the physical world.

We touch on some of the differences between ARKit, ARCore, and spatial mapping–based systems like 6D.ai, Magic Leap, and Hololens.

Apple's announcement of ARKit at WWDC 2017 has had a huge impact on the AR ecosystem. Developers are finding that for the first time a robust and widely available AR software development kit (SDK) "just works" for their apps. There's no need to fiddle around with markers or initialization or depth cameras or proprietary creation tools. Unsurprisingly, this has led to a boom in demonstrations (follow @madewitharkit on twitter for the latest). However, most developers don't know how ARKit works or why it works better than other SDKs. Looking "under the hood" of ARKit will help us to understand the limits of ARKit today, what is still needed and why, and help predict when similar capabilities will be available on Android and head-mounted displays HMDs; either virtual reality (VR) or AR.

 I've seen people refer to ARKit as SLAM, or use the term SLAM to refer to tracking. For clarification, treat SLAM as a pretty broad term; like, for example "multimedia." Tracking itself is a more general term, whereas odometry is more specific, but they are close enough in practice with respect to AR. It can be confusing. There are lots of ways to do SLAM, and tracking is only one component of a comprehensive SLAM system. ARKit was launched as a "lite" or simple SLAM system. As of this writing, Tango or Hololens' SLAM systems have a greater number of features beyond odometry, like more sophisticated mapping, 3D reconstructions, and support for depth sensors.

The term "AR cloud" has really caught on since my Super Ventures (*http://bit.ly/2ChCpoi*) partner Ori (*http://bit.ly/2TOp5Sk*) and I (*http://bit.ly/2Hx888z*) wrote two blogs on the topic. We've seen it applied to a great number of "cloudy" ideas that have some AR angle to them, but to me it specifically refers to the infrastructure to enable AR systems to connect with one another and to the larger world in general, not to the content.

CHAPTER 5

How the Computer Vision That Makes Augmented Reality Possible Works

Victor Prisacariu and Matt Miesnieks

Who Are We?

My name is Matt Miesnieks, and I'm the CEO of a startup called 6D.ai (*http://6d.ai/*), which is a spinoff of the Oxford University Active Vision Lab, where my cofounder, Professor Victor Prisacariu, supervises one of the world's best AR computer vision research groups. I've spent 10 years working on AR, as a founder (Dekko), investor (Super Ventures), and executive (Samsung, Layar). I have an extensive background in software infrastructure in smartphones (Openwave) and Wireline (Ascend Communications), as an engineer and sales vice president.

At 6D.ai, we are thinking slightly differently to everyone else about AR. We are solving the most difficult technical problems and exposing the solutions via developer APIs for customers with the most challenging AR problems. We are independent and cross-platform, and we sell usage of our APIs, not advertising based on our customer data. We believe that persistence is foundational, and you can't have persistence without treating privacy seriously. And to treat privacy seriously, it means that personally identifiable information (PII) cannot leave the device (unless explicitly allowed by the user). This creates a much more difficult technical problem to solve because it means building and searching a large SLAM map on-device, and in real time. This is technically easy-ish to do with small maps and anchors, but it's very, very difficult to do with large maps. And when I say small, I mean half a room, and large means bigger than a big house.

Fortunately, we have the top AR research group from the Oxford Active Vision Lab behind 6D.ai, and we built our system on a next-generation 3D reconstruction and relocalizer algorithms and neural networks, taking advantage of some as-yet unpublished research. The goal for all of this was to get multiplayer and persistent AR as close as possible to a "just works" user experience (UX), where nothing needs to be explained, and an end user's intuition about how the AR content should behave is correct. Here's what's special about how 6D.ai does AR:

- We do all the processing on-device and in real time. We use the cloud for persistent map storage and some offline data merging and cleanup.

- Maps are built in the background while the app is running. Updates from all users are merged into a single map, vastly improving the coverage of the space.

- The anchors and maps have no PII and are stored permanently in our cloud. Every time any 6D.ai powered app uses that physical space, the anchor grows and improves the coverage of that space. This minimizes and eventually eliminates any need to prescan a space.

- Maps are available to all apps. Every user benefits from every other user of a 6D.ai app.

- Our map data cannot be reverse engineered into a human-readable visual image.

- Our anchors greatly benefit from cloud storage and merging, but there is no dependency on the cloud for the UX to work. Unlike Google's system, we can work offline, or in a peer-to-peer environment, or a private/secure environment (or China).

It's a very small world. Not many people can build these systems well.

A Brief History of AR

Following is a summary of the key players who brought AR to consumer quality:

- Visual inertial odometry invented at Intersense in the early 2000s by Leonid Naimark → Dekko → Samsung → FB and Magic Leap and Tesla

- FlyBy VIO → Tango *and* Apple

- Oxford Active Vision Lab → George Klein (PTAM) → Microsoft

- Microsoft (David Nister) → Tesla

- Oxford → Gerhard Reitmeir → Vuforia

- Oxford → Gabe Sibley → Zoox

- Oxford + Cambridge + Imperial College → Kinect → Oculus and ML (Richard Newcomb, David Molyneux)

- Vuforia → Eitan Pilipski → Snap

- FlyBy/Vuforia → Daqri

One fascinating and underappreciated aspect of how great-quality AR systems are built is that there are literally only a handful of people in the world who can build them. The interconnected careers of these engineers have resulted in the best systems converging on monocular visual inertial odometry (VIO) as "the solution" for mobile tracking. No other approach delivers the UX (today).

VIO was first implemented at Boston, Massachusetts–based military/industrial supplier Intersense in the early 2000s. One of the coinventors, Leonid Naimark was the chief scientist at my startup, Dekko, in 2011. After Dekko proved that VIO could not deliver a consumer UX on an iPad 2 due to sensor limitations, Leonid went back to military contracting, but Dekko's CTO, Pierre Georgel, is now a senior engineer on the Google Daydream team. Around the same time, Ogmento was founded by my Super Ventures partner, Ori Inbar. Ogmento became FlyBy and the team there successfully built a VIO system on IOS using an add-on fish-eye camera. This codebase was licensed to Google, which developed into the VIO system for Tango. Apple later bought FlyBy, and the same codebase is the core of ARKit VIO. The CTO of FlyBy, Chris Broaddus, went on to build the tracker for Daqri, which is now at an autonomous robotics company, with the former chief scientist of Zoox, Gabe Sibley. Gabe did his post-doctoral work at Oxford (along with my cofounder at 6D.ai, who currently leads the Active Vision Lab).

The first mobile SLAM system (PTAM) was developed around 2007 at the Oxford Active Computing Lab by Georg Klein, who went on to build the VIO system for Hololens, along with Christopher Mei (another Oxford Active Vision graduate) and David Nister, who left to build the autonomy system at Tesla. Georg obtained his PhD at Cambridge, from where his colleague Gerhard Reitmayr went on to Vuforia to work on the development of Vuforia's SLAM and VIO systems. Vuforia's development was led by Daniel Wagner, who then took over from Chris Broaddus (ex-FlyBy) as chief scientist at Daqri. The engineering manager of Vuforia, Eitan Pilipski, is now leading AR software engineering at Snap, working with Qi Pan, who studied at Cambridge alongside Gerhard and Georg, and then went to Vuforia. Qi now leads an AR team at Snap in London with Ed Rosten (another Cambridge graduate, who developed the FAST feature detector used in most SLAM systems).

Key members of the research teams at Oxford, Cambridge (e.g., David Molyneaux) and Imperial College (Professor Andy Davison's lab, where Richard Newcombe, Hauke Strasdat, and others studied) further developed D-SLAM and extended the Kinect tracking systems, and now lead tracking teams at Oculus and Magic Leap. Metaio was also an early key innovator around SLAM (drawing on expertise from TU Munich, where Pierre Georgel studied), many of the engineers are now at Apple, but their R&D lead, Selim Benhimane, studied alongside Pierre and then went to develop SLAM for Intel RealSense, and is now at Apple.

Interestingly I'm not aware of any current AR startups working in the AR tracking domain led by engineering talent from this small talent pool. Founders from backgrounds in Robotics or other types of computer vision haven't been able to demonstrate systems that work robustly in a wide range of environments.

How and Why to Select an AR Platform

There are many platforms to choose from in AR, ranging from mobile AR to PCAR. Here are some technical considerations to keep in mind when starting to develop for AR.

I'm a Developer, What Platform Should I Use and Why?

You can begin developing your AR idea on whatever phone on which you have access to ARKit. It works and you probably already have a phone that supports it. Learn the *huge* difference in designing and developing an app that runs in the real world where you don't control the scene versus smartphone and VR apps, for which you control every pixel.

Then, move onto a platform like Magic Leap, 6D.ai, or Hololens that can spatially map the world. Now learn what happens when your content can interact with the 3D structure of the uncontrolled scene.

Going from one to the other is a *really steep* learning curve. Steeper, in fact, than from web to mobile or from mobile to VR. You need to completely rethink how apps work and what UX or use cases make sense. I'm seeing lots of ARKit demonstrations that I saw five years ago built on Vuforia, and four years before that on Layar. Developers are relearning the same lessons, but at much greater scale. I've seen examples of pretty much every type of AR apps over the years, and am happy to give feedback and support. Just reach out.

I would encourage developers not to be afraid of building novelty apps. Fart apps were the first hit on smartphones—also it's very challenging to find use cases that give utility via AR on handheld see-through form-factor hardware.

Performance Is Statistics

When first working with AR or most any computer vision system, it can be frustrating because sometimes it will work fine in one place, but in another place it will work terribly. AR systems never "work" or "don't work." It's always a question of whether things work well enough in a wide enough range of situations. Getting "better" ultimately is a matter of nudging the statistics further in your favor.

For this reason, *never* trust a demonstration of an AR app, especially if it's been shown to be amazing on YouTube. There is a *huge* gap between something that works amazingly well in a controlled or lightly staged environment and one that barely works at all for regular use. This situation just doesn't exist for smartphone or VR app demonstrations.

Let's summarize this:

- *Always* demonstrate or test a system in the real world. There's a *huge* gap between controlled and uncontrolled scenes. *Never* trust a demonstration video.
- What does work well mean?
  — No detectable user motion for init
  — Instant convergence
  — Metric scale <2% error
  — No jitter
  — No drift
  — Low power
  — Low BOM cost
  — Hundreds of meters of range with <1% drift (prior to loop closure)
  — Instant loop closures
  — Loop closure from wide range or angles
  — Low-featured scenes (e.g., sky, white walls)
  — Variably lit scenes/low light
  — Repetitive or reflective scenes

Here's a specific technical description of why statistics end up determining how well a system works. Figure 5-1 depicts a grid that represents the digital image sensor in your camera. Each box is a pixel. For tracking to be stable, each pixel should match a corresponding point in the real world (assuming that the device is perfectly still). However, the second image shows that photons are not that accommodating, and various intensities of light fall wherever they want, and each pixel is just the total of the photons that hit it. Any change in the light in the scene (a cloud passes the sun, the flicker of a fluorescent light, etc.) changes the makeup of the photons that hit the sensor, and now the sensor has a different pixel corresponding to the real-world point. As far as the visual tracking system is concerned, you have moved!

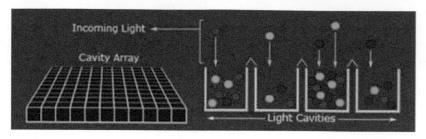

Figure 5-1. Everything to do with computer vision performance is a matter of statistics; it's the real world that isn't binary

This is the reason why when you see the points in the various ARKit demonstrations, they flicker on and off; the system must decide which points are "reliable" or not reliable. Then, it needs to triangulate from those points to calculate the pose, averaging out the calculations to get the best estimate of what your actual pose is. So, any work that can be done to ensure that statistical errors are removed from this process results in a more robust system. This requires tight integration and calibration between the camera hardware stack (multiple lenses and coatings, shutter and image sensor specifications, etc.) and the inertial measurement unit (IMU) hardware and the software algorithms.

If you're a developer, you should always test your app in a range of scenes and lighting conditions. If you thought dealing with Android fragmentation was bad, wait until you try to test against everything that might happen in the real world.

Integrating Hardware and Software

Interestingly, VIO isn't that difficult to get working; there are a number of algorithms published and quite a few implementations exist. But, it's *very* difficult to get it working well. By that I mean the inertial and optical systems converge almost instantly onto a stereoscopic map, and metric scale can be determined with low single-digit levels of accuracy. The implementation we built at Dekko, for example, required that the user made specific motions initially and then moved the phone back and forth for about 30 seconds before it converged. To build a great inertial tracking system requires experienced engineers. Unfortunately, there are literally only about 20 engineers on Earth with the necessary skills and experience, and most of them work building cruise-missile tracking systems, or Mars rover navigation systems, or other nonconsumer mobile applications.

As Figure 5-2 illustrates, everything still depends on having the hardware and software work in lockstep to best reduce errors. At its core, this means an IMU that can be accurately modeled in software, full access to the entire camera stack and detailed specifications of each component in the stack, and, most important, the IMU and camera need to be very precisely clock synchronized. The system needs to know exactly which IMU reading corresponds to the beginning of the frame capture, and which to the end. This is essential for correlating the two systems, and until recently was impossible because the hardware OEMs saw no reason to invest in this.

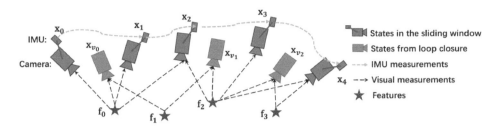

Figure 5-2. AR needs tight integration between software and hardware, which slowed down solutions on mobile phones

This was the reason why Dekko's iPad 2–based system took so long to converge. The first Tango Peanut phone was the first device to accurately clock synchronize everything, and it was the first consumer phone to offer great tracking. Today, the systems on chips from Qualcomm and others have a synchronized sensor hub for all the components to use, which means that VIO is viable on most current devices, with appropriate sensor calibration.

Because of this tight dependency on hardware and software, it has been almost impossible for a software developer to build a great system without deep support from the OEM to build appropriate hardware. Google invested a lot to get some OEMs to support the Tango hardware specification. Microsoft, Magic Leap, and others are building their own hardware, and it is ultimately why Apple has been so successful with ARKit, because it has been able to do both.

Optical Calibration

For the software to precisely correlate whether a pixel on the camera sensor matches a point in the real world, the camera system needs to be accurately calibrated. There are two types of calibration:

Geometric calibration
> This uses a *pinhole model* of a camera to correct for the Field of View of the lens and things like the barrel effect of a lens—basically, all the image warping due to the shape of the lens. Most software developers can do this step without OEM input by using a checkerboard and basic public camera specifications.

Photometric calibration
> This is a lot more involved and usually requires the OEMs involvement because it gets into the specifics of the image sensor itself, any coatings on internal lenses,

and so on. This calibration deals with color and intensity mapping. For example, telescope-attached cameras photographing far away stars need to know whether that slight change in light intensity on a pixel on the sensor is indeed a star, or just an aberration in the sensor or lens. The result of this calibration for an AR tracker is much higher certainty that a pixel on the sensor does match a real-world point, and thus the optical tracking is more robust with fewer errors.

In Figure 5-3, the picture of the various RGB photons falling into the bucket of a pixel on the image sensor illustrates the problem. Light from a point in the real world usually falls across the boundary of several pixels and each of those pixels will average the intensity across all the photons that hit it. A tiny change in user motion, a shadow in the scene, or a flickering fluorescent light will change which pixel best represents the real-world point. This is the error that all of these optical calibrations are trying to eliminate as best as possible.

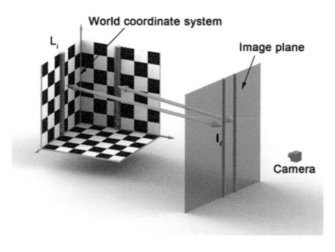

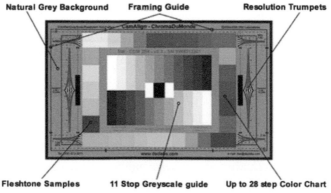

Figure 5-3. Optical calibration is critical for the system to know which pixel corresponds to a real-world point

Inertial Calibration

When thinking about the IMU (the combination of accelerometer and gyroscope in your device), it's important to remember it measures *acceleration*, not distance or velocity. Errors in the IMU reading accumulate over time, very quickly! The goal of calibration and modeling is to ensure the measurement of distance (double integrated from the acceleration) is accurate enough for X fractions of a second. Ideally, this is a long enough period to cover when the camera loses tracking for a couple of frames as the user covers the lens or something else happens in the scene.

Measuring distance using the IMU is called *dead reckoning*. It's basically a guess, but the guess is made accurate by modeling how the IMU behaves, finding all the ways it accumulates errors, and then writing filters to mitigate those errors. Imagine if you were asked to take a step and then guess how far you stepped in inches. A single step and guess would have a high margin of error. If you repeatedly took thousands of steps, measured each one and learned to allow for which foot you stepped with, the floor coverings, the shoes you were wearing, how fast you moved, how tired you were, and so on, your guess would eventually become very accurate. This is basically what happens with IMU calibration and modeling.

There are many sources of error. A robot arm is usually used to repeatedly move the device in exactly the same manner over and over, and the outputs from the IMU are captured and filters written until the output from the IMU accurately matches the *ground truth motion* from the robot arm. Google and Microsoft went so far as to send their devices up into microgravity on the International Space Station, or "zero gravity flights," to eliminate additional errors.

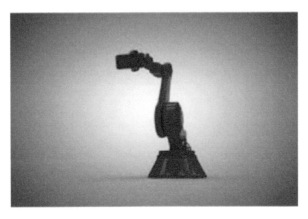

Figure 5-4. Inertial calibration is even more challenging and no use case ever needed it before (for consumer hardware)

This is even more difficult than it sounds to achieve real accuracy. Following are just a few of the accelerometer errors that must be identified from a trace such as the RGB lines in the graph shown in Figure 5-5:

Fixed bias
　　Nonzero acceleration measurement when zero acceleration is integrated

Scale factor errors
　　Deviation of actual output from mathematical model of output (typically nonlinear output)

Cross-coupling
　　Acceleration in direction orthogonal to the sensor measurement direction passed into sensor measurement (manufacturing imperfections, non-orthogonal sensor axes)

Vibro-pendulous error
　　Vibration in phase with the pendulum displacement (think of a child on a swing set)

Clock error
　　Integration period incorrectly measured

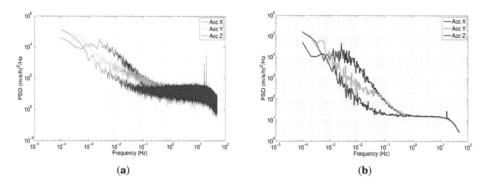

Figure 5-5. These are just a few of the errors that must be identified from a trace like the RGB lines in the graph

It's also challenging for an OEM to have to go through this process for all the devices in their portfolio, and even then, many devices might have different IMUs (e.g., a Galaxy 7 might have IMUs from Invensense or Bosch, and of course the modeling for the Bosch doesn't work for the Invensense, etc.). This is another area where Apple has an advantage over Android OEMs.

The Future of Tracking

So, if VIO is what works today, what's coming next and will it make ARKit redundant? Surprisingly, VIO will remain the best way to track over a range of several hundred meters (for longer than that, the system will need to relocalize using a combination of GPS fused into the system plus some sort of landmark recognition). The reason for this is that even if other optical-only systems become as accurate as VIO, they will still require more (graphics processing unit [GPU] or camera) power, which really matters in an HMD. Monocular VIO is the most accurate, lowest-power, lowest-cost solution.

Deep learning is really having an impact in the research community for tracking. So far, the deep learning–based systems are about 10% out with respect to errors, whereas a top VIO system is a fraction of a percent, but they are catching up and will really help with outdoor relocalization.

Depth cameras (Figure 5-6) can help a VIO system in a couple of ways. Accurate measurement of ground truth and metric scale and edge tracking for low-features scenes are the biggest benefits. However, they are very power hungry, so it makes sense to run them at only a very low frame rate and use VIO between frames. They also don't work outdoors because the background infrared scatter from sunlight washes out the infrared from the depth camera. Also, their range is dependent on their power consumption, which means that on a phone, very short range (a few meters). They are also expensive in terms of BOM cost, so OEMs will avoid them for high-volume phones.

Stereo RGB or fisheye lenses both help with being able to see a larger scene and thus potentially more optical features (e.g., a regular lens might see a white wall, but a fisheye could see the patterned ceiling and carpet in the frame, as well — Magic Leap and Hololens use this approach) and possibly getting depth information for a lower compute cost than VIO, although VIO does it just as accurately for lower BOM and power cost. Because the stereo cameras on a phone or even an HMD are close together, their accurate range is very limited for depth calculations (cameras a couple of centimeters apart can be accurate for depth up to a couple of meters).

The most interesting thing coming down the pipeline is support for tracking over much larger areas, especially outdoors for many kilometers. At this point, there is almost no difference between tracking for AR and tracking for self-driving cars, except AR systems do it with fewer sensors and lower power. Because eventually any device will run out of room trying to map large areas, a cloud-supported service is needed; Google recently announced the Tango Visual Positioning Service for this reason. We'll see more of these in the very near future. It's also a reason why everyone cares so much about 3D maps right now.

Figure 5-6. The future of tracking

The Future of AR Computer Vision

Six-degrees-of-freedom (6DOF) position tracking is already almost completely commoditized, across all devices; 2019 will see it ship as a default feature in mass-market chipsets and devices. But there are still things that need to be solved. Let's take a moment to examine them here as we look at the future of AR computer vision.

3D reconstruction (spatial mapping in Hololens terms or depth perception in Tango terms) is the system being able to figure out the shape or structure of real objects in a scene, as demonstrated in Figure 5-7. It's what allows the virtual content to collide into and hide behind (occlusion) the real world. It's also the feature that confuses people because they think this means AR is now "mixed" reality. It's always AR, it's just that most of the AR demonstrations that people have seen have no 3D reconstruction support, so the content appears to just move in front of all real-world objects. 3D reconstruction works by capturing a dense point-cloud from the scene (today using a depth camera) and then converting that into a mesh and feeding the "invisible" mesh into Unity (along with the real-world coordinates), and then placing the real-world mesh exactly on top of the real world as it appears in the camera. This means the virtual content appears to interact with the real world. As the 3D reconstructions become bigger, we need to figure out how to host them in the cloud and let multiple users share (and extend) the models.

 ARKit does a 2D version of this today by detecting 2D planes. This is the minimum that is needed. Without a ground plane, the Unity content literally wouldn't have a ground to stand on and would float around.

Figure 5-7. A large-scale 3D reconstruction

Figure 5-8 shows an early attempt to demonstrate occlusion by constructing a mesh using an iPad 2. It was the first app to demonstrate physical interactions between virtual content and the real world on commodity mobile hardware.

Figure 5-8. This app was built by the author's previous startup, Dekko

Figure 5-9 presents an example of 3D semantic segmentation of a scene. The source image is at the bottom. Above that is the 3D model (maybe built from stereo cameras, or LIDAR), and at the top is the segmentation via deep learning; now we can distinguish the sidewalk from the road. This is also useful for Pokémon Go so that Pokémon are not placed in the middle of a busy road.

Then, we need to figure out how to scale all this amazing technology to support multiple simultaneous users in real time. It's the ultimate Massively Multiplayer Online Roleplaying Game (MMORG, e.g., *World of Warcraft*, but for the real world).

Here are some other challenges that we need to address and solve:

- Everything up the stack
  - Rendering (coherence, performance)
  - Input
  - Optics
  - GUI and apps
  - Social factors

Figure 5-9. A large-scale 3D reconstruction

Mapping

Mapping is the "M" in SLAM. It refers to a data structure that the device keeps in memory that contains information about the 3D scene against which the tracker (a general term for the VIO system) can localize. To localize just means determining where in the map I am. If I blindfolded you and dropped you in the middle of a new city with a paper map, the process you go through of looking around, then looking at the map, then looking around again until you ascertain where you are on the map is the process of localizing yourself.

At its simplest level a SLAM map is a graph of 3D points that represent a sparse point-cloud, in which each point corresponds to coordinates of an *optical feature* in the scene (e.g., the corner of a table). They usually contain a considerable amount of extra metadata in there, as well, such as how "reliable" that point is, measured by how many frames has that feature been detected in the same coordinates recently (e.g., a black spot on my dog would not be marked reliable because the dog moves around). Some maps include "keyframes," which are just single frames of video (a photo, essentially) that is stored in the map every few seconds and used to help the tracker match the world to the map. Other maps use a dense point-cloud, which is more reliable but needs more GPUs and memory. ARCore and ARKit both use sparse maps (without keyframes, I think).

A sparse map might look something like the upper-right image in Figure 5-10. The upper left shows how feature points match the real world (colors are used to indicate how reliable that point is). The lower left is the source image, and the lower right is an intensity map, which can be used for a different type of SLAM system (semi-direct—which are very good by the way, but aren't yet in production SLAM systems like ARCore or ARKit).

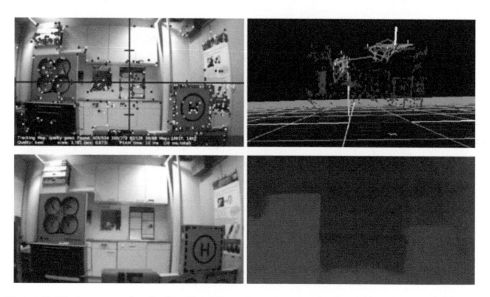

Figure 5-10. An example of what the AR system sees, overlaid on a human-readable image

So how does this work? When you launch an ARCore/ARKit app, the tracker checks to see whether there is a map predownloaded and ready to go (there never is in v1.0 of ARCore and ARKit). If there is none, the tracker initializes a new map by doing a stereo calculation, as I described earlier. This means that we now have a nice little 3D map of just what is in the camera's field of view. As you begin moving around and new parts of the background scene move into the field of view, more 3D points are added to the map and it becomes bigger. And bigger. And bigger.

This never used to be a problem because trackers were so bad that they'd drift away unusably before the map grew too large to manage. That isn't the case anymore, and managing the map is where much of the interesting work in SLAM is going on (along with deep learning and convolutional neural networks). ARKit uses a "sliding window" for its map, which means that it stores only a variable amount of the recent past (time and distance) in the map, and throws away anything old. The assumption is that you aren't going to ever need to relocalize against the scene from a while ago. ARCore manages a larger map, which means that the system should be more reliable.

So, the upshot is that with ARCore, even if you do lose tracking, it will recover better and you won't be affected.

ARCore and ARKit also use a clever concept called *anchors* to help make the map feel like it covers a larger physical area than it really does. I saw this concept first on Hololens, which, as usual, is a year or more ahead of everyone else. Normally, the system manages the map completely invisibly to the user or app developer. Anchors allow the developer to instruct the system to "remember this piece of the map around here, don't throw it away." The physical size of the anchor is around one square meter (that's a bit of a guess on my part; it is probably variable depending on how many optical features the system can see). It's enough for the system to relocalize against when this physical location is revisited by the user). The developer normally drops an anchor whenever content is placed in a physical location. This means that if the user then wanders away, before anchors, the map around the physical location where the content should exist would be thrown away and the content would be lost. With anchors, the content always stays where it should be, with the worst UX impact being a possible tiny glitch in the content as the system relocalizes and jumps to correct for accumulated drift (if any).

The purpose of the map is to help the tracker in two ways. First is that as I move my phone back and forth, the map is built from the initial movement, and on the way back, the features detected in real time can be compared with the saved features in the map. This helps make the tracking more stable by using only the most reliable features from the current and prior view of the scene in the pose calculation.

The second way the Map helps is by localizing (or recovering) tracking. There will come a time when you cover the camera, drop your phone, move too fast, or something random happens, and when the camera next sees the scene, it doesn't match what the last update of the map thinks it should be seeing. It's been blindfolded and dropped in a new place. This is the definition of "I've lost tracking," which pioneering AR developers were heard to say about one thousand times each day over the past few years.

At this point the system can do one of two things:

- Reset all the coordinate systems and start again! This is what a pure odometry system (without a map at all) does. What you experience is that all your content jumps into a new position and stays there. It's not a good UX.

- The system can take the set of 3D features that it *does* see right now and search through the entire map to try to find a match, which then updates as the correct virtual position, and you can keep on using the app as if nothing had happened (you might see a glitch in your virtual content while tracking is lost, but it goes back to where it was when it recovers). There are two problems here. First, as the map grows large, this search process becomes *very* time and processor intensive, and the longer this process takes, the more likely the user is to move again, which means the search must start again. Second, the current position of the phone never exactly matches a position the phone has been in the past, so this also increases the difficulty of the map search, and adds computation and time to the relocalization effort. So, basically, even with mapping, if you move too far off the map, you are screwed and the system needs to reset and start again!

Each line in the image shown in Figure 5-11 is a street in this large-scale SLAM map. Getting mobile devices to do AR anywhere and everywhere in the world is a huge SLAM mapping problem. Remember that these are machine-readable maps and data structures; they aren't nice and comfortable human-usable 3D street-view style maps (which are also needed!).

Figure 5-11. A large-scale SLAM mapping is a challenge for mobile phone–based AR

Also keep in mind that in our discussions when I refer to a "big" map, for mobile AR, that roughly means a map covering the physical area of a very large room or a very small apartment. Note also this means *for outdoor AR we need to think about mapping in an entirely new way.*

Robustly relocalizing against a large map is a very, very, very difficult problem, and in my opinion, as of this writing, no one has yet solved the problem to a consumer-UX level. Anyone claiming to offer multiplayer or persistent AR content is going to have their UX *very* limited by the ability of the second phone (e.g., Player 2) to relocalize from a cold-start into a map either created by Player 1 or downloaded from the cloud. You'll find Player 2 would need to stand quite close to Player 1 and hold their phone in roughly the same way. This is an annoyance for users. They just want to sit on the couch opposite you and turn on their phone and immediately see what you see (from the opposite side, obviously). Or, Player 2 would need to stand anywhere within a few meters of a prior position and see the "permanent" AR content left there.

 There are app-specific workarounds for multiplayer that you can also try, like using a marker or hardcoding a distant starting position for Player 2, and so on. Technically they can work, but you still need to explain what to do to the user, and your UX could be hit or miss. There's no magic "it just works" solution that lets you relocalize (i.e., join someone else's map) in the way ARKit and ARCore make VIO tracking "just work."

How Does Multiplayer AR Work?

For multiplayer to work, we need to set up a few things:

1. The two devices need to know their position relative to each other. Technically, this means that they need to share a common coordinate system and know each other's coordinates at every video frame. The coordinate system can either be a world system (e.g., latitude and longitude) or they might just agree to each use the coordinates from the first device to get started. Recall that each device when it starts generally just says, "Wherever I am right now is my (0,0,0) coordinates," and it tracks movement from there. My (0,0,0) is physically in a different place to your (0,0,0). To convert myself into your coordinates, I need to relocalize myself into your SLAM map and get my pose in your coordinates and then adjust my map accordingly. The SLAM map is all the stored data that lets me track where I am.

2. We then need to ensure for every frame that each of us knows where the other is. Each device has its own tracker that constantly updates the pose of each frame. So, for multiplayer we need to broadcast that pose to all of the other players in the game. This needs a network connection of some type, either peer-to-peer, or via a cloud service. Often there will also be some aspect of pose-prediction and smoothing going on to account for any minor network glitches.

3. We would expect that any 3D understanding of the world that each device has could be shared with other devices (this isn't mandatory, though the UX will be badly affected without it). This means streaming some 3D mesh and semantic information along with the pose. For example, if my device has captured a nice 3D model of a room that provides physics and occlusion capabilities, when you join my game, you should be able to make use of that already captured data, and it should be updated between devices as the game proceeds.

4. Finally, there are all the "normal" things needed for an online real-time multiuser application. This includes managing user permissions, the real-time state of each user (e.g., if I tap "shoot" in a game, all of the other users' apps need to be updated that I have "shot"), and managing all the various shared assets. These technical features are exactly the same for AR and for non-AR apps. The main difference is that, to date, they've really been built only for games, whereas AR will need them for every type of app. Fortunately, all of these features have been built many times over for online and mobile MMO games, and adapting them for regular nongaming apps, such as that shown in Figure 5-12, isn't very difficult.

Figure 5-12. Even an app like this needs the AR cloud and "MMO" infrastructure to enable the real-time interactions

What's the Difficult Part?

Imagine that you are in a locked, windowless room and you are given a photograph of a city sidewalk. It shows some buildings and shop names across the street, cars, people, and so on. You have never been here before, it's completely foreign to you, even the writing is in a foreign language. Your task is to determine *exactly* where that photo was taken, with about one centimeter of accuracy (Figure 5-13 illustrates an actual game that you can play that roughly simulates this). You've got your rough latitude and longitude from GPS and only roughly know which direction you are facing, and you know GPS can be 20–40 meters inaccurate. All you have to go on is a pile of photographs taken by someone else in roughly the same area recently, each marked with an exact location.

This is the problem your AR system must solve every time it is first turned on or if it "loses tracking" by the camera being temporarily covered or if it points at something that it can't track (a white wall, a blue sky, etc.). It's also the problem that needs to be solved if you want to join the AR game of your friend. Your photo is the live image from your device's camera, the pile of photos is the SLAM map that you have loaded into memory (maybe copied from your friend's device or one built in the past). You also need to finish the task before the user moves the camera and makes the most recent live image irrelevant.

Figure 5-13. For a sense of how difficult it is to relocalize, try playing the Geoguessr game (https://www.geoguessr.com), which is very close to the same problem your AR system has to solve every time you turn it on

To illustrate the problem, let's take two extreme examples. In the first case, you find a photo in the pile that looks almost exactly like the photo you have. You can easily estimate that your photo is fractionally behind and to the left of the photo in the pile, so you now have a really accurate estimate of the position at which your photo was taken. This is the equivalent of asking Player 2 to go and stand right beside Player 1 when Player 2 starts their game. Then, it's easy for Player 2's system to determine where it is relative to Player 1, and the systems can align their coordinates (location) and the app can happily run.

In the other example, it turns out that, unbeknownst to you, all of the photos in your pile are taken facing roughly south, whereas your photo faces north. There is almost nothing in common between your photo and what's in the pile. This is the AR equivalent of trying to play a virtual board game and Player 1 is on one side of the table and Player 2 sits down on the opposite side and tries to join the game. With the exception of some parts of the table itself (which you see in reverse to what's in the pile) it is *very* difficult for the systems to synchronize their maps (relocalize).

The difference between these examples illustrates why just because someone claims they can support multiplayer AR, it probably also means that there are some significant UX compromises that a user needs to make. My experience in building multiplayer AR systems since 2012 informs me that the UX challenges of the first example (requiring people to stand side by side to start) are too difficult for users to overcome. They need a lot of hand-holding and explanations, and the friction is too high. Getting a consumer-grade multiplayer experience means solving the second case (and more).

In addition to the second case, the photos in the pile could be from vastly different distances away, under different lighting conditions (morning versus afternoon shadows are reversed) or using different camera models, which affect how the image looks compared to yours (that brown wall might not be the same brown in your image as in mine). You also might not even have GPS available (perhaps you're indoors), so you can't even start with a rough idea of where you might be.

The final "fun" twist to all of this is that users become bored waiting. If the relocalization process takes more than one or two seconds, the user generally moves the device in some way, and you need to start all over again!

Accurate and robust relocalization (in all cases) is still one of the outstanding challenges for AR (and robots, autonomous cars, etc.).

How Does Relocalization Work?

So how does it actually work? How are these problems being solved today? What's coming soon?

At its core, relocalization is a very specific type of search problem. You are searching through a SLAM map, which covers a physical area, to find where your device is located in the coordinates of that map. SLAM maps usually have two types of data in them: a sparse point-cloud of all the trackable 3D points in that space, and a whole bunch of keyframes. As I mentioned earlier, a keyframe is one frame of video captured and saved as a photo every now and then as the system runs. The system decides how many keyframes to capture based on how far the device has moved since the last keyframe as well as the system designer making trade-offs for performance. More keyframes saved means more chance of finding a match when relocalizing, but this takes more storage space and it also takes longer to search through the set of keyframes.

So, the search process actually has two pieces, as illustrated in Figure 5-14. The first piece is as I just described in the example of the pile of photographs. You are comparing your current live camera image to the set of keyframes in the SLAM map. The second part is that your device has also instantly built a tiny set of 3D points of its own as soon as you turn it on, based only on what it currently sees, and it searches through the SLAM sparse point-cloud for a match. This is like having a 3D jigsaw puzzle piece (the tiny point-cloud from your camera) and trying to find the match in a huge 3D jigsaw, for which every piece is flat gray on both sides.

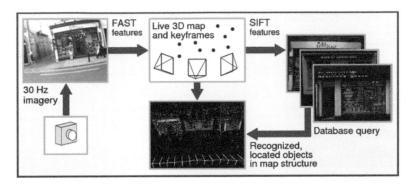

Figure 5-14. An overview of how most of today's SLAM systems build their SLAM map using a combination of optical features (sparse 3D point-cloud) and a database of keyframes

Due to the limited amount of time available before a user grows bored and the modest compute power of today's mobile devices, most of the effort in relocalization goes into reducing the size of the search window before having to do any type of brute-force searching through the SLAM map. Better GPS, better trackers, and better sensors are all very helpful in this regard.

What's the State of the Art in Research (and Coming Soon to Consumer)?

Although the relocalization method described in the previous section is the most common approach, there are others that are seeing great results in the labs and should come to commercial products soon. One method, called PoseNet (see Figure 5-15) involves using full frame neural network regression to estimate the pose of the device. This appears to be able to determine your pose to about a meter or so of accuracy under a wide range of conditions. Another method regresses the pose of the camera for each pixel in the image.

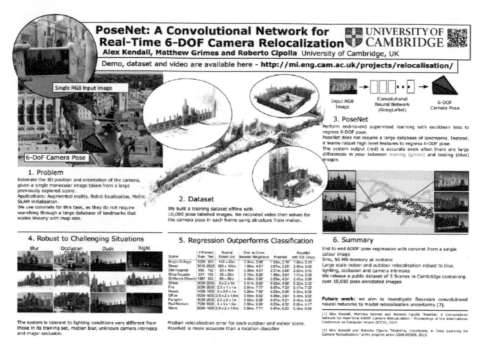

Figure 5-15. PoseNet is indicative of where systems are headed

Can the Relocalization Problem Really Be Solved for Consumers?

Yes! In fact, as of this writing, there have been some pretty big improvements over the past 12 months based on state-of-the-art research results. Deep learning systems are giving impressive results for reducing the search window for relocalizing in large areas, or at very wide angles to the initial user. Searching a SLAM map built from dense 3D point-clouds of the scene (rather than sparse point-clouds used for tracking) are also enabling new relocalization algorithms that are very robust. I've seen confidential systems that can relocalize from any angle at very long range in real time on mobile hardware as well as support a large number of users simultaneously. Assuming that the results seen in research carry over into commercial-grade systems, I believe this will provide the "consumer-grade" solutions we expect.

But these are still only partial solutions to fully solving relocalization for precise latitude and longitude and for GPS-denied environments, or parts of the world where no SLAM system has ever been before (cold-start). But I have seen demonstrations that solve most of these point problems, and believe that it will just take a clever team to gradually integrate them into a complete solution. Large-scale relocalization is on the verge of being primarily an engineering problem now, not a science problem.

Can't Google or Apple Just Do This?

Not really.

Google has demonstrated a service called Visual Positioning System (VPS; see Figure 5-16) for its discontinued Tango platform that enabled some relocalization capabilities between devices—sort of a shared SLAM map in the cloud. It didn't support multiplayer, but it made strides toward solving the difficult technical parts. It's never been publicly available so I can't say how well it worked in the real world, but the demonstrations looked good (as they all do). All of the major AR platform companies are working on improving their relocalizers that are a part of ARKit, ARCore, Hololens, Snap, and so on. This is primarily to make their tracking systems more reliable, but this work can help with multiplayer, as well.

Figure 5-16. Google has been developing its large-scale Visual Positioning Service for years

VPS is a good example of a cloud-hosted shared SLAM map. However, it is completely tied to Google's SLAM algorithms and data structures, and it won't be used by Apple, Microsoft, or other SLAM OEMs (who would conceivably want their own systems or partner with a neutral third party).

The big problem that every major platform has with multiplayer is that at best they can enable multiplayer only within their ecosystem—ARCore to ARCore, ARKit to ARKit, and so on. This is because for cross-platform relocalization to work, there needs to be a common SLAM map on both systems. This would mean that Apple would need to give Google access to its raw SLAM data, and vice versa (plus Hololens, Magic Leap also opening up, etc.). Although technically possible, this is a commercial bridge too far, as the key differentiators in the UX between various AR systems is largely a combination of hardware and software integration, and then the SLAM mapping system capabilities.

So, in the absence of all the big platforms agreeing to open all of their data to one another, the options are limited to the following:

- An independent and neutral third party acts as a cross-platform relocalization service
- A common open relocalization platform emerges

My personal belief is that due to the very tight integration between the SLAM relocalization algorithms and the data structures, a purpose-built dedicated system will outperform (from a UX aspect) a common open system for quite some time. This has been the case for many years in computer vision—the open platforms such as OpenCV or various open slam systems (orb slam, lsd slam, etc.) are great systems, but they don't provide the same level of optimized performance of focused in-house developed systems. To date, no AR platform company that I know of is running or considering to run an open slam system, though many similar algorithmic techniques are applied in the optimized proprietary systems.

This doesn't mean I believe open platforms don't have a place in the AR cloud. On the contrary, I think there will be many services that will benefit from an open approach. However, I don't think that as an industry we understand the large-scale AR problems well enough yet to specifically say *this* system needs to be open versus *that* system needs to be as optimized as possible.

Relocalization != Multiplayer; It's Also Critical for...

This section is looks at why multiplayer is difficult to implement for AR. In the previous section, we touched upon several issues, not least of which is the challenge of making relocalization consumer-grade. As we already discussed, there are other aspects that would be difficult to build, but they are all previously solved problems. But it's relocalization that really matters, and beyond just multiplayer. Here's a few of the problems that we must address:

"Cold start"
>   This refers to the first time that you launch an app or turn on your HMD, and the device must figure out where it is. Generally, current systems don't even bother to try to solve this, they just call wherever they start (0,0,0). Autonomous cars, cruise missiles, and other systems that need to track their location obviously can't do this, but they have a ton of extra sensors to rely on. Having the AR system relocalize as the very first thing it does means that persistent AR apps can be built because the coordinate system will be consistent from session to session. If you

drop your Pokémon at some specific coordinates yesterday, when you relocalize the next day after turning your device on, those coordinates will still be used today and the Pokémon will still be there. Note that these coordinates could be unique to your system, and not necessarily absolute global coordinates (latitude and longitude) shared by everyone else (unless we all localize into a common global coordinate system, which is where things will ultimately end up)

Absolute coordinates

This refers to finding your coordinates in terms of latitude and longitude to an "AR-usable" level of accuracy, which means that it's accurate to "subpixel" levels. Subpixel means that the coordinates are accurate enough that the virtual content will be drawn using the same pixels on my device as on your device if it were in the exact same physical spot. Usually subpixel is used for tracking to refer to jitter/judder so that the pose being accurate subpixel means that the content doesn't jitter when the device is still, due to the pose varying. It's also a number that doesn't have a metric equivalent, because each pixel can correspond to slightly different physical distances depending on the resolution of the device (pixel sizes) and also how far away the device is pointing (a pixel covers more physical space if you are looking a long way away). In practice, having subpixel accuracy isn't necessary because users can't distinguish whether the content is inconsistent by a few centimeters between my device and yours. Getting accurate latitude and longitude coordinates is essential for any location-based commerce services (e.g., the virtual sign over the door needs to be over the right building, as illustrated in Figure 5-17) as well as navigation.

Figure 5-17. This is what you get when you don't have accurate absolute coordinates (or a 3D mesh of the city)

Lost tracking

The last way in which relocalization matters is that it is a key part of the tracker. Although it would be nice if trackers never "lose tracking," even the best of them can encounter corner cases that confuse the sensors; for example, getting in a moving vehicle will confuse the IMU in a VIO system, and blank walls can confuse the camera system. When tracking is lost, the system needs to go back and compare the current sensor input to the SLAM map to relocalize so that any content is kept consistent within the current session of the app. If tracking can't be recovered, the coordinates are reset to (0,0,0) again and all the content is also reset.

How Is Relocalization Really Being Done Today in Apps?

The quick answer? Poorly!

Broadly speaking, there are five ways in which relocalization is being done today for inside-out tracking systems (it's easy for outside-in, like an HTC Vive because the external lighthouse boxes give the common coordinates to all devices that they track). Here is a description of each:

- Rely on GPS for both devices and just use latitude and longitude as the common coordinate system. This is simple, but the common object we both want to look at will be placed in different physical locations for each phone, as demonstrated in Figure 5-18, up to the amount of error in a GPS location (many meters!). This is how Pokémon Go currently supports multiplayer, but because the MMO back-end is still quite simple, it's actually closer to "multiple people playing the same single-player game in the same location." This isn't entirely accurate, because as soon as the Pokémon is caught, other people can't capture it, so there is some simple state management going on.

Figure 5-18. Here's what happens when you rely on GPS alone for relocalization—we don't see the object where it is "supposed" to be, and we don't even see it in the same place on two different devices

- Rely on a common physical tracking marker image (or QR code). This means that we both point our phones at a marker on the table in front of us, as depicted in Figure 5-19, and both our apps treat the marker as the origin (0,0,0) coordinates. This means the real world and the virtual world are consistent across both phones. This works quite well, it's just that no one will ever carry the marker around with them, so it's a dead end for real-world use.

Figure 5-19. This app uses a printed image that all of the devices use for relocalization in order to share their coordinates

- Copy the SLAM maps between devices and ask the users to stand beside each other and then have Player 2 hold their phone very close to Player 1. Technically this can work quite well; however, the UX is just a major problem for users to overcome. This is how we did it at Dekko for Tabletop Speed.

- Just guess. If I start my ARKit app standing in a certain place, my app will put the origin at the start coordinates. You can come along later and start your app standing in the same place, and just hope that wherever the system sets your origin is roughly in the same physical place as my origin. It's technically much simpler than copying SLAM maps, and the UX hurdles are about the same, and the errors across our coordinate systems aren't too noticeable if the app design isn't too sensitive. You just have to rely on users doing the right thing.

- Constrain the multiplayer UX to accept low-accuracy location and asynchronous interactions. Ingress and AR treasure-hunt type games fall into this category. Achieving high-accuracy real-time interactions is the challenge. I do believe there will always be great use cases that rely on asynchronous multiuser interactions, and it's the job of AR UX designers to uncover these.

It's worth noting that all five of these solutions have existed for many years, and yet the number of real-time multiplayer apps that people are using is pretty much zero. In my opinion, all the of the solutions fall into the bucket of an engineer being able to say, "Look it works, we do multiplayer!" but end users find it too much hassle for too little benefit.

Platforms

Building an AR app means choosing an AR Platform to build on. These platforms are a set of APIs and tools to enable the developer to create content which interacts with the real world. The two most widely available are Apple's ARKit and Google's ARCore (which evolved from an earlier project from Google called Tango which was software and custom phone hardware). Microsoft Hololens and Magic Leap both make AR developer platforms for their customer Head Mounted Display hardware. This next section discusses the main features of ARCore and ARKit and compares them from a developer's point of view.

Apple's ARKit

Specifically, ARKit is a VIO system, with some simple 2D plane detection. VIO tracks your device's relative position in space (your 6DOF pose) in real time; that is, your pose is recalculated between every frame refresh on your display, about 30 or more times per second. These calculations are done twice, in parallel. Your pose is tracked via the visual (camera) system by matching a point in the real world to a pixel on the camera sensor each frame. Your pose is also tracked by the inertial system (your accelerometer and gyroscope—the IMU). The output of both of those systems are then combined via a Kalman filter that determines which of the two systems is providing the best estimate of your "real" position (ground truth) and publishes that pose update via the ARKit SDK. Just like your odometer in your car tracks the distance the car has traveled, the VIO system tracks the distance that your iPhone has traveled in 6D space. 6D means 3D of XYZ motion (translation), plus 3D of pitch/yaw/roll (rotation).

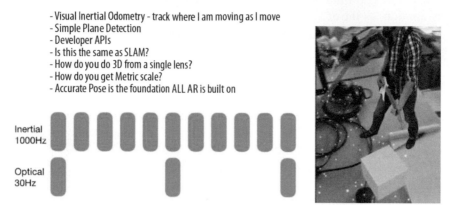

ARKit - What is it?

- Visual Inertial Odometry - track where I am moving as I move
- Simple Plane Detection
- Developer APIs
- Is this the same as SLAM?
- How do you do 3D from a single lens?
- How do you get Metric scale?
- Accurate Pose is the foundation ALL AR is built on

Inertial 1000Hz

Optical 30Hz

Figure 5-20. Apple's ARKit

The big advantage that VIO brings is that IMU readings are made about 1,000 times per second and are based on acceleration (user motion). Dead reckoning is used to measure device movement between IMU readings. Dead reckoning is pretty much a guess, just as if I were to ask you to take a step and estimate how many inches that step was. Errors in the inertial system accumulate over time, so the more time between IMU frames or the longer the inertial system goes without getting a "reset" from the visual system, the more the tracking will drift away from ground truth.

Visual/optical measurements are made at the camera frame rate, so usually 30 frames per second, and are based on distance (changes of the scene between frames). Optical systems usually accumulate errors over distance (and time to a lesser extent), so the farther you travel, the larger the error.

The good news is that the strengths of each system cancel the weaknesses of the other.

So, the visual and inertial tracking systems are based on completely different measurement systems with no interdependency. This means that the camera can be covered or might view a scene with few optical features (such as a white wall) and the inertial system can "carry the load" for a few frames. Alternatively, the device can be quite still and the visual system can give a more stable pose than the inertial system. The Kalman filter is constantly choosing the best quality pose, and the result is stable tracking.

So far, so good, but what's interesting is that VIO systems have been around for many years, are well understood in the industry, and there are quite a few implementations already in the market. So, the fact that Apple uses VIO doesn't mean much in and of itself. We need to look at why its system is so robust.

The second main piece of ARKit is simple plane detection. This is needed so that you have "the ground" on which to place your content; otherwise, that content would look like it's floating horribly in space. This is calculated from the features detected by the optical system (those little dots, or point-clouds, that you see in demonstrations) and the algorithm just averages them out as any three dots defines a plane. If you do this enough times, you can estimate where the real ground is. These dots form a sparse point-cloud, which we examined earlier in the chapter, which is used for optical tracking. Sparse point-clouds use much less memory and CPU time to track against, and with the support of the inertial system, the optical system can work just fine with a small number of points to track. This is a different type of point-cloud to a dense point-cloud, which can look close to photorealism (some trackers being researched can use a dense point-cloud for tracking, so it's even more confusing).

Some Mysteries Explained

Two mysteries of ARKit are: "How do you get 3D from a single lens?" and "How do you get metric scale (like in that tape measure demonstration)?" The secret here is to have *really good* IMU error removal (i.e., making the dead reckoning guess highly accurate). When you can do that, here's what happens:

To get 3D from a single lens, you need to have two views of a scene from different places, which lets you do a stereoscopic calculation of your position. This is similar to how our eyes see in 3D and why some trackers rely on stereo cameras. It's easy to calculate if you have two cameras because you know the distance between them and the frames are captured at the same time. To calculate this with only one camera, you would need to capture one frame, then move, then capture the second frame. Using IMU dead reckoning, you can calculate the distance moved between the two frames and then do a stereo calculation as normal (in practice, you might do the calculation from more than two frames to get even more accuracy). If the IMU is accurate enough, this "movement" between the two frames is detected just by the tiny muscle motions you make trying to hold your hand still! So it looks like magic.

To get metric scale, the system also relies on accurate dead reckoning from the IMU. From the acceleration and time measurements the IMU provides, you can integrate backward to calculate velocity and integrate back again to get distance traveled between IMU frames. The math isn't difficult. What's difficult is removing errors from the IMU to get a near perfect acceleration measurement. A tiny error, which accumulates 1,000 times per second for the few seconds that it takes for you to move the phone, can mean metric scale errors of 30% or more. The fact that Apple has worked this down to single-digit percent error is impressive.

Isn't ARCore Just Tango-Lite?

One developer I spoke to at around the time launch of ARCore jokingly said, "I just looked at the ARCore SDK, and they've literally renamed the Tango SDK, commented out the depth camera code and changed a compiler flag." I suspect it's a bit more than that, but not much more (this isn't a bad thing!). For example, the new web browsers (*http://bit.ly/2EWfEHa*) that support ARCore are fantastic for developers, but they are separate from the core SDK. In my recent ARKit post, I wondered why Google hadn't released a version of Tango VIO (*http://bit.ly/2UxBFTd*) (that didn't need the depth camera) 12 months ago, given that they had all the pieces sitting there ready to go. Now they have!

This is great news, as it means that ARCore is very mature and well-tested software (it's had at least two years more development within Google than ARKit had within Apple—though buying Metaio and Flyby helped Apple catch up), and there's a rich roadmap of features that were lined up for Tango (*http://bit.ly/2THBV53*), not all of which depend on 3D depth data, that will now find their way into ARCore.

Putting aside the naming, if you added depth camera sensor hardware to a phone that runs ARCore, you'd have a Tango phone. Now Google has a much easier path to get wide adoption of the SDK by being able to ship it on the OEM flagship phones. No one would give up a great Android phone for a worse one with AR (same as no one would give up *any* great phone for a Windows mobile phone with AR, so Microsoft didn't bother; it went straight to an HMD). Now people will buy the phone they would have bought anyway, and ARCore will be pulled along for free.

Many of the original ideas were aimed at indoor mapping. It was only later that AR and VR became the most popular use cases.

If we *do* consider the name, I thought it interesting that Tango had always been described along the lines of "a phone that always knows its location" (Figure 5-21). I've never met a single person who was impressed by that. To me, it positioned the phone as something more aligned with Google Maps, and AR was an afterthought (whether that was how Google saw it is debatable). *With the new name, it's all AR, all the time*, as demonstrated in Figure 5-22.

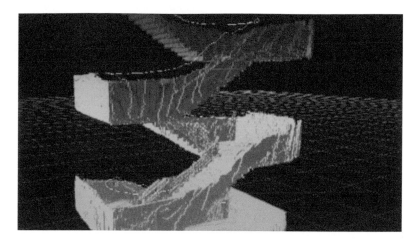

Figure 5-21. Tango started out mostly focused on tracking the motion of the phone in 3D space

Figure 5-22. Google ARCore is an evolution of Tango without the depth camera hardware

So, Should I Build on ARCore Now?

If you like Android and you have an S8 or Pixel, the answer is yes. Do that. If you like iPhones, don't bother changing over. The thing developers should be focusing on is that building AR apps *that people care about* is really challenging. It would be far less effort to learn *how* to build on ARKit or ARCore than the effort to learn *what* to build. Also remember the ARKit/ARCore SDK's are version 1.0. They are really basic (VIO, plane detection, basic lighting) and will become far more fully featured over the next couple of years (3D scene understanding, occlusion, multiplayer, content persistence, etc.). It will be a constant learning curve for developers and consumers. But for now, focus on learning what is difficult (*what* apps to build) and stick to what you know for the underlying technology (*how* to build it: Android, IOS Xcode, etc.). After you have a handle on what makes a good app, make a decision as to what is the best platform on which to launch with regard to market reach, AR feature support, monetization, and so on.

What About Tango, Hololens, Vuforia, and Others?

So, Tango was a brand (it's been killed by Google), not really a product. It consists of a hardware reference design (RGB, fisheye, depth camera, and some CPU/GPU specifications) and a software stack that provides VIO (motion tracking), sparse mapping (area learning), and dense 3D reconstruction (depth perception).

Hololens (and Magic Leap) have exactly the same software stack, but it includes some basic digital signal processing (DSP) chips, which they refer to as Holographic Processing Units, to offload processing from the CPU/GPU and save some power. Newer chip designs from Qualcomm will have this functionality built in, removing the need for custom DSP programming and reducing the cost of future hardware.

Vuforia is pretty much the same again, but it's hardware independent.

Each of these use the same type of VIO system. Neither Hololens, Magic Leap, nor Tango use the depth camera for tracking (though I believe they are starting to integrate it to assist in some corner cases). So why is ARKit so good?

The answer is that ARKit isn't really any better than Hololens, but Hololens hardware isn't widely available.

So, ultimately, the reason ARKit is better is because Apple could afford to do the work to tightly couple the VIO algorithms to the sensors and spend *a lot* of time calibrating them to eliminate errors and uncertainty in the pose calculations.

It's worth noting that there are a bunch of alternatives to the big OEM systems. There are many academic trackers (e.g., ORB Slam is a good one and OpenCV has some options) but they are nearly all optical-only (mono RGB, or stereo, and/or depth camera based; some use sparse maps, some dense, some depth maps, and others use semi-direct data from the sensor—there are lots of ways to skin this cat. There are a number of startups working on tracking systems. Augmented Pixels has one that performs well, but at the end of the day, any VIO system needs the hardware modeling and calibration to compete.

Other Development Considerations

Keep lighting, multiplayer features, and connection to other users and the real world in mind when developing.

Lighting

Both ARKit and ARCore provide a simple estimate of the natural lighting in the scene, as shown in Figure 5-23. This is one estimate for the scene, irrespective of whether the real world is smoothly lit with ambient light or full of sharp spotlights. ARKit hands control of intensity and color temperature back to the developer, whereas ARCore provides either a single pixel intensity value (Android Studio API) or a shader (Unity API). Both approaches seem from early demonstrations to give similar results. Subjectively, Google's demonstrations look a bit better to me, but that might be because Tango developers have been working on them for much longer than ARKit has been released. However, Google had already been showing what is coming soon (17:11 in this video) (*http://bit.ly/2HdVdJz*), which is the ability to dynamically adjust virtual shadows and reflections to movements of the real-world lights. This will give a huge lift in presence where we subconsciously believe the content is "really there."

Figure 5-23. ARCore and ARKit provide a real-time (simple) estimate of the light in the scene, so the developer can instantly adjust the simulated lighting to match the real world (and maybe trigger an animation at the same time)

Multiplayer AR—Why It's Quite Difficult

Earlier in this chapter, we examined what makes a great smartphone AR app (*http://bit.ly/2J6wSqE*) and why ARKit (*http://bit.ly/2UxBFTd*) and ARCore (*http://bit.ly/2NXZukR*) have solved an incredibly difficult technical problem (robust 6DOF inside-out tracking) and created platforms for AR to *eventually* reach mainstream use (still a couple of years away for broad adoption, but lots of large niches for apps today IMO). Developers are now working on climbing the learning curve from fart apps (*http://bit.ly/2EZhvuM*) to useful apps (though my nine-year-old son thinks the fart app is quite useful, thank you). The one feature I get more people asking about than any other is multiplayer. The term "multiplayer" is really a misnomer, as what we are referring to is the ability to share your AR experience with someone else, or many someone-else's, in real time. So, calling it "multiuser," "Sharing AR," "Social AR," and "AR Communication" are just as good terms, but multiplayer seems to stick right now, probably because most of the 3D AR tools come from gaming backgrounds, and that's the term gamers use. Note that you can do multiplayer asynchronously, but that's like playing chess with a pen-pal. As an aside, I can't wait for newer tools to come to AR that align with workflows of more traditional design disciplines (architects, product designers, UX designers, etc.) because I think that will drive a huge boost to the utility of AR apps. But that's for another book.

I personally believe that AR won't really affect all of our day-to-day lives until AR lets us communicate and share in new and engaging ways that have never been possible before. This type of communication *needs* real-time multiplayer. Personally, I think the gaming-centric term multiplayer restricts our thinking about how important these capabilities really are.

Multiplayer AR has been possible for years (we built a multiplayer AR app at Dekko in 2011), but the relocalization UX has always been a huge obstacle.

So, if multiplayer is the main feature people are asking for, why don't we have it? The answer, like so much AR functionality, means diving into the computer vision technology that makes AR possible. (We'll also need low-latency networking, maintenance of consistent world models, sharing audio and video, and collaborative interaction metaphors, as well, but this section focuses on the computer vision challenges, which aren't really solved yet.) Multiplayer AR today is somewhat like 6DOF positional tracking was a few years ago. It's not that difficult to do in a crude way, but the resulting UX hurdles are too high for consumers. Getting a consumer-grade multiplayer UX turns out to be a difficult technical problem. There are a bunch of technologies that go into enabling multiplayer, but the one to pay attention to is our old friend: relocalization. The other non-intuitive aspect of multiplayer is that it needs some infrastructure in the cloud in order to work properly.

How Do People Connect Through AR?

How do we support multiple users sharing an experience? How do we see the same virtual stuff at the same time, no matter what device we hold or wear, when we are in the same place (or not)? You can choose a familiar term to describe this capability based on what you already know: "multiplayer" apps for gamers, or "social" apps or "communicating" apps. It's all the same infrastructure under the hood and built on the same enabling technology. Really robust localization, streaming of the 6DOF pose and system state, 3D mesh stitching, and crowd-sourced mesh updating are all technical problems to be solved here. Don't forget the application-level challenges like access rights, authentication, and so on (though they are mostly engineering problems now).

Figure 5-24. "The Machines" game that Apple demonstrated at its keynote used a simple in-house developed multiplayer system (good demonstration, but not the AR cloud)

How Do AR Apps Connect to the World and Know Where They Really Are?

GPS just isn't a good enough solution—even the forthcoming GPS that's accurate to one foot. How do we get AR to work outside in large areas? How do we determine our location both in absolute coordinates (latitude and longitude) and also relative to existing structures to subpixel precision? How do we do achieve this both indoors and out? How do we ensure content stays where it's put, even days or years later? How do we manage so much data? Localizing against absolute coordinates is the really difficult technical problem to solve here.

Figure 5-25. This sort of thing isn't possible without the AR cloud

How Do AR Apps Understand and Connect to Things in the Real World?

How do our apps understand both the 3D structure or geometry of the world (the shape of things); for example, how does my Pokémon know that it can hide behind or bounce into the big cube-like structure displayed on the screen of my smartphone (Figure 5-26). How does it identify what those things actually are—how does my virtual cat know that the blob is actually a couch, and he should stay off couches? Real-time on-device dense 3D reconstruction, real-time 3D scene segmentation, 3D object classification, backfilling local processing with cloud trained models are the challenges here.

Like much in AR, it's not that difficult to build something that demonstrates well, but it's very difficult to build something that works well in real-world conditions.

You will probably hear about the AR cloud a lot in coming months: if you're confused, it's not you, it's them.

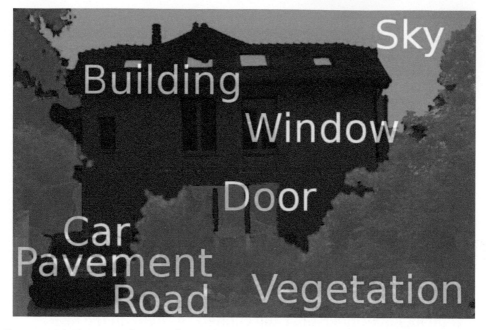

Figure 5-26. For your phone to figure this out as you walk past while capturing and managing the 3D data structures involved requires the AR cloud

Just when you thought you were getting your head around the difference between AR, VR, and MR, it all goes another level deeper. Vendors will use identical terms that mean completely different things, such as the following:

Multiplayer AR

> This could refer to a purely game-level way of tracking what each player does in the game itself with zero computer vision or spatial awareness. Or, it could refer to a way to solve some very difficult computer vision localization problems. Or, both of the above. Or they can mean something else entirely.

Outdoors AR

> This might just mean an ARKit app that has large content assets that look best outside, or it could mean something verging on a global autonomous vehicle 3D mapping system.

Recognition

> This might mean manually configuring a single marker or image that your app can recognize. Or, it might mean a real-time, general-purpose machine learning–powered global 3D object classification engine.

The AR Cloud

If you think about all of the various pieces of an app that sit in the cloud, I tend to split "the cloud" horizontally and separate those services into things that are "nice to have" in the top half, and "must have" in the bottom half (Figure 5-27). The nice-to-have things are generally related to app and content and make it easy to build and manage apps and users.

What I Envision When I Think About the AR Cloud

Your AR apps today without an AR cloud connection are like having a mobile phone that can only play *Snake*.

The bottom half of the cloud is, for me, the interesting part. An AR system, by its very nature, is too big for a device. The world is too large to fit within it, and it would be like trying to fit all of google maps and the rest of the web on your phone (or HMD). The key insight is that if you want your AR app to be able to share the experience or work well (i.e., with awareness of the 3D world it exists in) in *any* location, the app just can't even work at all without access to these cloud services. They are as important as the operating system APIs that let your app communicate with the network drivers, or the touchscreen, or disk access. AR systems *need* an operating system that partially lives on-device, and partially lives in the cloud. Network and cloud data services are as critical to AR apps as the network is to making mobile phone calls. Think back before smartphones—your old Nokia mobile phone without the network could still be a calculator and you could play *Snake*, but its usefulness was pretty limited. The network and AR cloud are going to be just as essential to AR apps. I believe we will come to view today's ARKit/ARCore apps as the equivalent to just having offline "Nokia Snake" versus a network-connected phone.

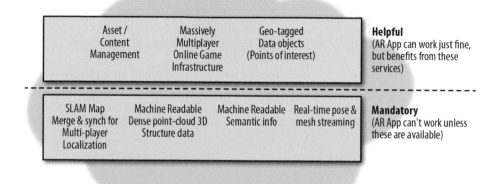

Asset / Content Management	Massively Multiplayer Online Game Infrastructure	Geo-tagged Data objects (Points of interest)	**Helpful** (AR App can work just fine, but benefits from these services)

| SLAM Map
Merge & synch for
Multi-player
Localization | Machine Readable
Dense point-cloud 3D
Structure data | Machine Readable
Semantic info | Real-time pose &
mesh streaming | **Mandatory**
(AR App can't work unless
these are available) |

Figure 5-27. The AR cloud can be stratified into two layers: the nice-to-have cloudy pieces that help apps, and the must-have pieces, without which apps don't even work at all

How Big a Deal Is the AR Cloud?

If you were asked what is the single most valuable asset in the tech industry today, you'd probably answer that it's Google's search index or Facebook's social graph or maybe Amazon's supply-chain system. I believe that in 15 years' time, there will be another asset at least as valuable as these that doesn't exist today. Probably more valuable when you look at it in the context of what Microsoft's Windows operating system asset (easily the most valuable technology asset in the 1990s) is worth in 2017 versus 1997.

Will one company eventually own (a huge profitable part of) it? History says probably. Will it be a new company? Also probably. Just as in 1997 it was unimaginable to think of Microsoft losing its position, in 2019 it seems impossible that Google or Facebook would ever lose their positions. But nothing is guaranteed. I'll try to lay out the arguments supporting each of three sides playing here (incumbents, startups, open web) in the last part of this chapter.

Earlier, we explored how ARKit (*http://bit.ly/2UxBFTd*) and ARCore (*http://bit.ly/2VY5BIH*) work. We discussed what's available today and how we got here. In the upcoming sections, we look at what's missing from ARKit and ARCore and how those missing pieces will work.

So, Just What Is This AR Cloud?

To get beyond ARKit and ARCore, we need to begin thinking beyond ourselves. How do other people on other types of AR devices join us and communicate with us in AR? How do our apps work in areas bigger than our living room? How do our apps understand and interact with the world? How can we leave content for other people to find and use? To deliver these capabilities, we need cloud-based software infrastructure for AR.

The AR cloud can be thought of as a machine-readable, 1:1 scale model of the real world. Our AR devices are the real-time interface to this parallel virtual world, which is perfectly overlaid onto the physical world.

Exciting, but remember: this is the v1.0 release.

Why All the "Meh" from the Press for ARKit and ARCore?

When ARKit was announced at WWDC this year, Apple chief executive Tim Cook touted augmented reality (*http://bit.ly/2XVIArm*), telling analysts, "This is one of those huge things that we'll look back at and marvel on the start of it."

A few months went by. Developers worked diligently on the next big thing, but the reaction to ARKit at the iPhone launch keynote was, "meh (*http://bit.ly/2SYldK9*)." Why was that?

It's because ARKit and ARCore are currently at version 1.0. They give developers only three very simple AR tools:

- The phone's 6DOF pose, with new coordinates each session
- A partial and small ground plane
- A simple average of the scene lighting

In our excitement over seeing one of the most difficult technical problems solved (robust 6DOF pose from a solid VIO system) and Tim Cook saying the words "augmented" and "reality" together on stage, we overlooked that you really can't build anything too impressive with just those three tools. Their biggest problem is people expecting amazing apps before the full set of tools to build them existed. However, it's not the *if*, but the *when* that we've gotten wrong.

What's Missing to Make a Great AR App?

Put succinctly, AR-first, mobile second (*http://bit.ly/2J6wSqE*).

Clay Bavor (*http://bit.ly/2VUbne8*) referred to the missing pieces of the AR ecosystem as connective tissue, which I think is a great metaphor. In my blog post on AR product design (*http://bit.ly/2J6wSqE*), I highlighted that the only reason for any AR app to exist (versus a regular smartphone app) is if it has some interaction or connection with the real world—with physical people, places or things.

For an AR app to truly connect to the world, there are three things that it must be able to do. Without this connection, it can never really be AR native. These capabilities are only possible with the support of the AR cloud.

Is Today's Mobile Cloud up to the Job?

When I worked in telecommunications infrastructure, there was a little zen-like truism that went, "There is no cloud, it's just someone else's computer." We always ended up working with the copper pairs or fiber strands (or radio spectrum) that physically connected one computer to another, even across the world. It's not magic, just difficult. What makes AR cloud infrastructure different from the cloud today, powering our web and mobile apps, is that AR (like self-driving cars and drones and robots) is a real-time system. Anyone who has worked in telecommunications (or on fast-twitch MMO game infrastructure) deeply understands that real-time infrastructure and asynchronous infrastructure are two entirely different beasts.

Thus, although many parts of the AR cloud will involve hosting big data and serving web APIs and training machine learning models—just like today's cloud—there will need to be a very big rethink of how do we support real-time applications and AR interactions at massive scale. Basic AR use cases such as streaming live 3D models of our room while we "AR Skype"; updating the data and applications connected to things, presented as I go by on public transport; streaming (rich graphical) data to me that changes depending on where my eyes are looking, or who walks near to me; and maintaining and updating the real-time application state of every person and application in a large crowd at a concert. Without this type of UX, there's no real point to AR. Let's just stick with smartphone apps. Supporting this for eventually billions of people will be a huge opportunity. 5G networks will play a big part and are designed for just these use cases. If history is any guide, some, if not most, of today's incumbents who have massive investments in the cloud infrastructure of today will not cannibalize those investments to adapt to this new world.

Is ARKit (or ARCore) Useless Without the AR Cloud?

Ultimately, it's up to the users of AR apps to decide this. "Useless" was a provocative word choice. So far, one month in, based on early metrics, users are leaning toward "almost useless." They might be a fun novelty that makes you smile when you share it. Maybe if you are buying a couch, you'll try it in advance. But these aren't the essential daily-use apps that define a new platform. For that, we need AR-native apps. Apps that are truly connected to the real world. And to connect our AR apps to one another and the world, we need the infrastructure in place to do that. We need the AR cloud.

The Dawn of the AR Cloud

Since Apple's WWDC conference in 2017, which fired the starting gun for consumer AR with the launch of ARKit, we've seen every big platform announce an AR strategy: Google's ARCore; Facebook's camera platform; Amazon Sumerian; and Microsoft continuing to build out its mixed reality ecosystem. We've also seen thousands of developers experiment with AR apps but very little uptake with consumers. In September 2017, I predicted that AR apps will struggle for engagement without the AR cloud (*http://bit.ly/2J7NP3T*), and this has certainly turned out to be the case. However, we are now witnessing the dawn of the cloud services that will unlock compelling capabilities for AR developers, but only if cloud providers get *their* UX right. It's not about being first to market, but first to achieving a consumer-grade UX.

Does anyone remember AR before ARKit and ARCore? It technically worked, but the UX was clunky. You needed a printed marker or to hold and move the phone carefully to get started, and then it worked pretty well. Nice demonstration videos were made showing the final working experience, which wowed people. The result: zero uptake. Solving the technical problem (even if quite a difficult technical problem) turned out to be very different to achieving a UX that consumers could use. It wasn't until ARKit was launched that a "just works" UX for basic AR was available (and this was 10 years after Mobile SLAM was invented (*http://bit.ly/2O1JDS2*) in the Oxford Active Vision Lab, which Victor Prisacariu (*http://bit.ly/2HdFkm8*), my 6D.ai (*http://www.6d.ai/*) cofounder, leads).

We are entering a similar time with the AR cloud. The term came about in a September 2017 conversation I had with Ori Inbar (*http://bit.ly/2TOp5Sk*) as a way to describe a set of computer vision infrastructure problems that needed to be solved in order for AR apps to become compelling. After a number of early startups saw the value in the term (and, more important, the value of solving these problems), we are now seeing the largest AR platforms begin to adopt this language in recognition of the problems being critically important. I'm hearing solid rumors that Google won't be the last multibillion-dollar company to adopt AR cloud language in 2018.

Multiplayer AR (*http://bit.ly/2F7PqTj*) (and AR cloud (*http://bit.ly/2J7NP3T*) features in general) has the same challenges as basic 6DOF AR: unless the UX is nailed, early enthusiast developers will have fun building and making demonstration videos, but users won't be bothered to use it. I've built multiplayer AR systems several times over the past 10 years and worked with UX designers on my teams to user-test the SLAM aspects of the UX quite extensively. It wasn't that difficult to figure out what the UX needed to deliver:

- Recognize that people won't jump through hoops. The app shouldn't require asking Players 2, 3, 4, and so on to "first come and stand next to me" or "type in some info." Synchronizing SLAM systems needs to just work from wherever the users are standing when they want to join; that is, from any relative angles or distance between players.

- Eliminate or minimize "prescanning," especially if the user doesn't understand why it's needed or receives given feedback on whether they are doing it right.

- After the systems have synchronized (i.e., relocalized into a shared set of world coordinates) the content needs to have accurate alignment. This means that both systems agree that a common virtual x,y,z point matches exactly the same point in the real world. Generally, being a couple of centimeters off between devices is acceptable in terms of user perception. However, when (eventually) occlusion meshes are shared, any alignment errors are very noticeable as content is "clipped" just before it passes behind the physical object. It's important to note that the underlying ARCore and ARKit trackers are accurate to only about three to five centimeters, so getting better alignment than that is currently impossible for any multiplayer relocalizer system.

- The user shouldn't need to wait. Synchronizing coordinate systems should be instant and take zero clicks. Ideally, instant means a fraction of a second, but as any mobile app designer will tell you, users will be patient up to two to three seconds before feeling like the system is too slow.

- The multiplayer experience should work cross-platform, and the UX should be consistent across devices.

- Data stewardship (*http://bit.ly/2TJifgZ*) matters. Stewardship refers to "the careful and responsible management of something entrusted to one's care," and this is the word we are using at 6D.ai (*http://www.6d.ai/*) when we think about AR cloud data. Users are entrusting it to our care. This is a growing issue as people begin to understand that their saved data can be used for things that weren't explained upfront or that it can be hacked and used criminally. However, people also are generally receptive to the bargain that "I'll share some data if I get a benefit in return." Problems arise when companies are misleading or incompetent with respect to this bargain rather than transparent.

So, putting aside all the application-level aspects of a multiplayer UI (such as the lobby buttons and selector list to choose to join the game), the SLAM-synch piece isn't just a checkbox, it's a UX in and of itself. If that UX doesn't deliver on "just works," users won't even bother to get to the app level a second time. They will try once out of curiosity, though, which means that market observers shouldn't pay attention to AR app downloads or registered users, but to repeat usage.

Enabling developers to build engaging AR apps is where AR cloud companies need to focus, by solving the challenging technical problems to enable AR-First apps that are native to AR (*http://bit.ly/2Cj3mYX*). This means (as I have learned painfully several times) that UX comes first. Even though we are a deep-technology computer vision company, the UX of the way those computer vision systems work is what matters, not whether they work at all.

The Bigger Picture—Privacy and AR Cloud Data

When it comes to Google's Cloud Anchors, visual image data is sent up to Google's servers. It's a reasonably safe assumption that this can potentially be reverse engineered back into personally identifiable images (Google was carefully vague in their description, so I'm assuming that's because if it were truly anonymous, they would have said so clearly).

This is the source image data which should never leave the phone, and never be saved to the phone or saved in memory (Figure 5-28). This is the type of personally identifiable visual image data that you *don't* want to be saved or recoverable from the AR cloud provider. Google says that it does not upload the video frames, but descriptors of feature points could be reverse engineered into an image (see Figure 5-29).

Figure 5-28. Image data that is viewable by a human should never leave the phone

For the future of the AR cloud's ability to deliver persistence and relocalization, visual image data should never leave the phone, and in fact never even be stored on the phone. My opinion is that all the necessary processing should be executed on-device in real time. With the user's permission, all that should be uploaded is the post-processed sparse point map and feature descriptors, which cannot be reverse engineered. An interesting challenge that we (and others) are working through is that as devices develop the ability to capture, aggregate, and save dense point-clouds, meshes, and photorealistic textures, there is more and more value in the product the more "recognizable" the captured data is. We believe this will require new semantic approaches to 3D data segmentation and spatial identification in order to give users appropriate levels of control over their data; this is an area our Oxford research group is exploring.

Figure 5-29 presents a sparse point-cloud for the scene in Figure 5-28 (our system selects semi-random sparse points, not geometric corners and edges, which cannot be meshed into a recognizable geometric space).

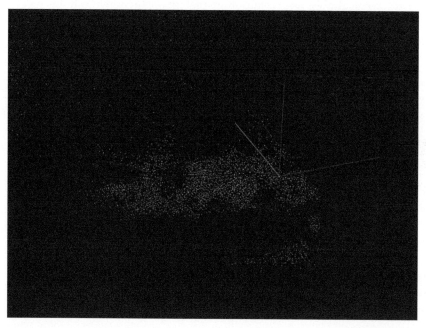

Figure 5-29. This point-cloud is based on the office image data shown in Figure 5-28

The second piece of the puzzle is the "feature descriptors," which are saved by us and also Google in the cloud. Google has previously said that the Tango ADF files, which ARCore is based on, can have their visual feature descriptors reverse engineered with deep learning back into a human-recognizable image (Figure 5-30) (from Tango's ADF documentation—"it is in principle possible to write an algorithm that can reconstruct a viewable image" (*http://bit.ly/2Tw6fjL*)). Note that I have no idea whether ARCore changed the anchor specification from Tango's ADF enough to change this fact, but Google has been clear that ARCore is based upon Tango, and changing the feature descriptor data structure is a pretty fundamental change to the algorithm.

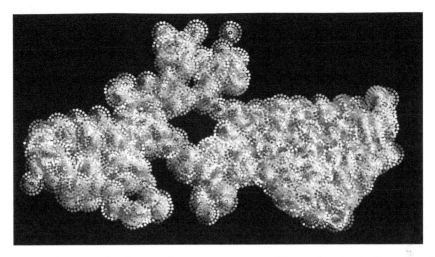

Figure 5-30. These are the feature descriptors generated for each point in the point-cloud (this is as far as 6D.ai's cloud-hosted data can be reverse engineered, based on applying the latest science available today along with massive compute resources)

This is critical because for AR content to be truly persistent, there needs to be a persistent cloud-hosted data model of the real world. And the only way to achieve this commercially is for end users to know that that description of the real world is private and anonymous. Additionally, I believe access to the cloud data should be restricted by requiring the user to be physically standing in the place the data mathematically describes, before applying the map to the application.

This reality regarding AR cloud data creates a structural market problem for all of today's major AR platform companies, given that Google and Facebook's (and others) business models are built on applying the data they collect to better serve you ads. The platforms such as Apple and Microsoft are silos and thus won't offer a cross-platform solution. They also won't prioritize cloud solutions for which a proprietary on-device P2P solution is possible.

The one factor that I had underestimated is that large developers and partners clearly understand the value of the data generated by their apps, and they do not want to give that data away to a big platform for that organization to monetize. They either want to bring everything in house (like Niantic is doing) or work with a smaller partner who can deliver technology parity with the big platforms (no small task) and who also can guarantee privacy and business model alignment. AR is seen as too important to give away the data foundations. This is a structural market advantage that AR cloud startups have, and it is an encouraging sign for our foreseeable future.

As ARKit announced the dawn of AR in 2017, we believe Google's Cloud Anchors are announcing the dawn of the AR cloud. AR Apps will become far more engaging, but only if AR cloud providers deliver a "just works" computer vision UX and address some challenging and unique privacy problems.

Glossary

These aren't precise technical descriptions of these terms; if you need that, you can find those on Wikipedia and countless online technical documents. Rather, this is an attempt to simplify the terms to make them understandable to a general audience.

SLAM (simultaneous location and mapping)
> This is a broad term that refers to a bunch of technical subsystems that help the AR device (and robots) determine where it is in the world. It includes things like tracking your position frame to frame (VIO is just one type of tracking) as well as building a specialized machine-readable map of the space to remember where you are long term (and relocalize if you become lost). SLAM usually is visual and based around cameras plus other sensors, but it's possible to build SLAM systems without cameras, using just (for example) radio signals like WiFi.

VIO (visual inertial odometry)
> A form of tracking that takes input from the camera and inertial sensors to track the position of the device in real-time.

6DOF (6 degrees of freedom)
> Refers to the position (x,y,z coordinates) *and* orientation (pitch, yaw, roll) of the device, together referred to as your pose. This can be in relative coordinates (where am I relative to where I started) or absolute coordinates (e.g., latitude, longitude, altitude, etc.).

Ground truth
> Your absolute "correct" pose. Usually measured against surveyed or measured data using highly accurate systems. It's a theoretical concept, as every measurement system has some small error from ground truth (e.g., even a laser-based measurement has microns of error). The aim is for AR systems to get close enough to ground truth that humans can't notice. Most of us treat GPS as ground truth, but we've all experienced how inaccurate it can be, and AR systems need to be so much more accurate.

IMU (inertial measurement unit)
> A term that refers to the combination of the accelerometer and gyroscope in your phone, which give measurements that can be fused with the camera output to help with tracking.

SIFT
> An accurate and robust feature descriptor for a SLAM system to recognize a point in space. It's a combination of a 3D coordinate plus a description of the pix-

---

els around that point (e.g., colors and lighting) so that the system can recognize it again in the next frame.

Point-cloud

A set of 3D points in space. Note that this doesn't include the feature descriptors, which are needed for relocalization and use in a SLAM system. Many people incorrectly assume a that point-cloud is all that's needed for a SLAM system. Instead, they need the map, which is a combination of the point-cloud and feature descriptors (plus possibly some metadata)

Kalman filter

A mathematical algorithm that predicts the next number in a series based on unreliable inputs. It's the way that inputs from the IMU and camera are fused into a pose and predicted a few frames ahead in time to account for processing time. Note that there's no such things as "the Kalman filter"; there are many types of varying complexity and every AR system will use their own version designed in-house.

PART IV

Creating Cross-Platform Augmented Reality and Virtual Reality

When Facebook bought Oculus Rift in 2014 for $2 billion, the investment industry became catalyzed with virtual reality (VR) validated as ushering in the dawn of a new age of computing. Slowly the market became inundated with Oculus alternatives in the war for the space on your face. Until that point, augmented reality (AR) was practically dominated by Vuforia, an image-based tracking solution. But with the Oculus acquisition, suddenly several companies and products in the immersive space quickly rose to recognition: Meta and Magic Leap for AR, Samsung GearVR and Google Cardboard, and then Hololens and Daydream among many others.

As an investor with Qualcomm Ventures, Steve Lukas was tasked with finding which companies would "win" in the VR/AR space; that's when a massive problem was identified: a software ecosystem that was limited and fracturing further with each headset release. This wasn't fully clear until 2016, when all of the platforms began releasing to the public. As is the usual case with a new industry, the most vocal proponents of VR caused an over-expectation of adoption uptake, and VR ended up selling in lower numbers than originally anticipated. This was consistent for every headset release, with each platform looking like it would be the one that would take the market mainstream, whether it was the full power of HTC Vive, the free Samsung GearVRs distributed with their new phones, the low cost and reach of Google Daydream, or the massive installed base of the PlayStation 4, which would make PlayStation VR the leader. We saw this same hype cycle with the introduction of mobile AR in 2017, with Apple's ARKit and Google's ARCore, which once again signaled a saving of the industry, only to fall short of analyst expectations time and again. Check the receipts.

Which companies were going to win in VR/AR? Conclusion: none of them, if they didn't solve the adoption problem. There are many factors limiting growth in *spatial computing*, but even if they were all solved today, the content problem is one that was going to get worse before it got better. The VR/AR industry in the early days still appealed to the niche: those with disposable income ($1,000–$3,000) on a device setup that provided only a few pieces of content to experience and enjoy. A promise of the future, while still stuck in the present. As it turns out, that number was a very small subset of the population willing to spend so much to gain so little in terms of entertainment and utility when compared to mobile phones, computers, and modern gaming systems.

This audience, being small as it was, would not grow until mainstream audiences jumped in. The early adopters had already made their purchases, and there weren't enough of them. With seven different platforms coming out in 2016, that small group of early adopters were split into seven slices, each camp with their own content eco-system. There was no standard for VR/AR development, as even the most available development engine of Unity still required SDK integrations for each target device as well as the unique design challenges inherent for each form factor.

Developing on only one eXtended reality (XR) device meant limiting your target audience to a small fraction of a small emerging market. The odds were high that the one device you selected would be superseded very shortly by a subsequent release if not altogether by a competitor's device, with both situations causing various degrees of obsolescence for the product you might have built.

Thus, versatility is strongly recommended for the early XR developer. Developers need to understand the difference between developing in general spatial computing versus developing for an actual device. You need to know where the separations exist and how to ebb and flow to new iterations of hardware as well as new device platforms altogether. This approach is intended to allow for device-agnostic development in order to future-proof your skillset as we watch new headsets come to market every few months over the course of the next dozen years.

To kick off, in Chapter 6, Steve Lukas gives some history and philosophy of cross-platform development theory, based on his time with Qualcomm Ventures and starting Across Realities. He goes over the conceptual approach and shows some examples of abstraction techniques in developing for XR.

Then, in Chapter 7, Vasanth Mohan of FusedVR provides a deeper look into cross-platform development tactics and strategy while walking you through some tutorials. In Chapter 8, Harvey Ball and Clorama Dorvilias finish out our examination with a brief history lesson and walkthrough of VRTK, an open source project meant to spur on cross-platform development.

Note that to keep everything platform agnostic and relevant regardless of development changes, within these chapters we are coding using pseudocode and posting screenshots. If you want to dive into working code for each project, check out all of our GitHub repositories, the links for which are provided at the end of each chapter.

This is just the beginning, and having a strong base foundation to develop for all platforms will be important at this stage of the XR life cycle.

CHAPTER 6

Virtual Reality and Augmented Reality: Cross-Platform Theory

Steve Lukas

Jumping straight into building a virtual reality (VR) experience can be very daunting. The same goes for augmented reality (AR), and brainstorming the simple decision as to whether the experience should be done in VR or AR is a good exercise. For the sake of simplicity, this chapter describes VR and AR experiences interchangeably as "immersive" because the majority of immersive content development utilizes the same principles. Where there is a nuanced difference between the two, we explicitly reference it.

The first step of learning immersive development depends on your perspective and what your goals are. You most likely identify with one or more of the following statements:

- I have no development experience.
- I have development experience in 3D graphics.
- I have an app idea in mind for VR.
- I want to learn how to build VR before thinking of an app idea.

If you have an idea of a project that you'd like to build, this is an advantage because you can then target specific milestones while learning your lessons as building blocks toward a completed product. Alternatively, if you want to learn what all of the tools are first, this will aid in the structure of your first app idea because you will understand the features and constraints of VR before committing to ideas that are unfeasible. Regardless, there is no wrong or better way of working, except to go with the system that operates best for you.

In this case, we break down the building blocks of constructing an immersive experience with a planned end game in mind. This chapter focuses more on high-level thinking. We discuss why cross-platform is important, provide a primer on the game engine, and offer some strategies on building toward a cross-platform framework.

Why Cross-Platform?

Tackling cross-platform could be seen as an advanced-level topic, but it is actually a foundational design solution that influences the entire architecture of any product that wants to go immersive.

In these early days of VR and AR, everything is still experimental—headset design, controller design, accessory schematics, and so on. We can identify more than 16 different headset and controller combinations for VR and AR, with more coming seemingly every few months. Until consistency is reached, content is being splintered across the ecosystem. With VR and AR, we are at the far end of a compatibility spectrum. On the near side, there are traditional television sets and mobile media devices, which can potentially play all flat screen content regardless of the manufacturer. In the middle, we have video game consoles, where each device shares some content (e.g., Fortnite, Minecraft) while also having some exclusive content (e.g., Uncharted on PlayStation, Mario on Nintendo, Halo on Xbox). Then, at the far end, we have VR and AR, for which platform-centric content in the early days has been more the norm (e.g., Robo Recall on Oculus Rift, FarPoint on PlayStation VR, Lego Brickheadz on Daydream).

There are multiple reasons for this. The wide variety of control paradigms offered with the different type of VR and AR headset setups has yet to achieve an agreed-upon set of standards. Thus, experiences are built to take advantage of each hardware's feature set and input methods. These can be categorized into the following:

- Tethered headsets with one or more controllers
- Mobile headsets with a controller
- Drop-in VR containers without a controller

This does not really cover the entire spectrum. The Oculus Rift launched with a gamepad and remote and subsequently released the Touch Controllers that shipped later the same year, offering at least three alternative control schemes beyond the traditional mouse and keyboard. Whereas the Oculus Go comes standard with a controller, the Samsung GearVR platform was shipped as a drop-in headset with gamepad support before releasing a tracked controller option a year later. As a result, it cannot be guaranteed that the owner of a platform will also own any of the inputs that did not originally ship with the platform. To reach the widest audience, we must address the core inputs available to each consumer. When building in adaptive input controls, this will help scale the product between the most available controls up to the most powerful.

Until VR and AR moves closer to the middle in terms of compatibility, it will be limited in the message it sends to mainstream consumers that "VR is ready," when those consumers cannot purchase a single headset and simultaneously get the majority of the top available content. The same goes for marketing: the return on investment for VR campaigns is limited due to the high cost of content development coupled with the limited audience base of a single headset.

Even though mainstream adoption is an industry goal, it might not be a specific developer's goal, nor is it their responsibility. Thus, there is the alternate school of thought in which a developer just wants to make the highest-level premium experience either as a hobby or to create a high-value application for a smaller audience. This can find success when developing for the enterprise market or in highly controlled environments like a VR arcade or installation. In all of these cases, focusing solely on one platform is probably fine to do, and thus this chapter might not hold as much value.

Still, designing for portability has an added advantage of avoiding vendor lock-in. By keeping a design largely platform agnostic, applications would be able to adapt to alternate hardware platforms very quickly with lower development cost. This could be advantageous when more suitable platforms launch as well as when better business opportunities might arise with competing VR and AR companies. It is also uncertain at this point which hardware platforms will survive the ever-changing tides of the emerging VR and AR industry, so this method reduces the risk of being bound to a single platform that might end up taking the smallest market share in the future.

In summary, the benefits of targeting cross-platform development include flexibility, a larger potential audience, and future-proofing by simplified porting over to new platforms. Besides all of this, cross-platform development can be very rewarding when seeing your work displayed on each new platform in a very short period of time.

Keep in mind that there is no current industry standard yet defined for cross-platform VR and AR development. Due to the nature of it, this will not likely change for quite some time. Still, there are a number of tools available to help, each with different techniques and benefits. That being said, you need to be aware that there are several approaches to handling cross-platform development, with no one solution being the only "right way" to do it. In this chapter, we present multiple identified solutions. As such, you should merely use these as guides or references to understanding different techniques in this evolving landscape, and ultimately, you should adopt the best practices that work for your own needs.

The Role of Game Engines

Although VR applications can be developed using C++, these days *game engines* are very popular for everything from rapid prototyping a game concept in a matter of hours to building a fully released triple-A product. What is a game engine? It's an industry term for a set of software that takes in a series of inputs (mouse, keyboard, touchscreen, etc.), applies logic to it (e.g., move character, jump, fire weapon), and produces a response, usually in the form of visual and audio feedback (e.g., score update, sound effects). The name "game engine" stems from its original design to primarily handle game applications, with the main benefit being that a lot of complex math and low-level code logic would be preprogrammed into the system. Additionally, game engines would also eventually become multiplatform compatible, establishing a common set of code design by developers while being deployable to different platform targets.

A major advantage of game engines that emerged was the ability to target all sorts of system architectures without having to learn multiple programming languages and platform-dependent APIs. Game developers could work freely in the game engine that they chose to learn and then deploy to new systems as they came to market.

With the rise of mobile applications, and especially with virtual and augmented reality, the need for 3D game engines became even stronger as many of the 3D world development challenges in virtual worlds were already solved by game engines. Thus, Unity and Unreal Engine quickly became the leading game engines for prototyping and authoring VR content.

Even though Unreal Engine has its own set of benefits, in this chapter we focus on Unity. Initially released in 2005, Unity has helped countless developers around the world to get started in building three-dimensional games, including everything from mobile to console to desktop. It has served as the backbone for 3D development for many developers while fostering an amazing community over the years as the company continues to develop its product for the ever-changing needs of new VR and AR feature sets.

Besides flexibility and ease of use, Unity benefits from strong integration partnerships with all of the major computing platforms, and, in some cases, Unity is even required if you want to use any game engine at all. One example is the Microsoft Hololens, which, as of this writing, cannot be targeted by any other commercial game engine. When looking at the most ubiquitous cross-platform development in VR and AR, Unity currently has the widest reach.

Game engine applications are built using an integrated development environment (IDE), which is a fancy term for what you likely know as a desktop app that runs on your computer. To follow along with the examples, we recommend that you download the Unity IDE (*http://bit.ly/2J5Ec5J*). Any current public release of Unity should do, but for compatibility purposes, we're using Unity 2018.1f1.

Unity is powerful and flexible. Its built-in tools and external plug-ins have significantly improved over time, responding to developer feedback to maintain a strong community. On the surface, Unity handles cross-platform development and deployment, but taking advantage of each platform's features requires a finesse that goes beyond basic control remapping. Unity takes care of a lot for the developer when it comes to the heavy lifting, but there are still exercises left for the developer to solve, which we go into further in this section.

Learning Unity from scratch is beyond the scope of this book, but many tutorials exist online, from Unity's website directly (*http://unity3d.com/*) as well as vast resources available on YouTube, Udemy, and PluralSight, among others.

Understanding 3D Graphics

If you've ever developed a 3D game in Unity, VR is a very small modification on top of it. It's practically one step to turn on VR for a minimum requirement to declare an app to be VR-enabled. If you understand how *virtual cameras* work in 3D graphics, you can skip to the next subsection.

The Virtual Camera

The virtual camera sits at the core foundation of VR. Traditionally, in the real world, we know a camera as a mechanical or electronic device that takes pictures and video. In a video chat between two mobile phones, each person is holding a phone in the real 3D world that transmits what the phone sees, in real time, to the other person's flat-screen device. A virtual camera inside the Unity game engine can be thought of in the same way, but instead of the camera being a real device placed in a real 3D world, the camera is placed in a virtual 3D environment. Thus, a live feed is provided to the flat-screen television or monitor. Moving the camera around the 3D world can be done traditionally with a gamepad or a keyboard and mouse combination, with the TV or monitor showing the character's updated viewpoint in real time.

In VR, a couple of things change here. First, the camera becomes attached to the user's head, so instead of using your hands to change your point of view, you would simply move your head. Second, the view is rendered twice: once for each eye, each given its own screen, with each eye's virtual camera position slightly offset from center so that the viewer will experience the *stereoscopic parallax effect*. This is all handled for the viewer in Unity with a simple toggle, but what this really means is that to develop for VR is to first develop for 3D. The VR can come afterward, which is extremely important for planning your hardware purchase strategy. To begin, all you really need is a laptop (or desktop if you're not the portable workaholic type). You can learn the basic mechanics of Unity and create a 3D world with keyboard input to move the camera around, and then attach the VR at the end to jump inside the experience. From there, you can adapt at will.

Most of the same goes for AR, obviously with some differences. For one, with mobile AR using the mobile phone, the mobile phone camera is held in your hand rather than mounted to your head. Still, the virtual camera feed is presented to the mobile phone flat screen (without the optical split for VR) in much the same manner.

Understanding the camera is extremely important because the change of the camera from a relatively fixed position in a video game to being completely movable in VR is a major change that affects how games are designed and optimized. For one, the graphics frame rate needs to be highly performant to reduce adverse effects on the brain, and, second, certain performance tricks and techniques (like unfinished areas of the world that users were never likely to see) are unavailable if the viewer has full freedom to explore the area.

Not all VR hardware is identical, even at the head level, so the next important topic is how control of the virtual camera is handled differently for each platform, which brings us to the following terms you need to know for VR: *three-degrees-of-freedom* and *six-degrees-of-freedom*.

Degrees of Freedom

Degrees of freedom, or DOF, refers to the variations of movement that are available to any tracked object. A tracked object is one that moves in a physical space and reports its position and/or rotation information to the game engine. This is done via a combination of sensor data, but most important, a tracked object's position and/or orientation in the real world can be represented in the virtual world, synchronizing the real and the virtual worlds.

Virtual reality headsets come in two flavors: three-degrees-of-freedom (3DOF) and six-degrees-of-freedom (6DOF). If you've tried VR, you might not have realized which one you've used and why certain headsets can cause discomfort more than others. If you've been in an untethered mobile VR headset powered by a phone, you most likely were in a 3DOF headset. If you could turn around and look behind you in VR, but you couldn't experience walking toward an object in the distance, you were probably in a 3DOF headset. The same goes if you crouched down and your view didn't change. This is because 3DOF tracking means that the rotation of the tracked object is being reported to the software, but the position is not. With rotational tracking, the game engine would have information on the headset's yaw, pitch, and roll (rotations along the x, y, and z axes, not necessarily respectively). This is commonly known as *3DOF tracking*. Google Cardboard, Samsung GearVR, Google's Daydream View, and the Oculus Go fall into these categories, and 3DOF tracking can be performed using the internal accelerometer, gyroscope, and magnetometer sensors present in most mobile phone chipsets.

The remaining 3DOF in a 6DOF headset are the x, y, and z positions along the x, y, and z axes (respectively). Because 3DOF experiences cannot move the camera using your head alone, the virtual camera either moves automatically (such as in a roller-coaster experience) or some form of movement is implemented through control input. This is known as *locomotion*, and we discuss this further in the next section. Due to brain and body discomfort, locomotion has a number of solutions, including teleportation and camera blur to alleviate any motion sickness side effects.

6DOF experiences feel more natural due to the complete 1:1 association between moving your head in all directions and having the visual experience match up. In these experiences, you can crouch to the floor to pick something up, tiptoe to get a better vantage point, or sidestep to catch a football. However, position tracking is a complex problem that requires an understanding of the tracked object relative to a real-world location in space. Visual sensors need to be placed either on the tracked object itself or on a fixed location facing the object. Although full tracking has its advantages, it can also come at a cost of movement freedom. Currently, the majority of 6DOF solutions are tethered to a computer, with a dangling cable acting as a leash that can cause trip hazards or it can get wound up or yanked from the machine if not properly managed. Advancements in technology such as the Vive Focus, Google Standalone Daydream, and Oculus Santa Cruz headset are bringing us closer to wireless freedom with full 6DOF capability, but the majority of deployed headsets are still 3DOF experiences.

Controllers are another factor for virtual reality. Controllers can be either tracked or untracked, and, like the headsets, tracking comes in both the 3DOF and 6DOF variety. Table 6-1 lists the major VR platforms available as of mid-2018.

Table 6-1. Available VR platforms

3DOF VR platforms	Input method
Mobile VR: Cardboard/phone drop-in	Gaze and hold position
Mobile VR: Cardboard/phone drop-in	Untracked
Oculus Mobile with headset touchpad	Headset touchpad, untracked. Clickable touchpad + 1 button
Oculus Mobile with Gamepad	Gamepad, untracked. Digital direction pad, analog controller, 6 face + 4 trigger buttons each
Oculus Mobile with controller	1 x 3DOF hand controller with clickable touchpad + 2 buttons
Google Daydream View	1 x 3DOF controller w/clickable touchpad + 1 button
6DOF VR platforms	Input method
Google Daydream: Mirage Solo	1 x 3DOF controller w/clickable touchpad + 1 button
HTC Vive Focus	1 x 3DOF controller w/clickable touchpad + 2 buttons
Oculus Rift with Xbox controller	Gamepad, untracked. Digital direction pad, analog controller, 6 face + 4 trigger buttons each

3DOF VR platforms	Input method
Oculus Rift with remote	Remote, untracked. Directional pad + 1 button
Oculus Rift with Touch controllers	2 x 6DOF controllers. Clickable joystick, 2 face + variable trigger + grip, each
HTC Vive	2 x 6DOF controllers. Clickable touchpad + 2 buttons + variable trigger, each
Microsoft mixed reality headset	2 x 6DOF controllers. Clickable touchpad + 2 buttons + variable trigger, each
6DOF AR platforms	
Microsoft Hololens	2 x positional 3DOF hands, detect hand + hand tap only
Microsoft Hololens	1 x clicker with 1 button only
Mobile AR: iPhone/Android	Touchscreen

Table 6-1 includes only releases currently available from the five major commercial VR and AR manufacturers: Facebook, Google, Microsoft, HTC, and Apple. (Sony has its PlayStation VR platform, as well, but its closed developer ecosystem is more difficult to break in to, and all of the platforms in Table 6-1 can be purchased and developed for by the average person in a matter of weeks if not days.) Reemphasizing that as much as cross-platform is a technical challenge, it is an even more difficult design challenge. There is a reason why it is mostly 360-degree video content that appears consistently on every platform, and that is because the interaction system of "sit and stare, look around" can be attributed to just about every one of the aforementioned platforms.

Taking a look at Table 6-1, it's not difficult to imagine that supporting 16 different headsets plus input combinations for VR and AR can appear quite daunting. However, these are challenges that are solved every day by anyone doing real-world space planning: accommodating children, strollers, wheelchairs, people of sizes great and small, short and tall, hearing impaired, visually impaired, and so on. The real world is constantly being engineered to accommodate the largest audience possible with wheelchair ramps, braille, subtitles, and more. With obvious limitations being applied where necessary ("you must be this tall to ride"), there is already an industry standard term for this: *accessibility*. Design principles of accessibility, when applied to VR, can be beautifully adaptable.

What this means is to consider the overall experience that you want to convey. What is it that you want players to do in this virtual environment? Is it a passive experience or an active one? What will they find satisfying? If the experience you are designing is purely a showcase for a piece of hardware such as hand tracking or a new controller interface, the emphasis will definitely be platform centric and might not be transportable to other systems. Keeping the high-level concept experiential rather than interaction based allows for the greatest freedom in experience design, and secondarily controller functions can be applied as soon as the world-building has been solved.

Portability Lessons from Video Game Design

One product strategy is that applications should be designed for high-end hardware with full capabilities and then be incrementally reduced to handle lower-end platforms. Products that do this incorrectly tend to suffer as a result of not being originally designed for the lower end during the original product design. Graphics issues aside, control schematics are substituted out and replaced in an attempt to simulate the high-end version of the input experience, which can really show. Several video games have moved from their original home console release down to a portable game format. One example is the original *Street Fighter II* game, for which a six-button layout was provided in the arcades (see Figure 6-1); three buttons at the top for variable punches, and three buttons at the bottom for variable kicks, each with a low/medium/high progression from left to right.

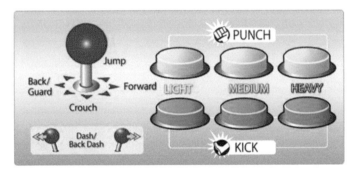

Figure 6-1. The original six-button arcade input experience for Street Fighter II

Upon home release for the original PlayStation, the four-button layout on the game-pad used two shoulder buttons to replace the remaining two face buttons, as illustrated in Figure 6-2.

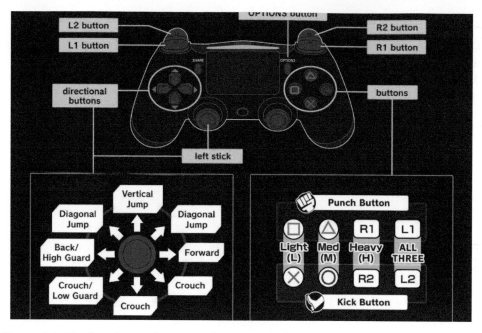

Figure 6-2. The four-button layout on the gamepad for the Sony PlayStation

The intuitive progression of strength level from left to right did not translate as smoothly, with the heavy buttons being moved to the right shoulder area and using the right thumb to press light or medium attack, and the right index finger to press for heavy attacks.

This was solved in future iterations of the franchise, such as *Marvel vs. Capcom 2*. This game was designed to be more port friendly, removing the medium attacks and reducing the main attack buttons to light and heavy, with the two remaining buttons in a new partner assist set of moves, thus falling outside of a linear model of strength across all six buttons and allowing the assist buttons to live independently of the other two without breaking the mental model. These assist buttons could now sit as the right two buttons of a six-button control, as shown in Figure 6-3, or they could be mapped to the shoulder buttons of a PlayStation controller.

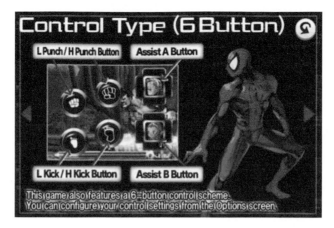

Figure 6-3. Scalable four plus two-button configuration for Marvel versus Capcom 2 adaptable to both 3 x 2 and 4 x 4 + 2 controller layouts

The main takeaway: think about the experience while factoring in some of the adaptation options available. What needs to happen in the experience, and then how do we accommodate the largest number of input schematics to feed into that control system? Answer those questions to take the first steps into scalable input design.

Simplifying the Controller Input

One of the earliest VR launch titles, *Job Simulator* by Owlchemy Labs, was built to be one of the most accessible VR games by having a very simplified input: one button for most major interactions. The goal of the gameplay was to explore the wonder of VR through a series of familiar tasks done within VR with a whimsical, fun approach as an added element of lightheartedness and enjoyment.

The developers at Owlchemy Labs have offered several insights and lessons-learned talks at conferences and online, and one of their main points given was that VR allows for the removal of many traditional controller inputs because those actions are now replaced by using our actual bodies in the real world. Whereas traditional video games control a protagonist's movements and actions by using one or even two directional joysticks, all of those movements could now be handled by turning your head and actually walking. Crouching or jumping could now be performed directly by the body instead of using buttons on a controller. This frees up the complex control schemes traditionally found on console games and allows the hand controllers to focus solely on manipulating items in the world.

By assigning a single trigger button to handle grabbing, throwing, and manipulating items, *Job Simulator* is one of the fastest games to pick up and play without any onboarding. Even more important, this applies to a large range of ages who have tried it, from 4 years old to 80 and older. The way they accomplished this was via one very genius approach: put the interactions into the world and allow those inputs to be manipulated by a player's hands. Pushing buttons, turning knobs, pulling open cabinet handles, and throwing objects were all done by simulating the real world, allowing a person's natural instincts to guide them through the experience. Instead of assigning a complex set of controls to the hand controllers, they became an extension of a player's own hands, and the user interfaces to learn were all within the world.

This disassociation allows for more thoughtful object design and more flexibility in having one set of controls interface with a wide variety of interfaces, such as a microwave, blender, sink, refrigerator, cash register, and even a car engine. In the long run, this approach is much more scalable.

We dive in now with a high-level solution to provide an example of how cross-platform development can make switching platforms easier in the long term.

Development Step 1: Designing the Base Interface

You can do object design in VR by thinking about how objects would work in the real world. Are there buttons attached to it like a remote control? Does it open and close like a box? Does it have a physical presence or is it a symbolic marker (like a ball of light)? Can it be picked up or is it attached to another object?

Consider all of the ways in which a person would interact with an object; for example, a light switch. When pushed, a light switch changes position and an action is performed, in this case a light is turned on or off. That light switch could be manipulated in multiple ways: it could be directly switched by a hand in proximity to the light switch, or you could take a stick, which would act as an extension to the hand, thereby pushing the switch semi-remotely. Alternatively, the light bulb power might also be controlled by a smart-home system, so an external force such as an app on a mobile touchscreen device could manipulate the light's on/off state.

Now let's translate that into what we know about different types of controls available for VR. With a 6DOF hand controller, you could directly put your hand next to the switch and click a button to flip it. Suppose that the controller was 3DOF and could not move its position in space but could rotate around. A laser pointer attached to the controller could act like a physical stick extension, and when the laser is pointing at the switch, clicking a button could activate the toggle. Without a controller, such as in a 3DOF head-tracked platform like a Cardboard device, the laser could be attached to the head, and looking directly at the switch and tapping a button could hit the switch. If there is no button on the Cardboard device, staring at the switch could initiate a short timer that measures how long the gaze is held, and when the timer reaches a predetermined length, the switch toggles itself. Finally, in a mobile device, the toggle could be tapped directly from the touchscreen or it could even be pulled up in an onscreen menu and controlled remotely like a smart-home app.

In this example, every single VR and AR platform can interface with the light switch in its own way, with the light switch responding to simple commands such as "turn on," "turn off," and "toggle."

You could take this further. Our light switch has two states: on and off. What if there were more states, such as a light intensity with a range of 0 to 100? Now, we would need a way of controlling the variable input. In the real world, we handle this with a dimmer switch. Instead of being a toggle that is flipped, the dimmer is often implemented as a sliding bar on the panel. Thus, the light switch needs an added button control, but this one would have the added feature of being able to be picked up and moved. Then, upon a button click, instead of the switch toggling the on/off state of the light bulb, the dimmer would toggle a state of being connected to the control or disconnected. In a connected state, movement of the controller (whether it be a hand controller, laser pointer, or head for a gaze attachment) would then move the slider and change the value of the light bulb's intensity in real time until it was disconnected. With a button or touchscreen, the "down/pushed" action would likely connect the object with the "up/released" action, disconnecting the object. In a gaze-and-stare approach, each gaze-and-stare action would need to be completely executed once for connect and once again for disconnect.

Without a controller, you could use your head to aim it by looking at the switch, and if there's no controller, a long stare could activate it. Ultimately the light switch would have a "button press" type of interface that would be activated by any number of control schemes in order to function.

We have now defined two interfaces, one for selection and one for grabbing, and we have shown how those work across all platform input types. We can extend this into more complex concepts such as the following:

- Ways of attaching objects in Unity: direct transform, fixed joint, and physics forces
- Two-handed manipulation of objects for movement and scale
- Secondary manipulation of objects, such as weapon reload or removing a bottle cork
- Restricting movement of a mounted object, such as a twisting doorknob

Unfortunately, delving into these in depth is beyond the scope of this chapter. But you can see how there are many ways to solve interface challenges.

With these two basic interface properties in place, you can populate a world environment with exploratory objects that can be interacted with regardless of which platform is used. The best part is that all of that work can be done without even leaving the computer and putting on a headset. When that's ready, we begin setting up how the platform integration is treated.

Development Step 2: Platform Integration

Platform integration involves taking an application and attaching the hardware pieces to it. This can be done directly, but the cross-platform design slows us down a little bit as we prepare a solid abstraction layer first. If you have already toyed around with building a prototype against a VR platform, this section is a good step two. If you have never written toward a VR platform, you can still follow along to understand the abstraction layers that we are setting up here.

There are two major parts to integrating with a platform.

- Attaching the head
- Attaching the control inputs

The head is typically straightforward and, in some cases, handled automatically by the game engine using the primary camera as the head input. Platform software development kits (SDKs) might provide their own custom scripts or object prefabs in Unity for attaching some base functionality to the head, such as rendering frames for the camera in mobile AR.

Attaching the control inputs can be much more complex based on the various interaction systems. For example, the HTC Vive system can use either OpenVR or Valve's SteamVR plug-in, whereas Oculus Touch controllers use OVRPlugin from Oculus. Google has its own code for the Daydream controller, which although having a similar configuration to the Oculus Go controller, uses a different input manager script. Examples provided for each platform tend to work directly with the custom SDK code to attach controller functionality, which is fine for learning, but for our purposes, we are going to integrate at a different level.

To be clear, the controller functionality comes in two parts: tracking the object position and/or orientation, and monitoring the button or touch inputs. Tracking object position/rotation is simple in Unity, and our code would attach to a virtual object that maps to the real-world object 1:1. It's the button/touch inputs that we are interested in for this exercise.

Let's first look at what a typical "Press menu button to open the menu" code path would look like in an example for a VR and AR platform SDK:

```
[ Frame Entrypoint: controller default ]
    For each frame:
        Did the user click down on a controller's menu button?
            If so:
                If the menu is not visible, open the menu
                    (make it visible)
                Otherwise, close the menu
```

This is very simple and straightforward. Why wouldn't we just do this? The actual code implementation of the line `Did the user click down on a controller's menu button?` is most likely platform dependent and built against SteamVR or Oculus Rift's controller API. It assigns a defined control to a specific button in the code, preventing customizability (suppose that an individual user wants to use a trigger button instead to pull up the menu) and lacks portability (the Daydream controller would not understand the API call.) Additionally, this code is written specifically to perform the single function of opening the menu. If new functionality were to be added, it would also need to be hardcoded in the same code block sequence here.

Alternatively, let's abstract this out:

```
[ Frame Entrypoint: controller menu behavior]
    For each frame:
        Is there a control input scheme to monitor? (such as 'open menu')
            If so, is there a mapped control in a state we should
                care about?
                If so, respond
```

Here, we have introduced the concept of a `control input scheme`. This would be an object that defines a set of functionalities that can be attached to this controller. In this case, an "open menu" function would be able to be set, unset, or toggled. Then, we would map one or more controls to it, and this code would have to be platform-dependent code, such as `map button_menu on SteamVR controller to functionality open_menu`. Then, the flow line `is there a mapped control` would look for the SteamVR controller's `button_menu` object and check to see whether it's in a state that matters for this functionality. These states could be "button down," "button up," or "button click." Then, if that button state sends a success, it would fire off the control to open or close the menu.

There are four scripts in play here. One is the controller mapping that checks for interactions on each frame. Call this the `ControllerModule`. This is simple and provides the logic to handle the frame loop and is purely platform independent. The second class is the control scheme class; let's call it `ControlScheme`. This defines the application-specific available functionality, and it would be built per application as needed. The third class is the control mapping scheme—for example, `MappingMenu ButtonToViveController`—which would be created once for each platform port to bridge the `ControlScheme` and the final class, which is the controller implementation. A class like this could be called `ViveController` and handle the checks for each button state on the controller, having zero knowledge of the application functionality and serving only as the interface to the controller itself. Together, they look like this:

```
[ ControllerModule ] - written once ever
[ ControlScheme ] - written once per application
[ ControllerMapping ] - written once per application per ported platform
[ ControllerImplementation ] - written once per platform controller
```

With this setup, the `ControllerModule` can then be written once as a piece of framework code. The rest of the classes would have a base functionality root class, with child classes implementing as needed.

`ControlScheme` would be the concrete implementation written once per interaction scheme for an application. Some examples besides interact would be to grab, draw, and select. All of these could have different response modes for the controller. Grab would be pick up, draw would dispense art into the world, and select could choose objects to manipulate.

`ControllerMapping` implementations would make the bridge connections between the control scheme and the controller implementation, defining what buttons on each controller would be attached to which pieces of functionality. In this setup, a user-definable controller mapping could also be created to allow the user at runtime to route which buttons they want to assign to what functionality.

Finally, the controller implementation would be written once per controller type on each platform. This would handle the platform-specific code to monitor button triggers, analog input, and so on.

So how does all this extra work help us? Let's now attach an "interact" functionality to the controller. This is the new flow chart:

```
[ Frame Entrypoint: controller that can interact ]
    For each frame:
        If there is a nearest hovered object:
            Is there a control input scheme to monitor? (such as 'interact')
                If so, is it in a state the object should respond to?
                    If so, respond
        Otherwise:
            Is there a control input scheme to monitor? (such as 'open menu')
                If so, is it in a state we should care about?
                    If so, respond
```

Not much has changed here, except now the frame script monitors for functionality attached to a hovered object. This script can now toggle a light switch if the appropriate button is selected, or toggle a menu otherwise. Note here that the control mappings could assign "interact" to a trigger while "open menu" stays attached to the menu button.

Let's go further and add the ability to grab an object. Note that if an object is grabbed, we might want to do something with that object like throw it, turn it, and so on, so logic for it appears first:

```
[ Frame Entrypoint: controller that can pick up an object ]
    For each frame:
        If there is a connected object:
            Is there a control input scheme to monitor? (such as 'shoot' or 'drop')
                If so, is it in a state the object should respond to?
```

```
                    If so, respond
        Otherwise if there is a nearest hovered object:
            Is there a control input scheme to monitor? (such as 'interact')
                If so, is it in a state the object should respond to?
If so, respond
        Otherwise:
            Is there a control input scheme to monitor? (such as 'open menu')
                If so, is it in a state we should care about?
                    If so, respond
```

Can you see the pattern? We can iterate through the control schemes and fall through to the basic controller functionality if there is any. This is scalable for creating controller functionality.

Additionally, let's take a look at how to adapt different controllers to this. If we wanted to port this app to Daydream, we would need a new `DaydreamController` script to handle the controller implementation and a new `MappingMenuButtonToDaydream` script to replace the other mapping. Other than that, we would be done.

Real-world example

Porting a prototype from Daydream to Oculus Go was interesting because the only difference in the two controller types seemed to be the trigger button. Thus, one prototype needed two customizable buttons: one to perform primary functions and one to perform the secondary function of toggling the primary function's mode. Then, we could switch out from paint mode to selection mode with one button while utilizing the primary button to actually do the painting or selecting. On the Go controller, the trigger was the most appropriate button to handle the primary function, leaving the touchpad click to do the secondary mode swap. On the Daydream controller, however, there was no trigger, and thus the primary input was the touchpad click, which was our secondary input on the Go controller! It made no sense to use the Go controller for the secondary input, so instead the Daydream controller used the app button for the secondary input to toggle the primary input mode. Although these made the platforms different, it was a simple matter of editing the mapping file to play with different options.

Example code is provided at this book's GitHub repository (*https://github.com/Creatin gARVR*).

Summary

The theory provided is meant to help kickstart high-level thinking in VR and AR design and to help get the most out of the technical information that follows. In this chapter, we explained the basics on game engines and 3D cameras, 3DOF versus 6DOF, and why the design approach should be considered at a holistic high level based on the goal of the experience. The concept of cross-platform abstraction will help allow your code to adapt to other platforms very easily, which is a core foundational element of multiplayer as well as real-time social experiences. This is because the world content would be consistent across the platforms without any issues given to asymmetric control inputs.

Besides the information in the following chapters, here are some additional cross-platform development resources that might be of help:

- Torch3d: collaborative VR and AR development tools
- BridgeXR: cross-platform toolkit in Unity
- Unity AR Framework: cross-platform AR framework by Unity
- Wikitude: cross-platform AR framework for Unity

In the next chapter, Vasanth provides more concrete examples of designing for VR and AR, including locomotion techniques as well as more information on the available control types.

As a former venture capitalist in the space, I've often been asked whether VR and AR are a fad that would go away. My answer has never changed: VR and AR are the inevitable future of computing. What's unknown is how long it will take for us to get there, be it 2 or 20 years. Still, every effort we can make to accelerate that growth will help us get to the future where we are naturally sharing the wonder of VR and AR with more of our friends and family. That's a future I'm excited about, and I hope that together we can arrive there soon.

CHAPTER 7

Virtual Reality Toolkit: Open Source Framework for the Community

Harvey Ball and Clorama Dorvilias

Virtual Reality Toolkit (VRTK) is an open source, cross-platform toolkit for rapidly building virtual reality (VR) experiences by providing easy-to-use solutions to common problems. VRTK focuses on two main areas of help for developers: *interactions* and *locomotion* techniques, offering a multitude of ways of solving these common problems.

What Is VRTK and Why People Use It?

VRTK is an open source codebase that allows users to drag and drop functionality. By being able to drag and drop Assets into Uniity 3D, with a few configurations, they can immediately open example scenes with ready-set fully functional essential gameplay mechanics such as locomotion, navmeshes, a variety of user interfaces, and physical interactions around which you can start building your game.

With the benefits of it being open source, anyone can immediately reduce their setup time and immediately begin customizing assets and the source code to manifest their ideas in Unity for rapid prototyping—at the very least.

The major benefits to this toolkit are that it's the only one of its kind that is readily adaptable to any hardware on which you plan to develop: Oculus + Touch controllers, HTC Vive, mixed reality (MR) headsets, mobile VR headsets. Because hardware accessibility can be a barrier to many aspiring or new VR creators, the default of its use includes a VR simulator. The VR simulator allows creators to be able to build fully functional immersive games in Unity along with previews that allow for keyboard inputs to substitute for controller use in navigating the experience.

The goal of VRTK is to bring as many creative people from as many diverse backgrounds as possible to try to solve the common problems that the new medium of VR brings. The faster solutions to these problems can be built, tried, and tested, the faster we can help accelerate the evolutionary process to find out what works and what doesn't work, because evolution is just a million mistakes until a bit of one thing works.

The way in which VRTK empowers such a large participation is to be totally free and open source (under the MIT license) to anyone who wants to use it, for any reason they want to use it, whether it's for learning the ropes of VR development or they're using it to make the next latest VR game, or even if they're a commercial entity making simulation solutions.

By making it completely free for anyone to use or to build for, the barrier for entry into VR development has been lowered massively so that those who want to turn their creative and wild ideas into a reality can have that opportunity with VRTK.

The History of VRTK

Over a weekend in April 2016, Harvey set out to take all of the knowledge gleaned from the SteamVR plug-in scripts and try to turn it into something that could make it easy for others to build something in VR. The script, which took only about two to three hours to write, was one script for Unity3d that was dragged and dropped into a scene with the SteamVR camera rig and immediately gave the ability to shine a laser pointer within the scene and teleport to wherever the tip was pointing. It also gave the ability to pick up items using a rudimentary fixed-joint-based grabbing system. This was great: you could build a scene, and with one quick drag and drop of an open source script, you could move around the scene and pick up things and throw them around. The next step was to share it with the world, so on an unknown YouTube channel with no more than 100 subscribers and hardly any regular views, a video was posted that showed how to use this VR script (*http://bit.ly/2EXqSv0*).

After a couple of days, the video had thousands of views, clearly indicating that there were a lot of people in a similar situation, eager to find tutorials on how to build content for VR. We quickly realized that if there was such a need and desire for this sort of content, this basic and flimsy script was not the best way for people to move forward. It was far too limiting, it was too coupled (meaning one script did everything so customizing it would be a total pain), and it wasn't really something people could work on together in a community.

Welcome to the SteamVR Unity Toolkit

After the success of this original single script, the SteamVR Unity Toolkit was born, which was a more concerted effort to try to build a reusable and extensible collection of scripts that made building for the HTC Vive easier and quicker not only for seasoned developers, but also for complete beginners who wanted to try but didn't know if they could do it. The SteamVR Unity Toolkit was a very appropriate name because it was basically a toolkit of scripts built in Unity3d that helped out when using the SteamVR plug-in, offering a collection of solutions such as teleporting, pointers, grabbing, and touchpad locomotion. Because it was all completely free and open source, it began gaining traction with people building content that was of interest to them in VR, some of this content would become some of the most well-known games in VR.

It was the age of the Wild West of VR development; no one really knew what problems would be thrown up by the medium, and no one really had the answers for the solution. The SteamVR Unity Toolkit became a GitHub repository where people could share their ideas for solutions by contributing to the codebase and getting their ideas out to other people in an effort to make it easier for other people to build their own VR experiences and games. In fact, the developer behind QuiVR contributed a number of cool features to VRTK, especially the bow-and-arrow example scene, which inspired a number of fun bow-and-arrow games to be built by budding developers.

As the number of developers using the SteamVR Unity Toolkit grew, it became more and more difficult to help out people with their individual problems. When there was only a handful of people using it, it was easy enough to jump on a Skype call with someone and sort out their issue, but when there's around a thousand people using something, this is never going to end well.

The community behind the toolkit had grown rapidly in such a short amount of time and it needed somewhere that it could freely communicate and incubate ideas together. The solution was a Slack channel that anyone could join and contribute to, seek assistance, and chat about ideas that could eventually become features of the toolkit for other people to use.

The Slack channel is still the heart of the community today, with more than 4,500 people worldwide working through problems and sharing ideas of how to make VR experiences more interesting for their audiences. It has become a place where people form real community bonds, online friendships, or partnerships into new ventures of building some really cool VR games.

People in the community felt so passionate about sharing their ideas, it cemented the SteamVR Unity Toolkit as being the tool of a community effort rather than the work of one person, which just helped it grow at an ever-increasing rate with more and more experiences being created.

It had grown to such a level that it had been noticed by some of the seasoned VR companies with Oculus reps asking what they could do to get it to work with their headset. Oculus was kind enough to provide a free Oculus Rift and Touch controller pack so that Harvey could get the toolkit working on a headset other than the Vive. Within a few days, it was a multiheadset toolkit with the added benefit that if something was built to work on the Vive, it would now also work seamlessly enough with the Oculus Rift. The toolkit had now also become a software development kit (SDK) abstraction layer that was sorely missing from the Unity3d product.

There was a small problem, though, with the toolkit working on the Oculus Rift: the name. SteamVR Unity Toolkit didn't really make sense anymore because it wasn't only for SteamVR so the community decided to rename the project to the Virtual Reality Toolkit, or VRTK for short.

The community carried it forward building more and more cool features such as climbing, arm-swinging locomotion, different types of grabbing mechanics, ranging from those that use physics to move objects around, to simpler techniques such as making the object a child of the controller.

But another problem was emerging: the toolkit had its origins built around how SteamVR was set up and how it worked. The Oculus SDK integration was really just an abstraction layer on top of the inner workings of SteamVR. Harvey realized that this was going to cause bigger problems down the line when other headsets and technologies would be released. It couldn't all hang on the underpinnings of SteamVR, because this would just be at a fundamental difference to how other headsets in the future could behave.

By this time, VRTK already did so much and so many people were happily using it to build all sorts of wonderful things, but it was clear that it needed to be rethought, reimagined, and rebuilt from the ground up in a fundamentally different way that wasn't tied to any particular piece of technology.

Because of the way VRTK had exploded in its popularity, there wasn't much time for sense-checking decisions or architectural foundations, and because it was based in a legacy of supporting SteamVR, it meant the codebase continued to grow around that concept. The more code that was added by an ever-expanding group of contributors, the more difficult it became to maintain and extend. By that point, it was clearly apparent that VRTK needed to be rewritten, right down to its fundamental design considerations.

VRTK v4

VRTK v4 was to be a completely new approach to the toolkit experience. Rather than prebuilt scripts that did a specific thing, it would be fundamental design patterns that could be composed in numerous configurations to provide functionality that was beneficial for VR (or any other use case for that matter). This was so important because it meant whatever changed with the technology in the future, the toolkit would be right there to support it. Developers could be building with ease for any fledgling hardware that was trying to succeed in the market meaning more games and experiences could support it, which would only help with the success of any evolutionary process.

The work on VRTK v4 started at the end of April 2018 with a completely new approach to the way the toolkit would work for developers. Also, its lack of a reliance on core Unity3d features meant that the future for the toolkit could, and aspired to, extend to other platforms such as Unreal Engine, WebVR, and Godot, to name a few. This premise was even more exciting for the potential of VRTK: if a developer could understand the fundamentals of VRTK and how to create solutions using it in Unity3d, there should be little to stop them from transferring that knowledge to another platform. The only blocker is learning how to use the interface of other platforms, but the capability to pick and choose the head-mounted displays (HMDs) and engine to build upon would be extremely beneficial to all developers alike.

One of the big passions of the VRTK team and community was making sure that VRTK and VR development was accessible to as many people as possible. VRTK is already being used at many hackathons, workshops, and educational institutes like high schools and universities to teach VR development to a new wave of creators. How could VRTK v4 also align the power of the new toolkit with educating those who might already be seasoned developers to those who had no experience at all but wanted to learn? Thus, the concept of a VRTK curriculum was devised. There was a question that needed to be answered, though: was it possible to have a collection of guides, tutorials, videos, and learning materials that were helpful to teach the power of VRTK but also in a consistent manner and provide various levels that depending on the user's expertise could have a feasible, understandable entry point?

The ability to bring a whole new medium to a world of new creators is a special opportunity. The advent of home computing in the 80s allowed bedroom programmers to create a video-game industry. Could VRTK help reignite such a movement but for VR? The passion to do so is certainly there, with the emphasis on education being on par with actually building the tools to do so. More important is to have much of the educational content also be free and open source so that it can be easily used and contributed to by anyone in the educational space.

The Future of VRTK

The future of VRTK is not just to provide a platform for beginners to start their development journey, but also to aid and rapidly improve the development process for seasoned developers, from indie to AAA houses. Providing reliable, tried-and-tested tools to prevent them from having to reinvent the wheel means new ideas can be prototyped quickly to determine whether their mechanics work. The ability to focus on content and not mechanics means that developers can put more effort into producing highly polished content furthering the appetite of the fledgling market but also with the underlying power of VRTK v4 means that these developers can further customize and extend the underlying solutions to provide even more unique experiences.

The ability to open up VR accessibility to corporations, as well, is an important mission for VRTK. To allow industries to quickly and cheaply trial VR solutions to everyday problems means that the commercial uptake of VR will be faster, resulting in more investment for this wonderful new medium to flourish and prosper.

It's with a heart of hope and love from the VRTK community that VRTK will continue to support the development of VR as a medium and even extend into the future to support other spatial computing sectors such as augmented reality (AR). The future is looking bright, and hopefully VRTK is able to make it much brighter.

The concept around VRTK v3 was to provide a single script that gave a specific piece of functionality. Although this made it easy to get something going by simply dragging and dropping a script, it meant that customizing the functionality component would require extending the script and potentially even writing large chunks of code. VRTK v4 aims to break usable functionality down into common components that have the responsibility of doing one specific job, and these small components are then combined to form a prefab that performs the same functionality that the single script did. These prefabs that contain the relevant components are wired up using events so that if any part of the execution path needs changing or amending, it can simply wire up new listeners on the events, which results most often in no coding actually needing to be done.

The benefit of these subcomponents in VRTK v4 is that a lot of reusable functionality can be spread across many different use cases, whether it's moving an object around or detecting a collision. It also means that the underlying core code in VRTK v4 has nothing to do with VR at all, so it can be used for any purpose, whether that's VR, AR, or even just a desktop or mobile experience. The prefabs that sit on top of the core code provide specific functionality, allowing for any new requirements to easily be catered for by simply composing the generic components together in a different mix to provide whatever is required.

Another issue within VRTK v3 was its origins in being built around the inner workings of SteamVR, meaning everything was basically a layer on top of a SteamVR setup for all of the other SDKs supported. Supporting things that had no clear similarity to SteamVR was very difficult. VRTK v4 has no foundations in any SDK and therefore is totally generic and should be able to support any number of devices with relative ease. A good example is something like moving the player around a scene; in V3 this was known as touchpad walking and would take the axis data from the Vive touchpad (or Oculus Touch thumbstick) and turn it into directional data. This worked fine, but it always expected that this directional information would come from the SDK in relation to a touchpad or equivalent. This meant that anything that simply wanted to inject directional information into the player movement script would need to go through the entire SDK pipeline to achieve it. In VRTK v4, because there is no reliance on that sort of intrinsic knowledge, it is very easy to just create an "Action" that emits a Vector2 containing the directional data and then operations can be performed on the Vector2 to mutate it along the way, such as multiplying elements of it like wanting to invert the y direction, the data can even be converted into another data type such as a float or a Boolean.

Because of new generic approach in VRTK v4 utilizing events to pass messages between subcomponents, it is much easier to create custom functionality without the need to write any code. There is also the benefit of being able to use a visual scripting tool to create functionality using simple drag and drop. This is a great step forward for those who are not coming from a coding background but still want to create unique experiences without the need to learn the underlying coding.

The Success of VRTK

Since the emergence of VRTK, there have been more than 30,000 downloads of the toolkit and has been used in a wide variety of projects ranging from solo indie devs to AAA game studios. Figure 7-1 shows just a fraction of the published titles that credit VRTK for rapidly reducing development time towards production available on all the major platforms, including the Oculus Store and Steam.

Made With VRTK

Many games and experiences have already been made with VRTK.

Figure 7-1. Here are some successful projects using VRTK

You can find a full list of published games that use VRTK online (*http://bit.ly/2CdDopG*).

Getting Started with VRTK 4

VRTK is a collection of useful scripts and concept demonstrations to aid building VR solutions rapidly and easily. It aims to make building VR solutions in Unity3d fast and easy for beginners and seasoned developers alike.

VRTK covers a number of common solutions such as the following:

- Locomotion within virtual space
- Interactions like touching, grabbing, and using objects
- Interacting with Unity3d UI elements through pointers or touch
- Body physics within virtual space
- 2D and 3D controls like buttons, levers, doors, drawers, and so on

Setting up the project

Following are the steps you need to take to set up your project:

1. Create a new project in Unity3d 2018.1 or above using the 3D Template.
2. Ensure that Virtual Reality Supported checkbox is selected.
   a. In Unity3d main menu, click "Edit," then "Project Settings," then "Player."
   b. In the PlayerSettings inspector panel, expand the XR Settings.
   c. Select the Virtual Reality Supported option checkbox.
3. Update the project to the supported Scripting Runtime Version.
   a. In the Unity3d main menu, click "Edit," then "Project Settings," then "Player."
   b. In the PlayerSettings inspector panel, expand Other Settings.
   c. Change Scripting Runtime Version to .NET 4.x Equivalent.
   d. Unity will now restart in the supported scripting runtime.

Cloning the repository

Here's how to clone the VRTK repository into your project:

1. Navigate to the project *Assets/* directory.
2. Git clone required submodules into the *Assets/* directory:

```
git clone --recurse-submodules https://github.com/thestonefox/VRTK.git

git submodule init && git submodule update
```

Running the tests

Open the VRTK/Scenes/Internal/TestRunner scene:

1. In the Unity3d main menu, click "Window", then "Test Runner".
2. On the EditMode tab, click Run All.
3. If all the tests pass, your installation was successful.

Setting up your environment

1. Download the latest version of VRTK from the GitHub repository (see Table 7-1) at *www.vrtk.io (https://www.vrtk.io)* (or *www.github.com/thestonefox/VRTK*).

Table 7-1. Supported SDKs

Supported SDK	Download link
VR Simulator	Included
SteamVR	https://www.assetstore.unity3d.com/en/#!/content/32647
Oculus	https://developer.oculus.com/downloads/package/oculus-utilities-for-unity-5/
Ximmerse*	https://github.com/Ximmerse/SDK/tree/master/Unity
Daydream*	https://developers.google.com/vr/unity/download

If you do not have access to a VR Headset, or want to build agnostically for prototyping purposes, an SDK is not required to run the preview of your game development on Unity 3D

a. VRTK is currently only accessible via the Command Line. If you are on a PC, open up your Command Prompt. On Mac, open Terminal.
b. Copy and paste the following command in the editor:

```
git clone --recurse-submodules
```

c. Press Enter and wait for the command to run before proceeding.
d. Enter the following command in the editor:

```
git submodule init && git submodule update
```

e. Press Enter and wait for the command to run.
f. Optional: Download the SDK for your desired hardware.
g. Import the VRTK 4 Assets Folder into your Unity 3D project.

h. Go to *Assets/VRTK/Examples*, then open any of the Example Scenes, press Play to see how the interactions look in your Game Scene.

Example scenes

A collection of example scenes has been created to aid with your understanding the different aspects of VRTK. This is a great place to begin if you're using VRTK for the first time—or even the 50 millionth time—because they also serve as a great starting point for rapid prototyping or basic project jump start.

The example scenes are environments that are readily set up for instant functionality with your SDK of choice. Each of these scenes are titled based on the type of functionality that the scene will demonstrate. The example scenes can easily be duplicated and customized into your project and they support all of the VRTK supported VR SDKs.

You can view a full list of the examples in *Examples/README.md* (*http://bit.ly/ 2NGlqAA*), which includes an up-to-date list of examples showcasing the features of VRTK.

To make use of VR devices (besides the included VR Simulator), import the needed third-party VR SDK into the project.

How to "check out" the VRTK v4 Examples Repository

Here are the steps needed to check out the VRTK v4 Examples Repository:

1. Currently, VRTK is accessible only via the command line. If you are on a PC, open your Command Prompt. If you're on a Macintosh, open your Terminal.
2. Copy and paste the following line into the editor:

    `git clone --recurse-submodules` *https://github.com/thestonefox/VRTK.git*
3. Press Enter and wait until complete.
4. On the new line, type the following command:

    `git submodule init && git submodule update`
5. Press Enter and wait until complete.
6. Optional: Download the SDK for your desired hardware.
7. Go to *Assets/VRTK/Examples*, open any of the Example Scenes, and then press play to see how the interactions look in your Game Scene.

Following is a current list of example scenes and interaction features (as of this writing):

Input scene

Displays the information being given by your controllers or keyboard inputs into the game.

Object pointer scene

Shows the raycast, using green lasers emitted by your controllers. You can point the lasers on various objects on the scene and see the different reactions your pointer can have when pointed on specific objects.

Straight pointer

The pointer is your basic straight laser emission. Best used for making UI selections, or interacting with objects.

Bezier pointer

A curve line emission that points to the ground—this is debatably the best user experience for teleportation.

Point-and-click teleport

Using a pointer, you can select an area that you wish to move to and in a "blink" you will be repositioned to that location.

Instant teleport

This is the use of a "black frame" that resembles a blink, in which the user will end up in the new location when the vision has returned.

Dash teleport

Point to an area you wish to teleport to, and it will then speed up the frames of the movement for the user to arrive there. This movement is an emerging and feels more natural than the instant teleport method.

Teleport scene

Shows different areas and area types that you can teleport to in the scene by clicking the Thumbstick to activate teleportation and pointing to the direction or point you want to move to with a click on the trigger button.

Interactable objects

Teleport around the scene to the various objects. Use the grip button on the controllers to see the various grab types on each of the objects. Here are a few examples of the type of interactions available at the time of release in the VRTK assets folder:

Precision grab

Grabs in a precise location of a given object. In the example of a gun, regardless of where the hand is located on the object, you can have it automatically be picked up in specific way to improve ease of use.

Gun grab

Grabs a gun shaped object will always have it positioned in a ready fire position in the hand when picked up in any angle.

Toggle grab

Allows you to release the button when an object is grabbed and maintain a grabbed position until you press the button again.

Two-handed hold

Holds objects in a functional position when both hands have grabbed it.

Pump

Allows use of a pumping action on an object to produce a specified effect.

Hinge joint

Moves only on a specific axis—for example, a door swinging open and closed.

Other interactions will include the scaling grab, two-handed precision grab, basic joint, customizable joints, character joints, pick and grabs, and so much more. For more information on the release of these assets, visit our website!

Scene Switcher

In play mode, you can select the CameraRig Switcher to alternate between different types of SDKs you are using for your experience or select a simulator. This is particularly useful, if not the most advantageous use of VRTK, as you can build for multiple headsets and preview how it would look in real time during the development stage for each one with just a click of a button.

How to set up a VRTK Core project from scratch

1. In your Unity 3D 2018.1+ project, open a blank scene.

2. Select the Virtual Reality Supported checkbox.

3. Go to Project Settings → Player → Other Settings. Under Configuration, change the Scripting Runtime Version to .Net 4x Equivalent.

4. When prompted, press Restart.

5. Download the VRTK.Unity.Core package from GitHub, and then drag and drop the Assets Folder into your Unity 3D project.

How to set up a Unity CameraRig

1. In your scene, go the "Hierarchy" tab, and then delete the Default Camera.

2. Drag the VRTK Camera Rig into your scene.

    a. Go to Assets → VRTK Unity.Core → CameraRig → [UnityXRCameraRig]. Drag the [UnityXRCameraRig] Prefab into your Hierarchy tab.[1]

3. Press play on the scene to preview the camera.

    Head anchor
        The parent game object referencing to the position of the headset.

    Left anchor
        Child game object referencing the left eye lens of the headset.

    Right anchor
        Child game object referencing the right eye lens of the headset.

How to set up a Tracked Alias

1. Drag the "Tracked Alias" prefab into your Hierarchy.

2. Go to Assets → VRTK.Unity.Core → CameraRig → TrackedAlias.

3. Tracked alias game objects are the child game objects that you can customize for the embodied user interactions tailored to the sensores that will be used in relation to the hardware type.

---

1 As of this writing, VRTK v4 is still in development. Refer to vrtk.io (*https://www.vrtk.io*) for the latest updates in documentation and tutorials, for getting started.

Play area alias
> In reference to the physical space that will be tracked by the hardware sensors for the experience

Headset alias
> In reference to the headset position

Left controller alias
> In reference to the left hand controller

Right controller alias
> In reference to the right hand controller

Scene cameras
> This game object references the various cameras that will be positioned in the experience (for either first or third person perspective)

Other tutorials available on the website at the time of this release will include:

- How to set up the Simulator
- Introduction to VRTK Actions
- How to set up a pointer
- How to set up teleporting with a pointer
- How to set up interactable objects (interactor/interactables)

CHAPTER 8

Three Virtual Reality and Augmented Reality Development Best Practices

Vasanth Mohan

Developing for Virtual Reality and Augmented Reality Is Difficult

And that is probably why you are reading this book in the first place.

But it is important to understand the sheer complexity before diving into development. So, let's break down first what makes development much more complicated than most fields.

Let's begin with the tools. Throughout this chapter, we work with the Unity game engine. Initially released in 2005, Unity has helped countless developers around the world to get started building three-dimensional games, everything from mobile to console to desktop. And although it has served as the backbone for 3D development for many people and has fostered an amazing community over the years, it is by no means perfect, especially as design paradigms for virtual reality (VR) and augmented reality (AR) are continually evolving. Since modern VR development kits first began releasing in 2013, Unity's built-in tools and external plug-ins have significantly improved, but certain tasks such as cross-platform development and multiplayer are still not quite as simple as enabling a button. Keep that in mind as you continue through this chapter.

Next, the hardware. More than the tools, the number of different pieces of hardware can tremendously increase complexity. From the Oculus Rift to PlayStation VR to an iPhone running ARKit, each device has its own set of restrictions that will need to be optimized on a case-by-case basis to meet the unique requirements of the device. Although this is nothing new if you are coming from a graphics or gaming background, each device has a unique set of buttons and tracking requirements that need to be integrated into how each specific app is developed.

And, lastly, maintenance. As mentioned before, VR and AR are evolving fields. As such, both the tools and hardware continue to change at outstanding rates. Unity releases a major change approximately every three months, and new headsets or tools for existing headsets can change even faster than that. This requires keeping your code up to date, sometimes even before releasing your experience. It might be time consuming, but it's necessary to ensure that your experience runs successfully for everyone.

Now, I know that is a ton of negative problems with the field, but there is a light at the end of the tunnel. VR and AR are the most *rewarding* development you can do, in my opinion. It might not be easy and there will surely be frustrating points along the way, but when you get to see people wearing a headset with a smile on their face, it is incredibly rewarding. And the reason why I began this chapter with that long introduction is to make it clear what the limitations are with development and really emphasize the constraints within which you will be working. There are workarounds for most of these issues via careful planning and by working with a design team to create a scope that delivers a compelling experience and hides all the aforementioned issues.

VR and AR development is *difficult*, so moving forward into this chapter, let's learn how we can make use of some tips and tricks to make it easier. With all that said, let's dive into three development practices that you can use within VR and AR.

Handling Locomotion

First up, we take a look at how to build a few different types of *locomotion mechanics* for both VR and AR. Locomotion can be extremely simple but is an incredibly important mechanic for any experience. It enables a developer to take an infinite world and make it traversable within a finite space; for example, your room. There are many ways to solve locomotion, and the type of locomotion you choose will often be determined by what your audience finds the most immersive. In this part, we build three different types of locomotion: *linear movement*, *teleportation*, and *scaled movement*.

Before we get building, I want to mention a few noteworthy loco-motion systems that we will *not* be building but could be valuable for future learning:

Redirected walking

A graphical technique that slightly distorts the image that is rendered to the headset in order to make the user thinks that they are walking in a straight line, when in reality they are walking in a curved path. You need a big area for this to trick the brain.

Dashing

Quickly moving the user to their destination over a short interval; for example, 0.5 seconds. The advantage is that the user has a better sense of immersion while mitigating potential simulation sickness.

Climbing

A user uses their hands to pull themselves in a desired direc-tion, often by holding onto a virtual object.

Controller Assisted On the Spot (CAOTS)

Using the positional tracked controllers while moving in place to move virtually. This tracking is used in the Freedom Loco-motion VR application listed for free on Steam.

1 to 1

If you can manage to fit everything necessary for your experi-ence within reach of a player, locomotion might not be neces-sary at all, as in *Job Simulator*. And this can be taken one step further in which the virtual room adapts to how big a player's space is, making an experience even more accessible.

Locomotion in VR

Before we begin, it's important to note that the type of locomotion that is integrated into an application is extremely dependent on the application itself. The upcoming implementations are the most common across VR games, but with that said, they might not be right for whatever you are trying to build. Nevertheless, these imple-mentations are valuable to know, especially as you are prototyping to see what works and what doesn't.

Linear movement (aka trackpad movement)

Other than Google Cardboard, all modern VR systems come with a controller of some kind, as shown in Figure 8-1, and all of these controllers come with either a joy-stick or trackpad.

Figure 8-1. Oculus Rift Controller (left) and HTC Vive Controller (right)

Knowing this, we can create a simple 2D movement system using the joystick or touchpad as input. If you are familiar with first-person-shooter games, this will be a very similar movement mechanism as with those games.

To begin, we first need to set up our player. For this, we use Unity's built-in physics simulation, which means that we will need to attach a *Rigidbody* component (see Figure 8-2) to our player. Some of the benefits of using a Rigidbody include easily adding forces and velocity to objects as well as simulating physics collisions between two objects. This is extremely useful for us because we want to use the velocity to move our player linearly as well as detect when the player is colliding with the ground.

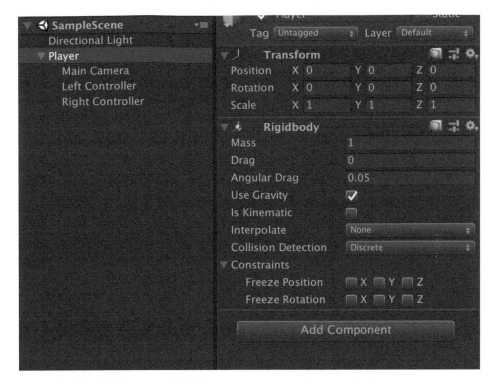

Figure 8-2. Rigidbody on our VR player

Next, we need to add a collider to define the bounds of our player. Here, I have some good news and bad news. The good news is that when we define the bounds of the player, the bounds don't need to be perfect. A simple capsule collider will suffice, which is a built-in collider for Unity, as illustrated in Figure 8-3, and is highly optimized for performance.

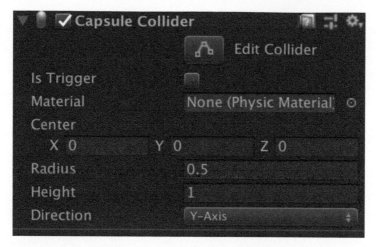

Figure 8-3. Unity's built-in capsule collider (added to a player)

The bad news is that for VR (and AR), unlike defining player collision bounds in a traditional video game, there is no one-size-fits-all-height for every single human that plays your game. There are a couple of potential fixes to this problem:

- Ask the players to stand still before they begin so that they can be measured for the duration of the session
- Assume that the current height of the player is their maximum height

Although neither fix is optimal, depending on your use case, one solution might be beneficial compared to the other. One thing to note is that in most VR toolkits (SteamVR, VRTK, etc.), the second solution is implemented by default. To see how they might implement it, take a look at this pseudocode (go to GitHub for the actual implementation):

```
public Collider capsule; // set from the Unity Interface
public Transform player; // set from the Unity Interface
void AdjustCapsuleHeight() {
    var playerHeightOffset = player.localPosition; //player's height from ground
    capsule.height = playerHeightOffset; //set the height
    capsule.localPosition.y = -playerHeightOffset / 2;
 //because capsule pivot is in the center
}
```

With the physics system set up, we can now dive into creating the linear motion. Just like with the capsule collider, following is pseudocode (again, you can find the working solution on GitHub):

```
public Rigidbody rigidbody; // set from the Unity Interface
public float speed; // set from the Unity Interface
```

```
void LinearMovement() {
    Vector2 trackpad = null;
    if (Input.GetTouch( LeftTrackPad )) { //check if left trackpad is touched
        trackpad = Input.GetLeftPad(); //set left trackpad 2D position
    }
    else if (Input.GetTouch( RightTrackPad )) { //check if right trackpad is touched
        trackpad = Input.GetRightPad(); //set right trackpad 2D position
    }
    if (trackpad != null) {
        rigidbody.velocity =
            new Vector3(trackpad.x, 0, trackpad.y) * speed;
 //set XZ velocity, so we don't start flying
    }
    else {
        rigidbody.velocity = Vector3.zero; //when not pressed, set to 0;
    }
}
```

And that is everything you need to set up some simple linear movement. Although this is a fairly simple movement mechanism to set up, it is by no means suitable for every audience. What we recommend is to provide this locomotion system as an option for the adventurous users (who make up a good portion of VR users) and then include our next locomotion system, teleportation, as a system for those who are more sensitive to simulator sickness.

Teleportation locomotion

Pretty much since the first Oculus Development shipped, teleportation has been one of the simplest, effective, and somewhat controversial solutions to traversing a large virtual space. On the one hand, it avoids a lot of the issues that other locomotion systems have with simulation sickness, making it the most accessible. But depending on the type of experience you are building, it can also lose the sense of immersion very quickly. That said, it is an amazing tool to keep in your belt because more often than not you will want to include it in your experience. So, let's build it!

There are a few different types of teleportations, but to keep the focus on what we're building, let's zero in on one of the most common types: Bézier (or curved) teleportation, as demonstrated in Figure 8-4. Here are two reason why curved paths are often commonly used:

- They limit how far players can travel, which limits players from traveling all the way across a level.
- It decreases the precision the player needs to end up in the desired location.

Figure 8-4. Curved teleportation

To begin, let's first do some setup. We want a few variables to customize our teleportation as well as a method to render our teleportation. Luckily, Unity has a built-in Line Renderer Component that is highly customizable to get the look and feel you want.

With that set up, we can focus on checking for input to start our teleportation. Depending on the platform on which you are developing, this code could look different, especially if you have 0, 1, or 2 controllers, the code will vary, but the concept is pick a button that will be comfortable for players to press often, such as the trackpad on the Vive controllers or trigger on the Oculus Rift. Whenever that button is held, show the curved path for the teleportation, and then when it is released, teleport to that location.

For more comfort, you can also choose to fade the player's view to black very quickly to increase the comfort of the teleportation (check the GitHub repository for a working solution):

```
public Vector3 gravity; //set in inspector as (0, -9.8, 0)
public LineRenderer path; //the component that will render our path
private Vector3 teleportLocation; //save the location of where we want to teleport
private Player player; //the player we will be teleporting
void Update() { //called every fame
    if (!CheckTeleport(LeftHand)) { //check the left hand
        CheckTeleport(RightHand); //if not teleporting with left hand try right hand
    }
}
bool CheckTeleport(Hand hand) { //check a hand to see the status of teleporting
    List<Vector3> curvedPoints; //the points on the teleport curve
    if (hand.GetPressed(TrackPad)) {
 //check if track pad ( button for teleport) is pressed
        if (CalcuateCurvedPath(hand.position, hand.forward, gravity
                        , out curvedPoints)) { //calculate teleport
            RenderPath(curvedPoints); //if calculate, render the path
            teleportLocation = curvedPoints[curvedPoints.Count - 1];
 //set teleport point
            return true;
        }
    } else if (hand.GetPressedUp(TrackPad)) { //time to actually teleport
        player.position = teleportLocation; //move the player instantly
    }
    return false; //we are not using this hand currently for teleporting
}
```

Now let's take a look at the actual teleportation code. The main method will be the CalculateCurvedPath, which takes the start point, direction, and effect of gravity and then outputs the curved path. With those inputs, we can run a simple physics simulation to calculate how long it takes for the curve to land on the ground. For simplicity, we assume the velocity to just be the normalized direction, although you can change this value to get different effects:

```
bool CalculateCurvedPath(Vector3 position, Vector3 direction,
//calcuates the teleportation path
                    Vector3 gravity, out Vector3 points) {
    int maxDistance = 500; //sets the max distance the path can travel
    Vector3 currPos = origin, hypoPos = origin, hypoVel = direction.normalized;
 //initialize variable to keep track off
    List<Vector3> v = new List<Vector3>(); //list of points
    RaycastHit hit; //gets raycast info at each step
    float curveCastLength = 0; //current distance traveled
    do { //loop
        v.Add(hypoPos); //add start
        currPos = hypoPos; //set start position as previous end postion
        hypoPos = currPos + hypoVel + (gravityDirection * Time.fixedDeltaTime);
 // calculate next point on curve
```

```
            hypoVel = hypoPos - currPos; //calulate the delta for the velocity
            curveCastLength += hypoVel.magnitude; // add velocity to distance
        }
    while (Raycast(currPos, hypoVel, out hit, hypoVel.magnitude) == false
  //check physics to see if we hit the ground
                && curveCastLength < maxDistance);
    points = v; //return points
    return Raycast(currPos, hypoVel, out hit, hypoVel.magnitude); //check if landed
}
void RenderPath(List<Vector3> points) {
    path.pointCount = points.Count;
    for ( int i = 0; i < points.Count ; i++) {
        path.points[i] = points[i]; //set all points in Line Renderer
    }
}
```

After the path is calculated, we can just assign all of the points to the line renderer, which will automatically render the line. One thing to note here is that you will want to go back to the input code and enable and disable the line renderer whenever the button is pressed and released, respectively. Otherwise, the first points assigned to the path will always stay there, which is a funny bug but probably not intended.

And with that, we have teleportation, a bit more complicated than linear movement, but it's definitely worth it within many experiences.

Locomotion in AR

We just covered one extremely important locomotion system for VR. The next locomotion system happens to work well within both VR and AR, but it is particularly impactful in AR because there aren't as many tools for locomotion given that it can appear a bit awkward if virtual objects change position due to locomotion, whereas in the real world they remain fixed. One way to get around this with AR is by using a visual trick that changes the perception of scale—and this is actually quite easy to achieve.

Giant (or Ant) mode

One of the biggest selling points of VR and AR is being able to experience new things, and a subpoint of that is being able to size things from a brand-new vantage point; that is, being really big or really small.

One way to make this happen is by increasing or decreasing the scale of each individual object in a scene—the problem with this approach is that the player is still human size and, as a result, the distance traveled by a player will still be human scaled.

Instead, to cover more (or less) ground and scale the distance traveled, it will often be better to scale the player. The way scale works in Unity (and in almost all game engines) is that the position and scale values of any objects nested under a parent object will be multiplied. To illustrate this, take a look at Figures 8-5 and 8-6.

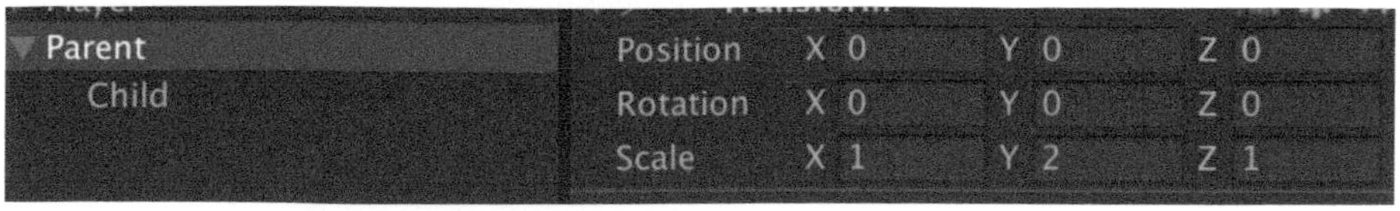

Figure 8-5. The parent object's transform parameters

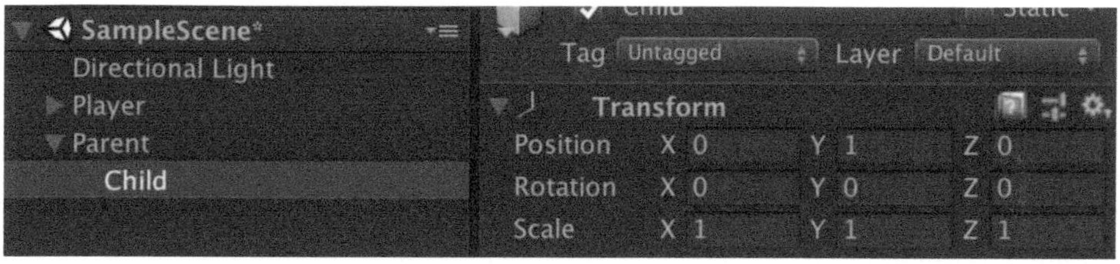

Figure 8-6. The child object's transform parameters

The Transform of the Child object will be:

Position
   The Child's (0, 1, 0) multiplied (dot product) with the Parent's (1, ,2, 1) = (0 , 2, 0)

Scale
   The Child's (1, 1, 1) multiplied (dot product) with the Parent's (1, ,2, 1) = (0, 2, 0)

Using that knowledge, we can apply this to our AR player. All we need to do is create a parent object with a scale bigger than (1, 1, 1), as demonstrated in Figure 8-7.

Figure 8-7. Scaling a VR player

And with that, we have created a giant scaled player if that scale is set to greater than (1, 1, 1), and an ant if that scale is less than (1, 1, 1). An important note to keep in mind is that you can set the scales for each axis to a different value, but this will lead to a *very* disorienting experience. I highly recommend that you keep all the scales exactly the same and as positive values to avoid weird behavior.

And that's it for locomotion. As VR and AR hardware change, different types of locomotion will be experimented with, and it is possible for some of these commonly used systems to go out of date in time. But being able to build any and all of these systems will be useful to start brainstorming new ways to handle new developments in the space.

Effective Use of Audio

When you hear the terms "VR" or "AR," which of your five senses come to mind? For most people, it is vision—being able to see the world and being able react to it. Audio almost always takes second or third place (behind touch). But in reality (and virtual reality) audio is equally important, if not more important, than the visuals of a world to create the ambiance. Imagine these three scenarios, you are sailing on the virtual ocean like the one shown in Figure 8-8, when suddenly you hear:

- Ambient disco music
- A heartbeat from behind you
- Nothing (the developer was feeling lazy)

Figure 8-8. The vast ocean

In each scenario, what happens next to you is independent of the visuals but extremely dependent on what you hear or what you don't hear. In short, audio isn't something to forget or ignore, so let's see how to implement it to get the most out of audio.

Audio in VR

In this part, let's take a closer look at how Unity allows developers to implement audio into its applications. The current methods have been traditionally used by 2D game developers. As a result, as VR developers we need to perform some additional steps to make the audio in VR environments sound more immersive.

Ambient versus 3D versus spatial audio

Within Unity, there are three main types of audio:

Ambient
> 2D audio that is independent of the location of the player. Think of this like distant bird chirps in a forest.

3D audio
> Audio that is tied to a 3D position and the volume drops off the further the player (audio listener) is from that position.

Spatial (binaural) audio
> Similar to 3D audio, the main difference being that the audio left and right channel intensity varies depending on how far away the object is from each ear, just as in real life.

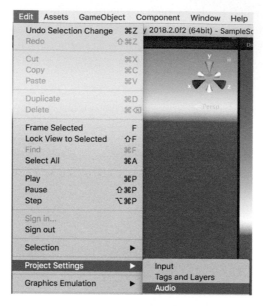

Figure 8-9. The path to Unity's audio settings

Each audio type has its place in VR development, but for the most realistic experience, we want to simulate audio using the spatial audio setting to get an effect very similar to real life.

There are several software development kits (SDKs) currently available for free, and most work cross-platform using Unity. For simplicity, here we use the Oculus Spatial Audio plug-in that is currently built in to Unity. As of Unity 2108.2, you can find these settings on the Edit tab (Figure 8-9), and then click Project Settings → Audio → Spatializer Plugin (Figure 8-10).

Figure 8-10. Unity's audio manager

After you set the Spatializer to Oculus, you can add an Audio Source to your scene (ideally, near your camera). When you do this, the Spatialize option becomes active, as shown in Figure 8-11.

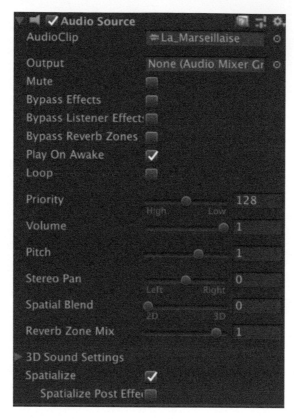

Figure 8-11. Unity's default Audio Source component

Click Spatialize on your audio source and then import any audio clip you have to test it out. To try it out, run your scene and then drag your audio source around near your camera. If you have headphones in, you will hear the audio go from your left ear to your right ear, and vice versa. If you enable VR, you will be able to test it by just rotating your head! Pretty neat, right?

Audio in AR

In most cases, developing for an AR headset will be very similar to mobile AR. However, in the case of audio, you will want to take a very different approach between the two. For an AR headset, I recommend developing audio in a similar style to VR headsets. However, for mobile AR, I recommend a completely different approach using *unspatialized* mono audio.

Mono versus stereo

Most audio files that you find online will be in a stereo format, which means that audio is recorded in two channels, one for your left ear and one for your right, which is great for headphone users. However, for mobile AR, it is best to take stereo files in your project and convert them to mono; that is, just having one channel. There are three reason for this:

- Most mobile users don't use headphones when using apps.
- Even if they use headphones, stereo audio—especially spatialized audio—can confuse players when they rotate their device and the audio changes even though their head didn't move.
- As an added bonus, mono audio takes up less space, which is important on any mobile device and especially important when developing using AR Studio or Lens Studio.

To deliver the best experience, I recommend that you use mono audio with a 3D audio source to change audio only when a player moves closer to an object.

To create a mono audio clip, you can use a program like Audacity to combine the left and right audio channels into a single averaged channel. This is an easy-to-use option within Audacity. After you export the clip, you can use that within a Unity audio source or any AR program of your choosing.

Common Interactions Paradigms

Newton's Third Law: For every action, there is an equal and opposite reaction.

When you apply this to VR and AR, for every action a user makes, there needs to be a response that matches the user's expectations. Whether that is throwing an object and seeing it go flying away, pulling a lever and opening a secret door, or simply turning your head and having the world update accordingly. All of these actions fall under the category of good game design, but, more important, all of these actions will make users feel fully immersed and avoid any potential for simulator sickness.

Moreover, another important lesson from game design is to never overwhelm users with too many input options. And the corollary to that is the developer must always guide users to learn all input options while still making the user feel like they are discovering new tools. Summarized, it means that no matter whether a user just downloaded your app or has spent 100 hours in it, they should always know what they need to do next.

What we build next is a couple of common input interactions that are seen across VR and AR titles: an *inventory system* for VR, and touchscreen real-world *raycast* for mobile AR.

Inventory for VR

An inventory system is often a must-have when creating an experience with a lot of interactive objects that a player needs to hold and carry around. Luckily, because we are building a virtual world, we have "infinite" space to place objects. So, let's take some space in front of the controller to hold our objects. To set this up, let's create some inventory slots (represented by the default spheres, as shown in Figure 8-12) and parent them under our controller (Figure 8-13) so that they always follow the controller.

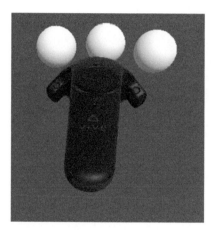

Figure 8-12. A prototype of inventory slots

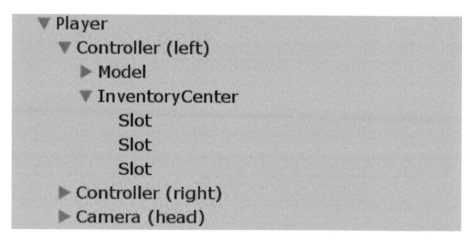

Figure 8-13. Setup for the inventory parented to the controller

With that setup, we can focus on our scripts. In total, we will need three: Inventory Manager, InvetorySlot, and InventoryItem. Let's look a little closer at each one:

InventoryManager

This will be the script that handles when the user presses the Application Menu button on the *left* or *right* controller to allow us to hide or show all inventory slots for that *respective* controller.

InventoryItem

This will be the script that is attached to any item that can be added and removed from the inventory.

InventorySlot

This will be the script that is attached to each slot to maintain its state.

Let's begin with `InventoryManager`. For this class, we need only to check whether the Application Menu button is pressed and, if so, show or hide the inventory slots for the controller. For a smoother effect, you could also animate the slots in and out, which is shown in the GitHub repository. After this is set up, we can just add this class as a component to each of our controllers:

```
public class InventoryManager : MonoBehaviour {
public Controller controller;
//which controller
public GameObject inventoryParent;
//parent of slots for this controller              void Update() {
//check every frame
              if (controller.PressDown(ApplicationMenu)) {
 // the first frame the button is pressed
               ShowInventorySlots(true);
            } else if (controller.PressUp(ApplicationMenu)) {
               ShowInventorySlots(false);
        }                  }                   void ShowInventorySlots(bool show) {
          inventoryParent.SetActive(show);
          //toggle whether shown or not based on bool parameter                  }
}
```

Next up, `InventoryItem`. Before we write this script, let's add all of the components we need to a test object; that is, a Rigidbody and Collider Component. To test this, we will need to also include an SDK, like VRTK, to be able to grab objects, and this will already be included in the GitHub repository.

After that is set up, it's time to write the code. The main method we will be using to trigger when the code starts running is `OnTriggerEnter`, a method that is triggered from the Rigidbody we attached earlier. This Rigidbody checks when any colliders attached to our object collide with any other collider. When that happens, the object can be referenced to see whether it is a slot. In this example, we check the name, but other viable ways to check are by the tag or by layer. If it is a slot, we can then assign our item to the inventory slot, which we will handle in the `InventorySlot` script:

```
public class InventoryItem : MonoBehaviour {
private void OnTriggerEnter(Collider other) {
             if (other.name == "Slot") {
   other.gameObject.GetComponent<InventorySlot>().SetItem(this, ItemReleased);
 //call the slot method
  SetSize(.01f); //set size to fit in slot
       }            }             void ItemReleased() {
 //callback for when item leaves slot
            SetSize(1f);
    //when item is released set size to normal
    }            void SetSize(float size) {
            transform.localScale = Vector3.one * size;
 //set a uniform size i.e (1,1,1)                   }
}
```

Last but not least is the code for each inventory slot. Although it might look like a lot of code, most of it is actually getting and setting variables during the two methods SetItem (called from InventoryItem) and OnTriggerExit, which is when the item is pulled out of the slot from the hand. Because we are also using OnTriggerExit in this class, we will also need to include a Collider and Rigidbody for each slot that we create within the Unity scene. And after each of these scripts is assigned to the right Game Object, our inventory system should be all set:

```
public class InventorySlot : MonoBehaviour {            public MeshRenderer renderer;
//the renderer to show the slot
public delegate void ItemReleasedAction();
//method signature for callback function
private InventoryItem currentItem;
//stores Current Item
private ItemReleasedAction currentReleasedCallback;
//callback for item
void SetItem(InventoryItem item, ItemReleasedAction releasedCallback ) {
//called from inventory item
            item.transform.parent = this.transform; //set the parent
            item.transform.position = this.transform.position;
 //center
            currentItem = item;
            currentReleasedCallback = releasedCallback;
            renderer.enabled = false;           }
 private void OnTriggerExit(Collider other) {
            if (other.GetComponent<InventoryItem> == currentItem) {
                currentReleasedCallback();
 //hand is grabbing item out of inventory
   currentItem = null;
   currentReleasedCallback = null;
   renderer.enabled = true;
           }
    }
}
```

And with that, here is a bare-bones structure of an inventory system. There are definitely a lot of improvements that we can make (some of which will be made in the GitHub), but this is meant to serve as a starting point toward a customized inventory in your experience.

Augmented Reality Raycasts

As a concept, this is extremely important for developing in AR. However, in practice, this only takes a few lines of code to implement, but there are also a few lines that can completely change the behavior of your augmentation if they are incorrect.

In computer graphics and also within Unity, a *ray* is defined by a starting point and a direction and then used as part of the calculations of a *raycast* to find the first physics collider (if there is one) with which the ray intersects.

In the context of AR, this can get a little confusing because an AR raycast is similar to this definition except an AR raycast will not detect a virtual object. Depending on how advanced the SDK is, it might be able to recognize and return the object, but more likely the SDK will return a point in virtual space that maps to a point in real world. Here is an example:

1. A user taps on the screen to place a virtual chair on the floor:

```
// FixedUpdate is called everytime the Physics engine updates
void FixedUpdate () {
                TrackableHit hit;
    //stores all raycast information if there is a hit
        // Does the ray intersect any objects excluding the player layer
        Ray ray = Camera.main.ScreenPointToRay(Input.touchPosition);
    //get location of touch
        if (Frame.Raycast(ray.origin, ray.direction, //ARCore example
            out hit, Mathf.Infinity)) {

            //Raycast was Successful - now do something!
        }
    }
}
```

2. A user taps on the screen to get more information about a virtual chair:

```
// FixedUpdate is called everytime the Physics engine updates
void FixedUpdate () {

    RaycastHit hit;
    //stores all raycast information if there is a hit
        // Does the ray intersect any objects excluding the player layer
        Ray ray = Camera.main.ScreenPointToRay(Input.touchPosition);
    //get location of touch
        if (Physics.Raycast(transform.position, transform.forward,
            out hit, Mathf.Infinity)) {
```

```
                    //Raycast was Successful - now do something!
        }
    }
```

3. A user wants to drag a virtual chair across the room.

And this last one is where things begin to get tricky. With a drag, you will need to combine using Unity's built-in physics raycast with an AR raycast. Specifically, in order of execution:

1. The user taps on screen.

2. Using Unity physics raycast, check to see whether the user tapped on an object to drag.

3. If it is a draggable object, do an AR raycast on each Update call to drag the object to a new position the user wants.

These are all fairly common AR interactions that users expect to have in their applications, so it is extremely helpful to keep raycasts in mind and why they might not be performing as desired while debugging.

Conclusion

We just covered some of several tips that are important for VR development. But before we close out of this chapter, I want to leave you with one final tip before you start off on your development journey for VR and AR.

If you ever become stuck or frustrated, just remember PRE:

Passion
    For whom, to do what, and why you are building your amazing project.

Resources
    There are countless resources online from online communities on Facebook and Slack to questions answered on Google. The chances are that someone faced something similar, too.

Experience
    You are building something unique that will let people experience something they never could have. Cherish that!

Yes, I know this acronym is cheesy, but if it helps you to complete your project, that makes it all the more worth it for everyone. And yes, VR and AR development is difficult, but as authors, we are all excited to see what each and every one of you can build and contribute to our awesome community!

PART V

Enhancing Data Representation: Data Visualization and Artificial Intelligence in Spatial Computing

During a time when "big data" companies have emerged with a large investment in working artificial intelligence (AI) models in production, it is essential for new and seasoned software engineers, designers, and technology business professionals in virtual reality (VR), augmented reality (AR), mixed reality (MR), and eXtended Reality (XR), or X Reality, to have a solid foundational understanding of the use and visualization of real-world data, user-generated data, and data constructed in embodied reality. In the following chapters, lead anthology book editor and University of San Francisco Deep Learning Diversity Fellow, Erin Pangilinan; Unity director of AI research department, Nicolas Meuleau; and Unity senior software engineer, Arthur Juliani discuss various aspects of immersive applications and experiences through the lens of data-driven principles. This part seeks to do the following:

- Define data visualization, AI, machine learning, and reinforcement learning paradigms and techniques through practical industry use cases that involve the human body, whether user generated in spatial computing, abstractions, or three-dimensional (3D) reconstructions of real-world data represented in spatial computing

- Offer resources and tips for those building with open source data and frameworks as well as opportunities for further exploration as spatial computing and machine learning advances

- Outline challenges in designing and developing for spatial computing, including highlighting specific nuances that are design challenges in AR given its overlay in the real world, and its distinction from VR

In Chapter 9, Erin Pangilinan defines data and machine learning visualization and its unique design opportunities in immersive technology. New design paradigms not conceived before with design for desktop and mobile platforms are made possible with spatial computing. She describes challenges with respect to the current ergonomic obstacles facing AR and VR, and offers resources and references to hands-on tutorials to get started creating data and machine learning visualizations in XR. Although this chapter is unable to fully cover and discuss data visualization startups with 2D dashboards analyzing user data (those like EaseVR, CognitiveVR, Retinad, etc. doing more involved analysis than simple heatmaps in Unity of XR applications), it references other aspects of embodied reality with use case examples across various B2B industry verticals visualizing data from the human body (particular to health technology—biotech not covered in Dilan Shah's discussion in Chapter 11), some of which are considered "big data" and render in real time at scale.

Chapter 10, by Unity staff Nicolas Meuleau and Arthur Juliani, describes existing AI paradigms, including reactive AI, deliberative AI, and reinforcement learning; how they are challenged by XR; and the answers they can bring. The applications involve behaviors such as animations, nonplayer characters (NPC) activities, and storytelling —behavior of the world. Meuleau focuses on behavior planning and automated animation as a part of Unity's offerings. You learn machine learning–based approaches, particularly reinforcement learning, and imitation learning methods involving player data of games in XR. Toward the end of the chapter, you learn about designing behavioral sets of demonstrations, both human provided or generated by another means (players playing games and, even more significant in AR and VR environments given a user's human body movements, gestures, we are able to use data to inform behavior of autonomous agents in simulation).

AI can be used to generate content that augments technical 3D artists in the game development pipeline as seen at Nvidia's talk at The Game Developer Conference (GDC) 2017 "Zoom, Enhance, Synthesize! Magic Upscaling and Material Synthesis using Deep Learning" (*http://bit.ly/2EmHCNr*), Deep learning algorithms such as style transfer were used in the creation of 360 degree films by Facebook (*http://bit.ly/2TwnMIs*), as screened during the Tribeca Film Festival 2017. Although these are not completely covered given the limited capacity for our scope here, software engineers and designers continue to show how to enhance their XR applications and experiences through cutting-edge AI algorithms and novel ways of representing and visualizing data (user or real-world data) in a new medium. AI outside of this part can be described more in detail in the chapter on SLAM and AR cloud authored by 6D.ai cofounders, Matt Miesnieks and Professor Victor Presacariu as well as Dieter Schmalsteig's work describing in detail the overlap between XR and visualization with regard to the data pipelines in VR and AR as it relates to spatial models, object detection, 3D tracking, and rendering.

CHAPTER 9

Data and Machine Learning Visualization Design and Development in Spatial Computing

Erin Jerri Malonzo Pangilinan

Introduction

Data and machine learning visualization are transforming the future of the workplace. Framing design principles is valuable. Companies such as VR Fund–backed company, Virtualitics, which was founded by Caltech PhDs, raise large rounds of funding based on good design principles. There are also many other data visualization independent consultancies popping up across all spatial computing platforms. Many of these are within the businesses service sphere with significantly large datasets, in the B2B verticals of fintech (finance tech), health technology, and biotech.

We begin this chapter by discussing the relevance of the topic to the users experiencing data and machine learning visualization applications. We then offer a framework to consider for identifying useful purposes that make the topic unique to spatial computing versus any other platform. We outline our goals to understand, define, and set data and machine visualization design and development principles in embodied reality. Then, we discuss various challenges with data and machine learning visualization in XR, describing various examples of industry use cases for data and machine learning visualization built on top of open source data and frameworks (though some interesting work has also been done with open source frameworks and proprietary data). Toward the end of this chapter, we highlight references to tutorials for creators of data and machine learning visualizations, whether you are new or a seasoned software engineer or designer accustomed already to working on web platforms (you can easily use in A-Frame in JavaScript or other frameworks) or in native development,

C# on Unity. There are a few figure examples that were created using C++ and Unreal Engine.

Understanding Data Visualization

Although whitepapers like the IEEE's "Cost-benefit Analysis of Visualization in Virtual Environments (VEs)" question the relevance and purpose of visualization in XR, asking "do we really need 3D visualization for 3D data?" Quite simply this chapter's basis assumes from the beginning that the use of VEs enables a better understanding of 3D data, given appropriate context, thoughtful design, and development.

First, we describe and define data visualization in XR and what makes it unique to other previous mediums. We look at the distinctions between interactive big data visualization versus pure infographic representation.

Considered the godfather of data visualization, statistician Edward Tufte writes that for centuries painters, animators, and architects have been attempting to represent data (2D and 3D) on a variety of displays (primarily in 2D space), using perspective and motion. Note that many static infographics lack motion or general understanding of perspective and thus do not qualify as "good data visualization" in spatial computing; the experience is mostly passive and does not enable rotation or other principles discussed later in this chapter. Data and machine learning visualizations enable users to see, explore, and better understand data. As said by Fernanda Viegas and Matt Wattenberg (Google's People and AI Researchers focused on data visualization) at NeuralIPS 2018, data visualizations transform data into visual encodings that help users educate, communicate, give insight, and better explore the data. Without visualization, data is just dead numbers on a page.

In his seminal book, *The Visual Display of Quantitative Information* (Graphics Press, 2001), Tufte writes that data visualization makes human understanding of large datasets more coherent. It serves a clear purpose to describe data represented in various forms; for example, as abstractions (pie charts, bar charts, etc.) and often as a term to describe 3D reconstructions of data as objects in 3D space (e.g., 3D reconstructed anatomical structures such as brain data, and flat slices of magnetic resonance imaging [MRI] files in an augmented and virtual environment). The data itself is comparative, relational, multivariate, and can allow the user to inquire specific questions or explore data generally to gain a better understanding of its qualities. Here are some of the key characteristics of interactive data visualizations in XR:

- It can plot and sort relational data through integrating descriptions to distinguish categorical data, whether it is qualitative data and can involve some statistical traits (focus on quantitative data).
- It involves information architecture that shows it as dynamic and provides interactivity to the user.

- It emphasizes aesthetics to help users understand data through good design, not just for the purpose of decoration.

Data is far less comprehensible without visualizations. As deep learning researchers put it, "data visualizations and visual analytics can be used to excel at knowledge communication and insight discovery by using encodings to transform abstract data into meaningful representations."[6]

Interactivity and animation on all platforms, desktop, mobile, and spatial computing help users make data more accessible and malleable with direct manipulation with various sets of inputs and controls.

Principles for Data and Machine Learning Visualization in Spatial Computing

Referencing the framework by deep learning researchers,[6] data and machine learning visualization creators in spatial computing should explore the five W's that will help give them a foundation to create successful applications experiences in spatial computing.

Creators should consider the design of their user experience by starting with the following: identifying their target users (Who) and where it is appropriate to use data visualization (When), the type of data visualization created (What), justify its existence as optimal in spatial computing and Why before they identify the method or (which type of visualization) that involves or does not involve machine learning before they begin selecting Where to house, process, visualize this data before selecting How (which languages to use for which platforms).

We explore more about approaches on methods and how to create the actual visualization at the end of this chapter, where we consider the holistic data-to-visualization engineering and design pipeline process.

Here is an example of those principles in practice. More specifically, the creator should consider these factors to be intentional about their visualization creation process:

Why
> *Identify the purpose, ask yourself why does this data or machine learning visualization make sense in spatial computing versus other computing.* The creator should consider the interaction of the so that the user can directly manipulate and unlock other insight to have an effective data visualization experience that would not be possible in other mediums.

Who

> *Specify target end users of the data or machine learning visualization spatial computing experience/application and what benefits they will gain from their experience in spatial computing* (e.g., surgeons monitoring brain data and other anatomical structure information). We will go into detail about this as we describe data categories and how the kinds of interactions depending upon the platform of choice have evolved over time for various visualizations in Figure 9-4.

What

> *Select scope and size of the type of data, how large it is, and how much they desire to visualize.* For specific MRI data of patients with cancerous tumors). Not all brain data is equal; for example, for larger datasets involving brain imaging, within the space of brainmapping and connectomics, researchers in Spain chose to visualize subset multidimensional data for a spatial computing visualization using Unity.[11]

Where

> *Select the most appropriate spatial computing platform to target either Head Mounted Display (HMD) or mobile display.* Consider various prototyping tools in 2D (see in resources section at the end of this chapter) on non-spatial computing (desktop and mobile) platforms if possible. The creator should understand the complexity of data so that they know if it must be pre-processed and where it is stored and housed (on the cloud using Amazon Web Services, in the format of JSON). This may or may not involve some prototyping (sometimes this involves using 3D with in 2D tools), before loading and visualizing data fully within XR.

How

> *Select what method to use when you create your data or machine learning visualization.* Basic visualizations do not require a ton of pre-processing, but for those that do (often ones that use Python) the whole pipeline must be considered. Select other programing languages you shall use for the platform selected to visualize the data (ex. C#, C++, JavaScript) and which Integrated Development Environment (IDE) program to use to (Unity, Unreal Engine, other game engine, your own proprietary engine to create, this book features examples predominantly from the first IDE).

Some data visualizations are made for practical use that aid marketing professionals, business analysts, and executives by being able to display and interact with data, leading them to better discrete business decisions. Others might be machine learning engineers, data scientists, or software engineers who seek to find optimization techniques, explore model interpretation and can make these discoveries through spatial computing visualization exploration. They can better see layers underlying more complex multidimensional data within spatial computing than other mediums. Here visualizations serve as solutions to "the curse of dimensionality," meaning to condense multidimensional data into a more comprehensible format.

On the other end of the spectrum, some visualizations often are miscategorized as data visualizations and actually fall into the spectrum of presentation and infographic design and are seen as "beautiful" artistic experimental pieces; they are perceived as created for the purpose of being purely decorative, or more for aesthetic value and appreciation than they are for practical use. We go into detail about this as we describe data categories in Figure 9-4 later in this chapter.

Why Data and Machine Learning Visualization Works in Spatial Computing

We delve into this topic deeper as we describe the evolution of data visualization design, how its purpose has improved and evolved with the introduction of spatial computing as medium its purpose, various categorizations of data and effective interaction designs.

The Evolution of Data Visualization Design with the Emergence of XR

Tufte goes on to say in his later book *Beautiful Evidence* that data visualizations provide producer and consumers of the creation to display evidence. He further explains that the basis of visualization design comes from underlying fundamental principles of analytical design, which are agnostic to "language or culture or century or technology of information display." Tufte elaborates:

> Powerpoint is like being trapped in the style of early Egyptian flatland cartoons rather than using the more effective tools of Renaissance visual representation.
>
> The principles of analytical thinking—and not from local customs, intellectual fashions, consumer convenience, marketing, or what the technologies of display happen to make available.[13]

Although this is true, some of the data visualization design best practices (which are primarily designed for paper, desktop, and mobile mediums) can be seen as obsolete and do not all directly apply in the medium of the XR spectrum because they account for designing primarily for only a 2D space with flat user interface (UI), even with 3D data, or a single window or screen. This limits the user and does not allow the user and producer to fully understand the data discoveries that can be unlocked with the potential of emerging technologies. These technologies can enhance analytical thinking, given the emergence of computational search and artificial intelligence (AI) displaying multidimensional data that can be more easily explored with new technologies.

Tufte, like many other data scientists and academics have criticized "bad" 3D data visualization such as 3D pie charts and instead offer more simple approaches to data visualization, stating that 3D geospatial data with a simple map on 2D paper suffices. They dismiss the use of any 3D visualization altogether, but this is misguided and backward. With the introduction of AR and VR, the UI of 3D geospatial maps has evolved much since the time that Tufte had created the paper 3D map. New conceptions of data are now encoded into the actual application experiences that improve the user's interaction with their data. For example, in WebVR, maps tend to look more like a game in which users can move in the z-plane, as depicted in Figure 9-1. Data visualizations can be "gamified" into mobile VR platforms (see Figure 9-2) on ARKit and MapBox.

Figure 9-1. A plot of the number of times people indicated that they disliked British television host Piers Morgan in a specific region, made in the webXR framework, A-Frame, which is viewable on a VR headset[1]

 This uses an old version of A-Frame (0.2.0). Some code might not achieve the desired results. If possible, upgrade to the latest version of A-Frame (which as of this writing is 0.9.0). All major browsers will begin supporting the WebXR specification in 2019. The old webVR API will be deprecated.

Figure 9-2. Data visualization mapping FourSquare check-ins using ARKit and MapBox by technologist Aaron Ng

Furthermore, AR and VR input enable new interaction paradigms that were not possible before in 2D space, which redefines human–computer interaction (HCI) as user interface via controllers, begin to directly load, and directly manipulate data with more sophisticated voice (via natural language processing [NLP] evolutions) and touch controls (haptics as they also continue to develop).

Much has been written about data visualization restricted to a 2D plane or 3D data that has been trapped in a 2D medium (which is very constraining for digging deeper into insights for those working in the fields of biotech and health technology, with data ranging from human anatomy in medical imaging microscopy, DNA molecular visualization, and protein visualizations) in 2D abstract data in a 3D space.

In his book, *Fundamentals of Data Visualization* (O'Reilly Media, 2018), University of Texas professor and trained biologist, Claus O. Wilke, emphasises *position* in XR as part of his discussion of data visualization. He talks about the importance of various elements (color and line) and so on. The focus for this chapter is on *positionality*, given XR's ability to place data as objects on the z-axis rotation.

2D and 3D Data Represented in XR

There are different types of data shown in data visualization within desktop, mobile, and spatial computing platforms. The categorical data shown in Figure 9-4 ranges from static to dynamic on various platforms. The types of data that are represented often in XR include the following:

- Abstractions of 2D data seen in 3D within XR (often seen as bar charts and line charts)
- 3D data from 2D data (anatomical structures such as brain fMRI imaging that is reconstructed several times over to look 3D and fit into 2D space)
- 3D data represented in 3D space, within XR (DNA molecular visualizations seen in XR)

After you select the type of data you are working with, you can visualize that data.

Some data makes less sense to visualize than other data. For example, Tufte references 3D pie charts as backward. Wilke continues this and specifically points toward effective data visualizations in XR that are all about the *context*.

Wilke says, "...it makes sense to use 3D visualizations when we want to show actual 3D objects and/or data mapped onto them."

2D Data Visualizations versus 3D Data Visualization in Spatial Computing

Although Tufte has been widely quoted against the incorrect usage of 3D data visualization (namely abstract data out of context like pie charts, which he believes add no substantial difference than a 2D visualization) and fancy animations, other scholars like Wilke show that there is some value in 3D data visualization and in spatial computing because they understand its ability to engage the user with their data in ways that are not constrained in a 2D screen. 3D data visualization by itself, without appropriate thought for the type of content and how it is represented, does not suffice. Interaction for the sake of interaction would make some sort of artistic piece, but it would not necessarily make an experience of data visualization and not necessarily involve data. There must be careful consideration into the design choices in XR. The recommendation to avoid it altogether, however, is short sighted. If we avoided 3D data visualization in 2D and 3D spaces, we would have recommended against the creation of great visualizations such as distill.pub, which shows clear purpose and enhances the understanding of data by the Google Brain team. We would have also dismissed a growing number of visualization examples (some of which are featured in this chapter) and more outside of this chapter that are too many to name. One of Google Brain's more popular machine learning visualizations that allows users to better understand their complexity through "dimensionality reduction" is called t-SNE, and Principal Component Analysis (PCA) was popularized.

These demonstrate how engineers can deepen their understanding of data by applied machine learning engineers and data scientists. To negate an entire dimension and medium because of poorly designed visualizations and avoid them altogether shows a lack of challenge in thought. This type of thinking restricts our minds to being limited to backward tooling that keeps humans at a distance from technology and farther away from data that can aid humanity. Instead, we need to utilize technology to become closer to our data and solve humanity's problems. Therefore, 3D data visualization in spatial computing should be encouraged but with proper design principles kept in mind. As Tufte says, "We should preserve the data through integrity." This is possible in a new medium; we only need to push the boundaries of our mind's imagination and make them relevant by updating our design, usability, and standards for preserving data integrity.

Interactivity in Data Visualizations in Spatial Computing

Another defining characteristic of data visualization is its emphasis on aesthetics. As Tufte puts it, "Graphical excellence is valued," data visualization is not about art for art's sake, which is common for many infographic designs that lack dynamic interaction; this is secondary. Any artistic thoughts such as color theory should be applied to help make data easier to understand (i.e., Viegas' talk that reminds us to consider color blindness and color choice for codifying various keys, maps, and categories).[15] Affordances in spatial computing allow the user in spatial computing the freedom to do more in a 3D environment, unlike 2D desktop and mobile experiences. Even with 3D data in desktop and mobile, the microinteractions are limited to a single view and screen.

Tufte writes that data visualization should "induce the viewer to think about the substance rather than about methodology graphic design and the technology of graphic production or something else." At the time that Tufte wrote this, spatial computing was not enabled as a technology used for data visualization as it is now and is not necessarily something that he would have taken into account.

In a 3D space, designers and software engineers should think about the substance of what they are creating and also how to create it given a new medium. By understanding how data visualization is formed, we can better understand human perception, why design works, and create more effective data visualization products in a whole new medium. The viewer is also able to appreciate how they can control their data more intuitively and how it deepens their understanding of the substance *because* of the methodology of design aesthetics (graphic design) *and* the technology of graphic production (how it is created in spatial computing). These novel interactions, which are possible only in spatial computing, unlock new insights because of being able to view and manipulate data in 3D space unlike previous design paradigms. The creation of 3D content, for example, on 2D screens is often half backward, given the lag time involved in rotating 3D data onto a screen projection that in the real world is sometimes better for quicker feedback loops through actual creation of 3D objects (i.e., sculpting mediums and paper prototyping), and data and machine visualization in spatial computing is no exception.

Spatial computing enables more mechanisms to directly manipulate data and offer spatial computing creators the ability to study new design paradigms in HCI to further enable a deeper understanding of human cognition as well as improve the ability to understand and reveal new insights of data for the viewer or user.

Many researchers in neuroscience, health technology, and biotech reveal that they can advance their understanding of the human brain and neurodegenerative disease through their ability to reconstruct, manipulate, and interact with 3D data. This data, when locked onto a 2D screen, lacks any means that would allow for more direct manipulation. This is still a preferred method of interaction rather than having another abstraction via a keyboard, mouse, or other tool a barrier in between. Spatial computing helps to speed up user productivity and unveil new insights that would not be possible had they interacted with data merely in a 2D manner with desktop and mobile.

Animation

Animation is not necessarily essential for experiences that are interactive upon input from the user. However, lack of responsiveness to input from the user borders on the line between data visualization and infographic. Animation alone, with what Tufte calls "dequantification,"[13] and removing data and quantitative data would be less along the lines of data visualization and infographic and might be more of an artistic piece that is often used in the world of eye candy and is often grouped with data visualization, which is not necessarily an accurate or appropriate description. Mere 3D reconstructions cannot by themselves be classified as data visualizations; that would be overly simplistic and more along the lines of the category below that of an infographic. Visualizations lacking descriptive data labels are not data visualizations. Data visualizations without significant responsive UX design or animation remain static and do not utilize the spatial computing medium and might as well be considered art pieces rather than visualizations. Stock data line charts in spatial computing are often criticized like 3D pie charts that Tufte despises. These types of visualizations are seen as miniscule improvements in spatial computing because they are perceived as adding unnecessary and extraneous decoration in spatial computing. It is how the line chart is designed, displayed, and visualized, however, that should be evaluated as a measure of success of the visualization, not the medium to dismiss entirely or the type of visualization itself alone that should be considered alone. We must also evaluate how the user interacts with the experience to find it useful to better understand data insights.

The dismissal of the use of data and machine visualization in spatial computing again happens because best practices for data visualization software design and engineering have been lacking. We must focus on the benefits of spatial computing and its ability to have a user view from all angles and rotate their data more naturally as they would do with 3D objects in the real world. Successful data visualization can be achieved when we give good thought to both purposeful functionality that benefits the end user, whose workflow is augmented in a 3D space as opposed to a 2D screen with a sensible human interaction for the end user.

Virtualitics and 10K systems (Figure 9-3) each have well-designed maps that are good demonstrations of XR data visualization in context, much like other 3D not in spatial computing (deck.GL, etc.).

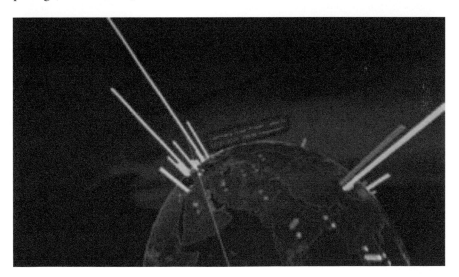

Figure 9-3. 10K systems, for example, had a great map visualizing solar data showing how VR data visualization works effectively in context and is more than an abstract concept

Failures in Data Visualization Design

Some new software engineers and designers have created poor data visualization in spatial computing that have repelled users from this medium altogether due to a gross lack of care for understanding and applying simple and fundamental principles for designing in this medium. As Tufte notes, "There are right ways and wrong ways to show data, there are displays that reveal truth and displays, that do not." Tufte, Edward (Visual and Statistical Thinking, 45)

The following are some common traits of bad data visualizations in XR:

- They do not load data in a coherent and easy to understand manner.
- They primarily use flat UI that could otherwise be displayed in a 2D space and not in XR and offer no interactivity.
- They contain too much noise, making data unclear to understand—which is the opposite purpose of what data visualizations is intended to enable.

A lot of data visualizations in XR fail because they don't use an actual 3D space and medium. This space provides users with capabilities not available with 2D UI (i.e., limited to a single screen or paper sheet in real life). Bad data visualizations in spatial computing fail to show a clear purpose as to why this data is better represented in spatial computing and do not properly allow users the ability to interact with their data efficiently.

On one end of the spectrum, some data visualizations remain static in their aesthetics, whereas others have too much information cluttering the 3D space such that it does not have a clear focus for the user to easily control their data with simple touch-controller interactions (voice right now is too much of an early stage, which many hope in the future will change as NLP and AI advance with XR).

Good Data Visualization Design Optimize 3D Spaces

Many data visualization applications in XR do not utilize 3D space and often have flat UIs. In Apple's Human Interface Guidelines (HIG) (*https://apple.co/2ThmReX*), it is recommended to fully use the space and avoid overly complex UI controls:

> **Use the entire display.** Devote as much of the screen as possible to viewing and exploring the physical world and your app's virtual objects. Avoid cluttering the screen with controls and information that diminish the immersive experience.

Data visualization should be intuitively designed, and users should not need a manual and cumbersome UI to understand how to use it—which data are x and y, and so forth. Unfortunately, many fintech data visualization applications fail this design concept and users are left confused. Instead of saving users time to gain an understanding of the data they are immersed in, they are left struggling to figure out odd ways of controlling data with overly complicated menus in a new medium. Many spend more time clicking through 10 to 15 menus to locate the data they should be able to load in three simple interactions.

Ultimately, this poor design detracts users from adopting data applications in any immersive and emerging technology. In John Maeda's book, *Laws of Simplicity* (MIT Press, 2006),[8] he states that design should ultimately save users time by simple UI.

"Savings in Time Feel Like Simplicity"

This universal design principle applies to paper, desktop, mobile, *and* the spatial computing spectrum as a whole. The elegance of simplicity in design is still valued in a brand-new medium and good data visualization conveys thoughtful design through a positive user experience (UX) in its accessibility and ease-of-use as well its ability to augment the user's ability to better understanding of data.

Data Representations, Infographics, and Interactions

We briefly mentioned the types of data within spatial computing earlier in this chapter. In this section we make clearer distinctions of subcategorizations and characteristics of data on various platforms and how they are created.

Figure 9-4 displays the overlap between static and dynamic data visualized across a range of platforms, with both 2D and 3D data in print and mobile form, and interactive dynamic visualizations in mobile, desktop, and within spatial computing.

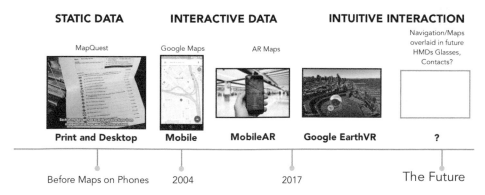

Figure 9-4. Categories of types of data visualization in 2D and 3D displayed within print, mobile, desktop, and spatial computing

What Qualifies as Data Visualization?

Data visualization can be separated into two specific camps: one that is more of an abstract, and another a literal representation of data via a 3D reconstruction, which involves a heavier preprocessing step, especially in medical imaging.

Types of data visualizations

As noted earlier, there are various types of data that qualify as data visualization, which we can categorize into these areas:

- Abstractions of data—line charts, pie charts, graphs—ranging from basic data (x, y) plotted in the z-plane of real-world data
- 3D reconstruction based on real-life data (biotech, health technology reconstructions of human biology) with animations and interactivity

Many other applications in the AR space, particularly Microsoft Hololens head-mounted display (HMD) take a 3D reconstruction of an object such as a human brain MRI and declare this is a data visualization. Although this is a data representation of real-world data in AR or VR as opposed to an abstraction of data such as a pie chart, line chart, graph, and so on, it is often confused with 3D objects themselves that are easily downloadable through TurboSquid or Sketchfab. But this does not necessarily qualify as data visualization, because some are mere loose interpretations or drawings of human anatomy but not connected to real-world data and are sometimes without any user interaction. Some of these assets are mere 3D reconstructions and, as such, are not to be categorized (because they are often miscategorized) as a data visualization; the majority of these are merely an artist's interpretation from the naked eye and not necessarily based on real-world data. This distinction draws the line between graphical excellence and engineers who separate design and art from engineering. Data visualization often is the result of the two fields that are cause for great productions of awesome experiences in spatial computing, but we must distinguish also between "art for art's sake" and looking pretty, while others actually being influenced by the substance and content of the actual data, which qualify as real data visualization.

Too often, "pretty" experiments in data visualization hardly qualify as data visualization and are instead more so artistic expressions.

Defining Distinctions in Data Visualization and Big Data or Machine Learning Visualizations

Data visualization reveals insights to understand unstructured data *and* structured data. Many big data companies handle large datasets, sometimes in the terabytes to petabytes scale, as described by Uber's open source Deck.GL team (*http://bit.ly/2UtS0sg*) with its WebXR presentation at the Silicon Valley Virtual Reality (SVVR) meetup and Facebook's At Scale Conference. Applications and experience that involve big data in real time and the complexity of information architecture as well as the amount of compute make it distinct from simple infographic bars and charts that are not big data visualizations, but simple data visualizations or representations that can be easily created without respect for the limitations of what an HMD can render in real time. 3D data visualizations in the deep learning space (a branch of machine learning) are similar but also distinct to those in the XR space given that they can involve large amounts of data visualized and are 3D in nature and not all data visualizations in XR may involve visualizing a large size or scope of data.

Additionally, "big data" as a term itself is often interchangeably used to define as large because it measures quantitative data by millions of users, but that is not always the case. Much of health technology data is considered big data or used for machine and data visualizing and might not be necessarily large in number of users, but is measured by size by itself.

How to Create Data Visualization: Data Visualization Creation Pipeline

The data visualization creation pipeline from native development and web development involves preprocessing data (which is often tedious work done among data engineers, especially for image processing in the medical space). This is known as Extract, Transform, and Load (ETL), in which we ingest data and transform and convert it to the proper formats for visualization in an HMD. Figure 9-5 presents both examples of the workflow.

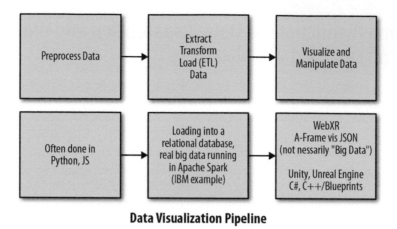

Data Visualization Pipeline

Figure 9-5. The data visualization pipeline, showing where raw data loads, transforms, and is visualized

WebXR: Building Data Visualizations for the Web

WebXR has introduced several web frameworks over the past couple of years, ranging from Facebook's React 360 (formerly known as ReactVR, based on the prominent ReactJS frontend framework) and the more popular A-Frame, to build virtual reality experience. A-Frame, created by Diego Marcos and Kevin Ngo (with the support of Mozilla), became a popular framework in the open course community. Web developers have created data visualizations with ReactJS, d3.JS (the go-to data visualization library created by Mike Bostock). Any frontend software engineer starting with little experience in VR can begin to create data visualizations with open source data. In Figure 9-6, data in JavaScript Object Notation (JSON) is embedded into an A-Frame scene that loads into a web page. It is not necessarily one that is considered a "big data visualization," but a data visualization nonetheless, which users are able to view within a VR headset within a browser.

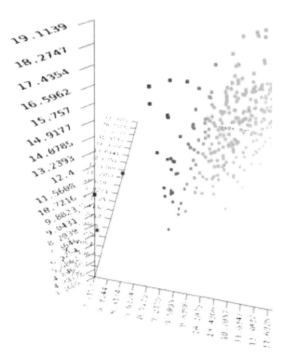

Figure 9-6. Zac Canter plots sea surface temperature data in WebXR using A-Frame

Data Visualization Challenges in XR

Across the spatial computing spectrum, the concept of input is one of the most exciting, unique, and cutting-edge design problems. Voice is less of a focus due to the lack of maturity with sophisticated NLP from Siri and Cortana being able to pull big datasets in real time at the moment, which many anticipate to change in the coming years. It is the current limitations (but also anticipated evolutions to come) in controllers, haptics, and voice that software engineers and designers aim to tackle with new experiments and solutions. Although the focus here is less on voice, controllers in VR and the advances in computer vision techniques for improving haptics in AR, both now provide affordances for users that have not been possible in VR over the past decades, and AR over the past few years. This evolution in HCI raises new challenges for designers and software engineers in immersive and emerging technology, with various use cases for AR, VR, or MR in the spectrum of XR.

Here are some challenges across the spatial computing spectrum particular to each type of platform given its limitations and interactions that we expect to change in the future as the medium advances as a whole:

AR

> There are two types to consider here: MobileAR (hich has almost no interaction, so it does not make sense to do a ton here) and PCAR (still ergonomically uncomfortable and not commercial ready for most HMDs).

VR

> VR restricts users from the real world and puts them in a closed environment while in an HMD. Because of this, many UX designers and consumers feel that HMDs are unusable and inaccessible. Part of this is due to technical limitations with optics even if claimed to be consumer ready. Because of this accessibility challenge in ergonomics, many applications are shorter experiences in length to avoid fatigue.

Data Visualization Industry Use Case Examples of Data Visualizations

In this section, I provide references to a few examples of well-designed data visualizations that load large datasets in real time in AR and VR but which are still not without their own design limitations.

Figure 9-7 shows IBM's data visualizations, which utilize open source data framework, Apache Spark to load data (including open source data, particularly Twitter Sentiment analysis) in real time.

Figure 9-7. IBM's data visualization in Microsoft Hololens using open source data framework (http://bit.ly/2NET0a8)

In his talk at GDC 2017 "Immersive Data Visualization: AR in the Workplace," Rosstin Murphy, formerly of IBM, presents his research on using AR to visualize, analyze, and manipulate big data in the workplace. His goal is to do the following:

> [U]se AR to augment the data scientist's toolbox and improve the speed and depth of their analyses. Exploring VR interaction in a business context showed promise, but revealed objective challenges to VR in a work environment. These challenges include the time cost of switching between VR gear and mouse and keyboard, juggling a 3D virtual environment alongside conventional 2D desktop interfaces, and choosing the right hardware controller model and 3D interaction algorithms...AR technology, though still in its infancy, elegantly solves many problems.

More specifically, in Murphy's struggles with ergonomics and ease of use as he transitions from Jupyter notebook on his PC desktop in reality to change data values typing on a keyboard while wearing a Hololens headset on his head. The heavy weight of the Hololens is a barrier to entry for many to consider HMDs usable. Direct manipulation because of a lack of integrated UI with Cortana (voice) and other visual menus (UI in AR) to adjust the data, and the restriction of data manipulation is still somewhat indirect as Murphy made these changes on desktop. This makes the current state of AR (which we expect to change in the future) difficult for user adoption.

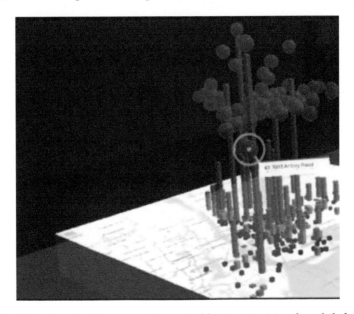

Figure 9-8. A data visualization example created by Rosstin Murphy while he was at IBM, which overlays data on a map

3D Reconstruction and Direct Manipulation of Real-World Data: Anatomical Structures in XR

Many data visualizations are 3D reconstructions that load data in real time that comes in the form of anatomical structures, which can be directly manipulated and edited within spatial computing. This distinct spatial computing interaction increases the overall efficiency of workflows for various B2B verticals.

As a part of the University of California, San Francisco, leader and neuroscientist Adam Gazzaley and Tim Mullen, in Gazzaley's lab, Neuroscope, created a visualization called "Glass Brain" that is frequently used in the demonstration of the various modules for the Meta 2 AR HMD.

A Closer Look at Glass Brain

Utilizing Unity3D, the Glass Brain data visualization is composed of the brain structure, both tissue and fiber tract architecture, obtained from high-resolution (MRI and Diffusion Tensor Imaging [MRI-DTI]) brain scans. Real-time brain activity and functional interactions among networks are superimposed on the brain structure using high-density electroencephalography (EEG). This is a great example of data visualization loading in real time. The captured visualization, which you can see in Figure 9-9, is that of percussionist Mickey Hart.

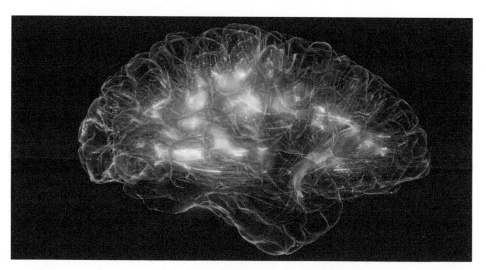

Figure 9-9. Glass Brain (http://bit.ly/2H1YPOE) frequently appeared in the Meta 2 demonstrations by founder and CEO, neuroscientist Meron Gribetz (more information available at the University of California San Francisco's Neuroscape (http://bit.ly/2Hl4JK9))

TVA Surg Medical Imaging VR Module

The University of Toronto also has real Digital Imaging and Communications in Medicine (DICOM) images (uncolored) reconstructed from human brain MRI scans and other medical images of human anatomical structures.

Medical Holodeck—DICOM

Medical Holodeck, founded by Swiss radiologists who created a tool that allows radiologists and other medical professionals to take their DICOM images into VR and be able to cut down the amount of time spent with image segmentation (often done manually via some basic machine learning algorithms). This is a tedious task in the overall pipeline in data engineering involving parsing data and rotating slices of various MRI images in MATLAB, which is comparable to kerning and tweaking every microchange needed with the plethora of fractured ecosystem of 3D desktop tools. Medical Holodeck enables radiologists, medical professionals, and researchers to instead focus on the substance of their problems in their work involving the actual medical issues at hand that they are seeking to analyze, such as locating tumors, making more precise incisions for surgery, finding other correlations to various pathologies, and increasing efficiency for the overall research pipeline for drug discovery by enabling a few design interactions in spatial computing that are more direct. Similar approaches are found by Stanford radiologists in a variety of case studies, as is eloquently documented by Dilan Shah in Chapter 11 of this book.

Data Visualization Is for Everyone: Open Source–Based Data Visualization in XR

Anyone can utilize open source data to create their first data visualization. If you are just getting started in data visualization, there's no need to feel intimidated. You can find myriad datasets on Kaggle (now owned by Google) and various other areas (depending on the tech vertical) that allow any new developers to create meaningful data visualizations. Timothy Clancy also managed to create his own data visualization attempting to index a segment of various chunks of pages on the internet and created a great data visualization in Unreal Engine, which you can see in Figure 9-10.

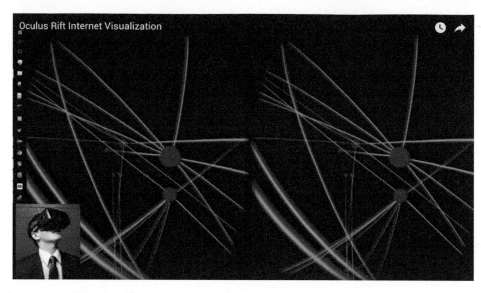

Figure 9-10. Timothy Clancy's data visualization showing a subsample of indexing various pages of the internet using Unreal Engine (http://bit.ly/2VOKyIi)

In 2016, Unreal Engine also hosted a hackathon with Wellcome Trust data from the UK (biotech data), where the winner, Hammer Head VR, made a VR browser analyzing the fruit fly genome, as depicted in Figures 9-11 and 9-12.

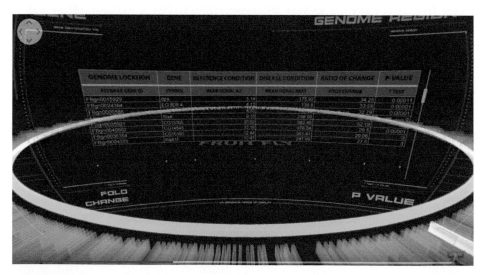

Figure 9-11. This data visualization created from a project made at Unreal Big Data hackathon has some flat UI with tables displaying data derived from the fruit fly genome

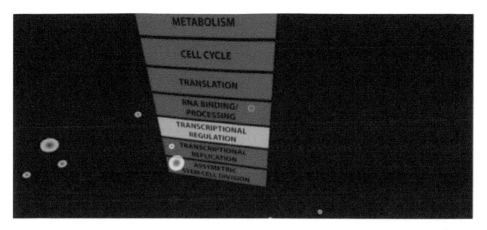

Figure 9-12. This data visualization made in Unreal Big Data hackathon project by HammerHeadVR uses spheres that light up in green when it is "hovered over" as it would be on the web, when the user interacts with the menu via a VR controller

Protein Data Visualization

The 10K platform from Dynamoid (see Figure 9-13) also created a dynamic UI to be able to view the open source Protein Data Bank (PDB) as a reference for various DNA proteins in its VR application which allows users to be able to look up, drop in, view, proteins with a few and resizing capabilities running in real time. Unlike many other health technology and biotech applications that often are static 3D data reconstructions with zero interaction or simple technical 3D art (OBJ or FBX files of a contrived view of an MRI scan or DNA protein), 10K systems dynamically pull based on real data used by practitioners in the field.

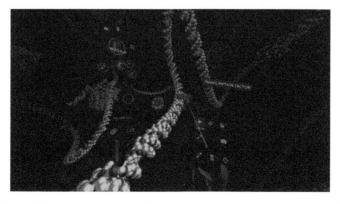

Figure 9-13. The 10K platform founded by Dynamoid's Laura Lynn Gonzalez, demonstrating how to display data visualization in VR effectively in context

Hands-On Tutorials: How to Create Data Visualization in Spatial Computing

Now that we have a framework for good design of data visualization across various data types, platforms, and HMDs, we can learn how to create dynamic data visualizations in spatial computing.

The remainder of this chapter describes various references by new and seasoned software engineers on various approaches on how to make a data visualization in spatial computing ranging from web and native platforms, on A-Frame, ReactJS, D3.JS (WebXR) using JavaScript (JS) and Unity using C#.

To gain a better understanding of data visualization using big data, some of the best examples can be found by data scientists and leading machine learning engineers showcasing 3D data, such as that shown in Figure 9-14, due to the curse of dimensionality reduction, namely various Principal Component Analysis (PCA) and t-SNE visualizations. Although we recognize that these are not in spatial computing as a medium, they provide a solid foundation to understanding visualizing multidimensional, complex, and sometimes very large datasets, which provides new creators with some fundamental principles that they can apply to creating new visualizations in spatial computing.

Figure 9-14. Machine learning journal distill.pub has many interactive machine learning visualizations that help researchers better understand their data

For a good starting point toward understanding these two types of data visualizations commonly used in the machine learning community, refer to Google's Projector TensorFlow and YCombinator-backed ML Journal work, distill.pub with work also by Ian along with Google machine learning leader, Chris Olah.

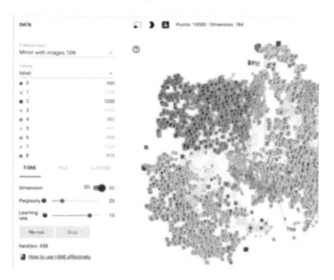

Figure 9-15. Fernanda Viegas and Matt Wattenberg's tool with Google machine learning framework TensorFlow, visualizing Principal Component Analysis (PCA) and other visualizations

In the Windows universe, C# is the language of choice and thus porting data visualizations to Microsoft Hololens AR HMD, commonly used for various B2B use cases. We would like to note that AR is not limited to this HMD alone. The amount of independent developer content created on mobileAR with the introduction of ARKit on iOS and ARCore on Android is detailed in Chapter 5 by 6D.ai cofounders Matt Miesnieks and Professor Victor Prisacariu.

Although data and machine learning visualization is less prominent in mobileAR, we are aware that some projects are beginning there that might merge with future HMDs and glasses. We anticipate even more future releases of AR HMDs and glasses, including new developer kit versions of Microsoft Hololens, Magic Leap, Apple, others from China and Israel, and even others that we might not know about that are in the pipeline estimated for a 2020 release or later (beyond the initial release date of this anthology).

How to Create Data Visualization: Resources

Revisiting the principles in the beginning of this chapter, creators must consider a number of steps that will help them specify the best approach for effective data visualization in spatial computing.

One great example for getting started in WebXR comes from Mustafee Saifee, who created a framework that combines A-Frame with React (for DOM manipulation) and D3 (for data visualizations) to generate visualization in VR, one of which you can see in Figure 9-16.

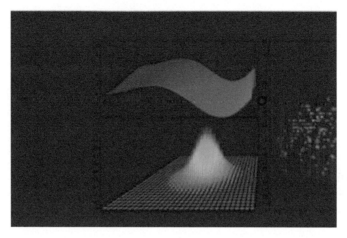

Figure 9-16. VR-Viz provides a high-level react component to generate 3D visualization in webVR using ReactJS, A-Frame, and D3.JS

This is one of many examples that you can find on blockbuilder and other WebXR resources that demonstrate a good grasp of solid design principles for building spatial computing data visualizations successfully.

Conclusion

I hope this chapter has demystified data in XR and provided examples of techniques, best practices, and practical tools to create beautiful and functional data visualizations optimized for this medium.

Although this chapter focused primarily on data visualization and only tangentially touched upon machine learning visualization due to this book's inherent length limitations, it is highly encouraged to view our supplemental GitHub repository and tutorial references to continue with hands-on material to get started with creating data and machine learning visualizations in spatial computing.

Refer to our resource list for various types of data and machine learning visualizations.

Like most spatial computing standards, WebXR is still evolving, but software engineers and designers can already get started with these existing open source frameworks to create their first data and machine learning visualizations.

References

1. Almossawi, Ali. "Where is Piers Morgan Disliked the Most?" Almossawi. *http://bit.ly/2TdGB34.*

2. Clancy, Timothy. "Oculus Rift Internet Visualization." YouTube, September 7, 2015. Video. *https://youtu.be/GpFVWFUHLcI.*

3. Chen, Min, K. Gaither, N. W. John, and B. McCann. "Cost Benefit Analysis of Virtual Environments." EuroVis, 2017. *https://arxiv.org/pdf/1802.09012.pdf.*

4. Gonzales, Laura Lynn. "10KS." STEAM. Video. *http://bit.ly/2XCi2LW.*

5. Hinton, Geoff. "Visualizing Data using t-SNE." *Journal of Machine Learning,* 2008. *http://bit.ly/2SHKnws.*

6. Hohman, Fred, Minsuk Kahng, Robert Pienta, and Duen Horng Chau. "Visual Analytics in Deep Learning: An Interrogative Survey for the Next Frontiers." Institute of Electrical and Electronics Engineers (IEEE). Transactions on Visualization and Computer Graphics, 2018.

7. Johnson Ian. "How to Use t-SNE Effectively." *Distill.pub,* October 13, 2016. *https://distill.pub/2016/misread-tsne/.*

8. Maeda, John. *Law of Simplicity: Simplicity, Design, Technology, Business, Life.* Cambridge, MA: MIT Press, 2006.

9. Murphy, Rosstin. "Immersive Data Visualization: AR in the Workplace." Game Developer Conference. November 2, 2016. *http://bit.ly/2NET0a8*

10. Ng, Aaron. "Downtown LA. My July 4th weekend FourSquare checkins visualized in AR. (ARKit + Unity + Mapbox + Swarm)." Twitter, July 13, 2017. *http://bit.ly/2SImGnC.*

11. Papachristodoulou, Panagiota. "Sonification of Large Datasets in a 3D Immersive Environment: A Neuroscience Case Study." The Seventh International Conference in Advances in Computer-Human Interactions (ACHI), 2014.

12. Schmalsteig, Dieter, When Visualization Met Augmented Reality." Keynote, IEEE Vis Conference, 2018, October 23 Berlin, Germany. *https://www.youtube.com/watch?v=qtar1Q2ZPYM.*

13. Tufte, Edward. *Beautiful Evidence.* Cheshire, CT: Graphics Press, 2006.

14. Tufte, Edward. *Visualizing Display of Quantitative Information.* Cheshire, CT: Graphics Press, 2001. *http://bit.ly/2TjKDap.*

15. Viegas, Fernanda and Wattenberg, Martin. "Visualization for Machine Learning." *Neural Information Processing Systems* (NeuralIPS), 2018. *http://bit.ly/2TncTYT.*

Resources

More information on the topics discussed on this chapter can be found in the following sections for you to pursue.

Data Visualization Tools

A-Frame (https://aframe.io/)
A web framework to create visualizations and other XR applications and experiences, created by Diego Marcos and Kevin Ngo with support of Mozilla.

Bl.ock builder (https://blockbuilder.org/)
A visualization prototyping tool created by Ian Johnson

D3.js (http://www.d3js.org)
A library created by Michael Bostock

Observable (https://beta.observablehq.com/)
A tool created by Michael Bostock

VR-Viz (https://github.com/mustafasaifee42/vr-viz)
A-Frame based React component of data visualization in VR and AR created by Mustafa Saifee

Machine Learning Visualization Tools

- Google (*https://projector.tensorflow.org/*): Embedding Projector
- Distill.pub: Articles about machine learning

Data Journalism Visualizations

- Pudding: Pudding.cool
- New York Times Data Visualization
- You can find additional tutorials at our supplemental GitHub repository (*http://www.github.com/*)

Glossary

Human Computer Interaction (HCI)
> A term used to describe the interaction between human users and computing

User Interface (UI)
> A term used to describe the visual representation of an application

Affordances
> A result of good design that does not allow the user to have a manual of instructions to know how to use intuitively

t-SNE
> From leading AI researcher, Geoff Hinton, Stochastic Neighbor Embedding (SNE), a type of machine visualization

CHAPTER 10

Character AI and Behaviors

Nicolas Meuleau and Arthur Juliani

Introduction

Virtual reality (VR) brings to life the promises of a more immersive sensorial experience than the previous forms of digital entertainment allow (movies, video games, interactive novels, etc.). A more immersive experience means a more emotional and a more impactful experience. Many of us remember their first immersion in VR with emotion. Many have witnessed the surprise, wonder, and enthusiasm that a first dive in virtuality can induce on others. There is arguably no other medium that can generate emotions of that intensity in just a few seconds. This fact has been recognized by the community that is now taking advantage of this emotional power to produce VR applications in domains as sensitive as personal training and therapy.[22, 40]

By using geolocalization and merging elements of reality with elements of virtuality, augmented reality (AR) and mixed reality (MR) define a new playground for artists, storytellers, and game developers to explore. This is still mostly uncharted territories, but the observed infatuation for primitive AR experiences such as Pokémon Go R gives us a glimpse at the huge potential of this medium to generate fun and play. The possibility of treasure hunting in your home city (of which Pokémon Go R is a primitive form) or defending your street against players from another team by placing artillery batteries on the roof of your own house will surely appeal to a large audience of gamers and nongamers. Professional applications of AR also come in numbers, from desktop replacement solutions, to field operation tools and *in situ* visualization tools. The excitement around AR can be measured by the number of startups and established companies currently developing AR apps, even though no AR device has yet been able to reach a large consumer base.

VR, AR, and MR—gathered under the acronym "XR"—are very promising media, and this chapter is here to help you put in place a first application of these technologies.

Over the past five years, artificial intelligence (AI) has become a buzzword. This was driven by impressive successes of machine learning in general and its subdivision, deep learning, in particular,[11, 26, 37] in the domain of data mining and robotic perception (computer vision, natural language processing [NLP], motion recognition, etc.) as well as in content generation (e.g., images, sounds, animations). It renewed the interest for this discipline beyond the wildest dreams of many long-term professionals. Possible applications of AI and machine learning in XR are many, and previous chapters already covered some of them (i.e., Chapter 5 by Matt Miesnieks and Professor Victor Prisacariu, which looks at vision and recognition). The purpose of this chapter is not to cover all of the potential applications of AI and machine learning to the development of XR apps. Instead, we adopt the opposite approach that begins from a problem—generating behaviors in virtual and semi-virtual environments—and then reviews the available technical approaches.

Historically, research and development in the domain of XR have been promoted mostly by the gaming community. This is illustrated by the fact that video game engines such as Unity and Unreal currently power a large majority of XR apps produced around the world. There are obvious technical and cultural reasons behind this fact. Among them is the similarity of the technical issues faced in video-game and XR development: the constraints of real time with limited resources; the stress on creating experiences rather than solving problems; and the possibility to create illusions—that is, to make the user believe the system has a capability when it is in fact just mimicking it. As a consequence, the XR community is looking at AI solutions from the video-game industry to bring their creations to life. Similarly, we begin our study by looking at game AI techniques and discuss their ability to tackle the challenges of XR. It will bring us to stress some of their limits and then discuss existing alternatives and current research efforts to bring game AI to its next level. On this trip, we must express opinions about the most promising approaches and where the research effort should go. These opinions are directed by several years of experience deploying decision-making and machine learning systems in other fields of industry, notably in autonomous robotics. But like any opinion, they can be subject to disagreement.

This chapter dives into the available technical approaches for generating behaviors in video games and XR. Before entering the heart of the matter, we frame the discussion by briefly debating the notion of behavior (in the section "Behaviors"). We stress that behaviors can be considered at different scales in terms of time and space, from low-scale sensory-monitor tasks to high-scale activity planning. Behaviors can also be attached to different types of entities: obviously to a single nonplayable character (NPC), but also to a group of NPCs or to the entire game world when we consider storytelling and interactive narration. You will see that the scale at which we consider the behavior has more influence on the nature of the problem we face—and so on the technical approach to adopt—than the object to which we apply the behavior.

The first major section of this chapter, "Current Practice: Reactive AI," surveys the state-of-the-art techniques that currently power most game AIs. The current practice is simple: the game developers must write "by hand" all the behaviors that the controlled entity exhibits at runtime. The lowest level of sophistication is a completely scripted and immutable sequence of actions that is executed no matter what happens at runtime. More evolved applications use a reactive architecture in which the actions executed depend on the observations made by the agent, with different game events triggering different behaviors. Nevertheless, developers need to design and implement the relation from observations to actions entirely by hand. Seeing the former (fixed-action sequence) as a particular case of the later (observation-dependent actions), we gather both under the name *finite-state machines* (FSM) and behavior trees (BT) to help the developer organize knowledge in a more readable and maintainable way than plain code. They are merely visual programming languages.

The main reason why this paradigm dominates game development is because it allows total control by the developers of the behaviors displayed in the game.[7] As stressed in many places, reactive AI is very good at describing how to do things. However, it does not provide any help in deciding what we should do. We believe that, for different reasons, both AR and VR put this model to the challenge. As a consequence, we need to examine the other alternatives available in academic AI for game and XR developers.*reactive AI*. In this paradigm, actions are produced one at a time as a function of the state of the environment, and the decision rules are entirely designed by the developers. The AI does not exhibit any real problem-solving or decision-making capability, it just repeats what it has been told to do. Given this, we can write reactive AI just in plain code (e.g., C#, C++, Java). However, behaviors are usually complex structures that we want or need to test, debug, improve, and augment as the application is being developed. Plain code is cryptic, and the AI designer might not be an expert coder. For these reasons, tools have been developed to help the designer structure the behaviors.

It leads us to the second large section of this chapter, "More Intelligence in the System: Deliberative AI," which is about *deliberative AI* and automated planning. In this paradigm, the AI is empowered with real problem-solving and decision-making abilities. Behaviors are generated by solving well-defined problems that are framed using models of the environment. Developers must create these models—which we call *planning domains*—in such a way that the desired behaviors are generated but do not get to fix by hand every aspect of the behaviors. This approach avoids lots of the limits of reactive AI. In particular, it is very good at deciding what to do. Although it is common in the domain of autonomous robotics, this approach has been largely neglected by the game AI community, and only a very small fraction of commercial products uses this technology at this time. This can be explained by the loss of control that comes with this approach. More than being a competitor, we believe that it should be seen as a complement to reactive AI. Automated planning should be used to solve the difficult decision problems, whereas reactive AI should be used to describe the details of how to execute decisions. Another explanation for this lack of interest is the large amount of work that is required to create a functioning reactive AI system, making the entire approach not economically viable for many small studios. In that regard, the efforts carried on at Unity Technologies to provide ready-to-use deliberative AI tools could have a crucial impact on the market. Deliberative AI works by solving problems, which is equivalent to searching a large solution space for the optimal solution. Every search algorithm has limits in terms of the size of the problems it can handle before affecting the game/XR fluidity by consuming too much time. To relieve these limits, we can turn to a third AI paradigm: machine learning.

Machine learning is at the center of most of the buzz around AI nowadays, particularly the branch called deep learning. The spectacular achievements of this technology in the domain of data mining and robotic perception—understanding the output of a suite of sensors—has opened the way to the wildest speculations about the future impact of AI on technology and society. The branch of machine learning that focuses on decision making and behavior generation is called *reinforcement learning*. In this paradigm, the AI learns to perform the right behavior by trial and error, interacting with the video game. It is guided in this process by a virtual reward that is provided each time the AI achieves a goal. The links between this discipline and video games has historically been tight. The research community has recognized the relevance of video games as a test bed for reinforcement learning algorithms. Simple arcade video games are now commonly used to evaluate the performances of new reinforcement learning algorithms in academic publications. It seems to indicate a great future for machine learning techniques being used to generate behavior in games and XR.

The goal of this chapter is not to provide an exhaustive and in-depth survey of all game-AI techniques. A chapter would not suffice. The References section of this chapter includes a survey of the field of game AI,[3, 27] and a deep dive into the current research.[32, 33, 34] The goal of this chapter is to give a high-level survey of the available approaches for tackling the challenges of XR and to stress their strengths and weaknesses. Moreover, we do not limit our study to "official game AI," but also borrow concepts from academic AI. We hope this vision will guide the early XR developers toward making the right design choices when it comes to designing behaviors.

Behaviors

When we look up the word "behavior," we quickly find the following definition: "The way in which one acts or conducts oneself (…)." So, the behavior is constituted by the sequences of actions performed by the subject. We stress that behind this sequence of actions there is a series of decisions to act in that way. So, we see the behavior of the sequence of decisions to act that an entity exhibits.

This is a very broad definition, particularly because it can be understood at many different scales. To illustrate this, consider an example from autonomous robotics. A robot control architecture usually comes in three large modules: *perception*, which has the task of understanding the input from the suite of sensors the robots is equipped with, and to build a consolidated world model from it; *decision*, which has the goal of deciding the next action to perform; and *control*, which tries to execute the decisions taken as faithfully as possible.

This chapter focuses on the issues associated with the development of the decision layer. The decision layer is itself divided in a hierarchy of modules making decisions at different time and scale. For instance, in a self-driving car, the decision layer typically comprises three modules: *navigation*, which plans for the entire trip (like the navigation app on your phone or in your car); *behavior*—to be understood here in a more restricted sense than in the rest of the chapter—which decides tactical actions such as lane changes and waiting at a stop sign; and *motion planning*, which tries to drive the car while staying on the road and avoiding obstacles such as potholes. A similar architecture can (and should) be used for video-game NPCs. For instance, we could stack up four layers of decision: deciding about quests and long-term goals, activity planning, navigation, and animation. Figure 10-1 provides an example of hierarchical decision-making architecture for an NPC. The decision is distributed over several modules working at different scale and frequency.

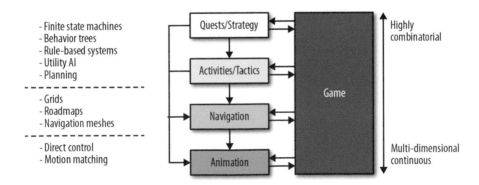

Figure 10-1. A hierarchical control architecture for an NPC in a video game or XR application (left: the techniques commonly used to address different levels of decision-making; right: the nature of the problem space evolves from continuous to combinatorial optimization as we climb up the hierarchy)

You can find an introduction to these techniques in the References section.[27]

Each decision module in Figure 10-1 works at a given scale in terms of time and space (decreasing scale as we go from quests to animations). The most important and usable point about these architectures is that the different modules do not need to work at the same frequency. In general, the higher in the architecture, the lower the frequency at which decisions must be made and revised. In a video game or XR, only the animations must be decided at 60 frames per second because a different pose of the character must be rendered at each frame. There is arguably little interest in running the navigation system faster than 10 frames per second: the user will not perceive that the NPC replans its route to its destination 10 times per second instead of 60. Similarly, higher-level decision modules can work at decreasing frequency as we climb up in the architecture.

This is a very natural phenomenon to which we all abide: the frequency at which we revise our decisions and make new plans decreases with the scale at which we reason. We do not revise our career plans every minute, but we do replan our actions several times a minute to adapt to the situation when we are just packing up our bag to get to work. This is actually good news from the AI programmer's perspective because it releases the pressure and increases the resources for all the tasks except at the lowest levels. This principle is well known and commonly exploited in the autonomous robotics community, which is familiar with the concept of a series of subprocesses working in parallel and at different frequencies. However, this is most often ignored in the game/XR development community that often painfully tries to make all kinds of decisions at the same frequency as the game is rendered.

Another important point about the decision-making hierarchies as represented in Figure 10-1 is that the nature of the problems we face to generate good behaviors changes as we move through the architecture. Low-level tasks that are close to sensory-motor skills are usually framed in multidimensional continuous spaces. Motion planning in robotics and animation generation in video games and XR involve a large number of continuous variables and can be framed as high-dimensional continuous optimization problems. Conversely, high-level activity planning is mostly about searching highly combinatorial discrete (noncontinuous) spaces. They typically involve a collection of discrete objects, locations and/or concepts, and the main difficulty is the huge number of ways in which these can be combined. For instance, if we decide to drop an object from our backpack and store it at a location for later use (maybe because we need space in the bag), there can be a large number of combinations of objects and storage locations to be considered. Things become worse if the time of the day influences storage capability, or if the object to be added into the bag must be factored in the decision. Each added variable multiplies the complexity by the number of options available for this variable, creating an exponential growth. This phenomenon is commonly called a *combinatorial explosion*. This shift from multidimensional continuous spaces to highly combinatorial discrete spaces as the scale increases is observable is many domains of human activity.

Before closing this introductory section, we also stress that the subject of the behavior —that is, the entity that exhibits the behavior—can take many shapes. The obvious case is that of an NPC in a role-playing game (RPG). However, you can also consider the squad of enemy NPCs in a first-person-shooter (FPS) game, or the entire enemy army in a real-time strategy (RTS) game, as the subject of the behavior. Pushing further, we see storytelling as a set of actions performed by the entire game world (or, if you prefer, a scenario management module that can act at the scale of the whole game world). Indeed, most of the tools and technical approaches available for interactive narration are similar to those used for individual NPCs.[20, 35, 46] Finally, any actor produces actions and thus has a behavior. So, if a game object representing a real-world object that is normally inanimate can take actions, it is concerned with the content of this chapter.

Current Practice: Reactive AI

If you open a book about game AI, or attend the AI Summit of the Game Developer Conference (GDC), you will read and hear a lot about FSMs, BTs, and rule-based systems. These three techniques, and different combinations of them, power the AI behind the majority of the current production in video games. They all fall within the same AI paradigm called reactive AI, which we alluded to earlier and discuss further in this section.

You can find a survey of reactive AI tools at the end of this chapter.[3, 27, 6] Figures 10-2 and 10-3 show how a simple enemy behavior called *wander-chase-shoot* is implemented using two among the most popular techniques: FSMs and BTs. The essence of these techniques is summarized in the last sentence: behaviors are implemented using these tools. That is, it is up to the developer to design every aspect of the behavior that the AI will exhibit. The tools are here to help organize the knowledge in a more or less graphical way and to make the decision rules more intelligible to humans than plain code. But they do not have any real problem-solving abilities and do not help in any design decision. In this respect, they are merely visual programming languages. Their merit is to provide a way to implement complex actions in an intelligible way.

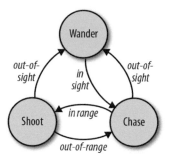

Figure 10-2. A finite state machine implementing the wander-chase-shoot behavior

The system shown in Figure 10-2 starts in the Wander state, in which it explores randomly the environment in search of its enemy; that is, the player. When the player comes into sight, the AI transitions to the Chase states in which it tries to get as close as possible to the player. When the player is in range, the AI moves to the Shoot state in which it attacks the player. If any of the conditions—player-in sight and player-in-range—becomes false, the AI returns to the corresponding state (Wander and Chase, respectively).

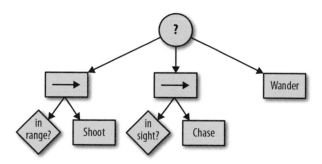

Figure 10-3. A behavior tree implementing the wander-chase-shoot behavior

The system shown in 10-3 starts in root node of the tree (the top round node). This node is a Select node. As such, it executes all of its children in turn, from left to right, until one of them returns success. If none of the children succeed, it returns a failure; otherwise, it returns a success (in short, it implements a logical OR and a priority rule). The rectangle nodes containing a dark arrow are Sequence nodes. They also try to execute all of their children from left to right, but they succeed only if they can get to the end of the sequence without encountering a failure of a child (so, they implement a logical AND and a sequencing rule). The diamond-shaped nodes are Condition nodes. They check a given condition and return success only if the condition turns out to be true. Finally, the gray rectangle nodes are the primitive actions of the wander-chase-shoot behavior.

The reason the game industry lends so much importance to this paradigm is that it provides total controllability of the AI. Many people—including us—see game design as some form of art. Like any artists, game developers want to have control over their creation. Because reactive AI provides total control, it was largely adopted as the default solution. However, total control comes with several downsides that we examine in the following subsections.

Adaptability

The first point is that, because they have been designed by hand, reactive behaviors are often specialized for a certain situation and not easily adaptable to important changes. An extension of a video game that brings a new gameplay element that can or should affect the NPC behavior might require a deep rewriting of the AI. *Utility AI* is a technique that has been introduced partly to compensate for this.[12, 27] It consists of implementing some basic decisions based on numerical computation instead of a fixed rule. Consider, for instance, a Select node of a BT (Figure 10-3). It encodes strict and always-respected preferences among the available options (left child always preferred to right child). Utility AI replaces this strict ordering of choices by a numerical computation: for each available alternative, we compute a utility score that depends on several numerical factors. In a tactical shooter, these factors can be, for instance, the number of enemies in the scene, the distance to the closest enemy, the amount of ammunition available, the existence of a reachable cover, and so on.

The point is that these factors are continuous and they are hardly controllable and observable. As result, the AI will be more adaptable and less predictable. Note that the utility computation—that is, the core decision rule—is still implemented by the designer. We are still in the domain of reactive AI, but decision is adaptable to the current situation, through meta-decision rules that are entirely designed by a human actor. In this approach, utility computation is an approximate way to evaluate the opportunity of each available action, and it is up to the developer to provide accurate estimates. In his article "Simulating behavior trees: A behavior tree/planner hybrid approach,"[13] Daniel Hilburn describes how simulation is used instead of user-defined computation to evaluate available alternatives.

Complexity and Universality

There is only so much complexity that a human brain can handle. The amount of knowledge that must be entered in the AI to achieve a satisfyingly complex behavior is often prohibitively large. One of the most difficult aspects of designing a reactive AI system is ensuring that all of the situations that the system will encounter at runtime are covered by a proper behavioral rule. Consider, for example, writing an AI to drive a car through a four-way-stop intersection (a problem borrowed from autonomous robotics). Designing the basic rule is easy: wait until you have the right of the way and the intersection is clear, then proceed to crossing the intersection. Now, we have to cover particular cases: if a driver displays an aggressive behavior and tries to cheat the stop sign, be safe and let him pass; if a fire truck is approaching from the rear, at full speed with all sirens on, try to free the way for it by proceeding carefully through the intersection. Then, we can ask ourselves: what should I do if I have both a stop-sign cheater and a fire truck incoming? Answering this question might require considering other factors; that is, defining more particular cases that would require particular rules. This is an example of combinatorial explosion that doomed reactive AI in real-world applications.

Feasibility

This is the strongest limit of the reactive AI approach. Designing all aspects of the behavior by hand requires knowing the solution to all of the problems the AI will need to solve. In some cases, deriving the optimal solution to a problem (or a good enough solution) cannot be done just by providing behavioral rules; it requires some amount of problem solving. Consider, for instance, navigation; that is, the task of finding the shortest path from an origin location to a destination. It is commonly solved using a shortest-path algorithm such as A*, which is an instance of the planning systems discussed in the next section. Shortest path is solved by exploring possible futures, predicting the outcome of different sequences of action to be able to pick the best. This reasoning depends on the current state of the environment and the goal of the AI, and it involves a fair amount of problem solving. It is just unfeasible to solve shortest-path problems in a generic way by using a fixed, predefined set of rules. In practice, game developers use reactive AI tools to design most of their behavior, but they delegate navigation tasks to a specialized module that uses a different paradigm. This argument applies to other aspects of reasoning beyond navigation. Other examples are provided in the beginning of the next section. In all of these cases, reactive AI is just not a viable solution.

These known limits of reactive AI become critical when we move from video games to XR. For different reasons, both VR and AR put this paradigm to the challenge more than games do. In AR, the difficulty comes from the unpredictability of the environment. An AR scene is built based on a real-world scene, by adding virtual elements in it; therefore, it is uncontrollable and unpredictable. There is little doubt that when the AR apps become common, they would be put to the test in the most original environments by the users. This contrasts strongly with video-game scenes that are entirely designed by hand and thus totally controllable and predictable (if we exclude the limited case of procedurally generated game levels).[41]

Obviously, it is easier to design by hand an AI that is adapted to a scene that we totally control rather than partially. In other words, AR challenges more the limits of reactive AI in terms of adaptability, complexity, and universality than video games do. In the case of VR, the argument is different. Like a video game scene, a VR scene is totally controlled by the designer. The problem here is in the user's expectations.

Because the sensory experience and the immersion are improved considerably when we move from games to VR, most users expect every aspect of the experience to step up similarly. "AI bugs"—AI behaviors that do not make sense to the user—can be acceptable, sometimes funny, and often exploitable in video games. However, game developers seem afraid to repeat these mistakes in VR worlds. This is reflected by the low number of actual NPCs encountered in VR games (other than enemy NPCs that are merely moving targets for the player to shoot).

Before examining existing alternatives to reactive AI, we remark that, so far, this section discussed only the highest-level and largest-scale aspect of behaviors (refer back to the section "Behaviors"). We already stressed that the navigation task is commonly solved using dedicated shortest-path algorithms that do not fall into the reactive AI paradigm. What about the lowest level in the hierarchy of Figure 10-1; that is, animation generation? In fact, the situation is very similar to that of large-scale behavior. The current practice is to use animation clips of a few seconds and representing a single gait. Clips are organized into large animation controllers, which are FSMs with one clip attached to each state.[22] Transitions between clips represent change of gait and are triggered by player input in the case of a playable character (PC) or by the higher-level behavior modules in the case of NPCs. Transitions from one animation to another is managed through animation blending, which involves several numerical parameters. The most common practice is to set and tune these parameters by hand, which is a daunting task.

This falls indeed in the reactive AI paradigm: the animation system does not anticipate more than one frame ahead in the future, and all decision rules are designed by the human developer. Recently, goal-based approaches have been proposed in which the AI is entitled to decide the next character pose based on its current pose and its goal.[4] Similar goal-based approaches from general behavior generation are discussed in the next section.

More Intelligence in the System: Deliberative AI

The trade-off between controllability and autonomy is central in the discussions around game AI: AIs that display some form of decision power are (obviously) less controllable than totally handcoded AIs. We saw in the previous section that the most common practice is to sacrifice autonomy to controllability, using reactive AI tools. We also saw that it cannot be applied to all problems that an artificial agent can encounter. Some decisions require predicting and anticipating the effects of different sequences of actions. This is the case of navigation that cannot be performed without a shortest-path algorithm; in other words, a problem solver. Other examples of "difficult" problems include the following:

Resource management

Particularly when it is mixed with a navigation problem. For instance, an agent must navigate to a destination, but motions consume resources that come in limited amount. Resources can be replenished in different locations of the environment. So, the agent needs to integrate a few stops to replenish resources on its way to the destination. Finding the shortest path to the destination includes making the shortest detour to replenish resources. This reasoning must integrate the structure of the environment, including the location of the resource refill stations and the destination. It is very difficult—if possible, at all—to design general decision rules by hand for this problem.

Intelligent exploration

Scouting an enemy character requires reasoning about the state of knowledge— what is known and unknown at the current time—and planning how exploration moves will modify this state. For instance, the AI will decide to make a detour through a nearby hill because the view from the top of the hill provides information about the current locations of enemy units. Again, this type of reasoning must integrate information about the structure of the environment, including which locations are observable from each location. It is poorly solved by a fixed-decision rule.

Tactical planning

Examples include managing a squad of NPCs so that they try to trap the player, blocking all of their exit paths from the game scene. This is again too dependent on the configuration of the problem to use predefined rules.

These tasks (and others) require some form of search and problem-solving ability in the AI. They are tackled by automated planning tools,[9, 10] which implement the deliberative AI paradigm discussed in this section.

Here are the two key points of the deliberative AI paradigm:

- We focus on producing sequences of actions rather than single-shot decisions. This is appropriate to the type of aforementioned decision problems. These problems are characterized by the fact that an action is interesting only with respect to the actions that will follow it. To clearly understand the difference with reactive AI, consider the problem of navigating to a destination. If we always move straight in the direction of the goal, we can become stuck into a corner-shaped obstacle. In some situations, we need to move away from the goal to get around an obstacle. A shortest-path algorithm such as A*[27] understands this and can make a move away from the goal and around the obstacle. This move is interesting only as the first step of a sequence that can lead us to the goal. Taken in isolation, it does not achieve any goal. The real output of the algorithm is the complete path to the goal; that is, the plan, of which the executed decision is only the first step.

- Decisions are produced automatically, by solving a well-defined problem rather than hardcoded by the developer. In other worlds, the AI has real decision-making power, backed up by problem-solving abilities. In this respect, it is a perfect complement to reactive AI in that it helps decide what to do in a given situation. It also helps avoid part of the complexity that arises from the need of universality discussed previously. Automated planners use a model of the decision-making problem they face. To elaborate, using again the example of navigation, a shortest-path algorithm can model the navigation problem as a roadmap; that is, a discrete network (or graph) in which nodes are called waypoints, connectors between nodes represent possible motions, and there is a cost associated to each connector. (This is an example; some navigation systems use a different model of the problem.) As long as a navigation problem can be modeled in this way, the planner is able to solve it. Thus, planners are universal within the (limited) scope of their domain model.

As we said, the most common example of a planner is a navigation system that computes the shortest path between two locations in the game world. Any introductory game AI book gives a survey of these algorithms; see for instance [3, 30]. The basic principle is called *search*. Given a starting location, represented for instance as a waypoint in the roadmap, they expand several possible future trajectories toward the goal and pick the best one. Algorithmic tricks allow you to perform this search efficiently and to avoid considering sequences of actions that can be proven to be nonoptimal. But the basic principle is still very simple: we (implicitly) enumerate the possible plans and pick the best.

Search is not limited to shortest-path problems. Figure 10-4 shows an example of how you can use it to decide general behaviors. The idea is to extend the notion of location by considering general planning states. The planning state summarizes all of the information that is relevant to the decision problem at a given time. In a navigation problem, it consists only of the location of the agent (x and y coordinates) because this is the only information that is relevant to the decision problem of finding a shortest path to a given and fixed destination. If the problem also involved some form of fatigue, so that the agent grows tired along the way and must stop in designated places to rest, the current fatigue of the agent is also included in the planning state. Similarly, motions between waypoints are generalized by planner actions.

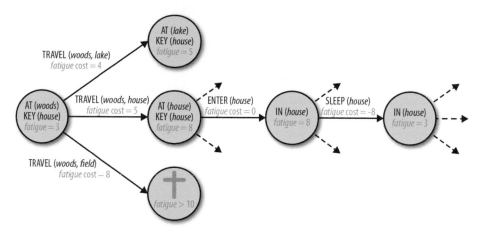

Figure 10-4. The search space of an automated planning algorithm (partial)

Figure 10-4 shows the first steps of expanding future trajectories from a given starting state. The AI starts in the leftmost state, where the agent is in the woods, its fatigue level is set to 3, and it owns a key to the house. From there, several Travel actions are possible, each involving a different fatigue cost. Actions that would cause the agent to die of exhaustion, such as travelling to the fields, lead to a terminal "dead" state. Other Travel actions change both the location and the fatigue of the agent. If the agent decides to go to the house, it can use its key to enter the house, making him in the house instead of at the house. Because we are in a video game, keys are consumed when they are used. So, entering the house also has the effect of removing the key from the agent possession. After it's in the house, the agent is allowed to sleep, which resets its fatigue to 0.

In the same way as motions change the location of the agent, actions change its state. However, they can semantically represent very different activities than locomotion. In our example, the Sleep action has the effect of resetting the agent's fatigue to zero while leaving its location unchanged. Other actions such as Travel will modify both the agent's location and fatigue. Formally, planner actions have conditions that must be true in the current state before they can be applied. They also have effects, which is the list of changes they bring to the state. In our example, the Sleep action can be executed only when the agent is at home (At (house)), and it has the effect of setting the agents fatigue back to 0 while leaving other aspects of the state unchanged. The action of traveling from location A to location B has the condition that we must start at location A, and the effect of not being at location A anymore but being at B, instead. Automated planning works by searching the graph representing the planning problem, similar to Figure 10-4, for a shortest/cheapest path between the current state and a goal state specified by the developers.

Automated planning is a systematic goal-based approach to generating behaviors. See the References section for a survey of this field.[9, 10] There are many variations to the basic scheme we just described, including the following:

Temporal planning

This allows a fine reasoning about the duration of actions, and the simultaneous execution of multiple actions that do not conflict.

Planning under uncertainty

This models and reasons about the uncertainty in the effects of actions. Instead of a single set of effects, an action has several effect sets with different probabilities attached to them. For example, attacking an enemy might have multiple effects (success or failure) with given probabilities, scouting a location from a distant observation point can lead to finding the enemy units or not. The possibility to model the uncertainty attached to action outcomes is crucial in some domains. In the example of a tactical shooter, an AI that cannot handle uncertainty will assume that every attack either always succeeds or always fails. In both cases, it will lead to a bad behavior (being overly confident in the first case, and being too conservative in the second). A proper behavior is obtained only by considering the different possible outcomes of actions, and balancing the risk with the benefit of different options.

Partial-order planning

This produces a plan in which actions are not totally ordered in a sequence. For instance, a branch of techniques produces plans in the form of sequences of sets of actions (as opposed to sequences of actions).[2] These plans are executed in the following way: first all actions in the first set are executed in any order that is convenient, then all actions in the second set are executed in any order, and so on. The planner guarantees that actions in the same set can be executed in any order without it affecting the result.

Hierarchical planning

This attempts to solve in a single tool several layers of decision making (refer to Figure 10-1). The most used tool in this approach is called hierarchical task network (HTN).[29] It allows a hierarchical decomposition of behavior as observed in BTs, while automating all core decision-making using planning.

 Note that the techniques behind these extensions can differ significantly from the basic state–space search outlined here.

The first game to use automatic planning for the highest levels of the behavior hierarchy was F.E.A.R. The planner was called Goal-Oriented Action Planning (GOAP).[30] It was used for enemy AI, and it made a strong impression on the gamers community.[18] Despite this, the entire deliberative AI approach had very shallow penetration in the game industry.[5] Not surprisingly, it has been applied mostly to tactical and strategic games that contain difficult decision and optimization problems whose solutions require some form of deliberation. HTNs received some attention from the community, notably for their similarity with the widely popular BTs.[19] Despite these attempts, the deliberative AI paradigm still represent a tiny minority of all commercial game AIs. There are several reasons to explain this:

Controllability

We already largely discussed this point. Reactive AI provides total control, which is great for authoring games and XR (although painful). Planners are less easy to control, but they can solve difficult problems out of reach of hand-written rules. Instead of having to choose between one approach or the other, we strongly recommend using a mix of them. We encourage developers to design a clean modular architecture and use different techniques and approaches in different modules.

As long as there is no difficult decision problem to solve, reactive AI provides a great way to generate the behaviors we want. You should use deliberative AIs (only?) for the difficult-to-solve problems. For instance, a planner in which each action is implemented by a particular BT is an architecture that can make a lot of sense in many situations. Similarly, a BT can contain a planning node that addresses a limited but hard-to-decide subproblem.

Run-time complexity

One of the main issues with problem-solving techniques such as the state–space search described earlier is their execution time. The complexity increases with the size of the problem (the size of the map in a navigation problem, the number of NPCs to control in a tactical shooter, etc.). Depending on its position in the architecture of Figure 10-1, the planner has different constraints on the frequency at which it must produce decisions, and there is always a problem that is big enough to break this limit. In other words, some problems are too big to be solved at the desired frequency. We note that when they are too slow to be used in real time, you can use planners offline—at the time of developing the game or XR app—to produce in advance a plan that can later be converted into a reactive decision rule to be used at runtime.[21] We discuss in the next section how you can use machine learning to further enhance the problem-solving power of a planner when it is used offline.

Difficulty to implement

Automated planning makes the promise of great AI behaviors, but it comes with a cost. Planning algorithms have a certain complexity and require some resources to develop, putting them out of reach of small teams without an expert AI programmer. In the academic world, planning domain description languages have been developed to allow reusing the same planner/solver in different domains. The idea is to define a language in which we can express (planning) problems of different nature and then to create a solver that can handle any problem expressed in that language (in the same way as the shortest-path algorithm can handle any problem represented as a roadmap). This approach is widely used by the autonomous robotics community, notably by NASA, which controls several (semi-)autonomous devices of very different nature and size using the same planners. We believe it is a key for producing general, reusable deliberative AI tools for video games and XR, and that it deserves more attention from this community.

Difficulty to adopt

Moving from reactive to deliberative AI is a radical shift in the AI designer workflow: instead of fixing behaviors, the designer must design problems whose solutions generate good behaviors. Because they cannot directly edit the behaviors but instead need to go through the task of domain modeling, many people will feel like an additional layer of complexity has been added on the way. However, there is a theoretical argument pointing to the fact that—at least for complex problems—declarative AI might actually be easier to use than reactive AI.

In short, this argument goes as follows. The world has structure, at least to a human eye. When we are asked to describe a problem, we are usually able to do it in a relatively compact and structured way. Notably, we can assess multiple hypotheses of independence between different variables. For instances, consider the problem faced by a photocopier repair technician who needs to design a schedule for a day. He needs to decide which of his customers he will visit and what operations he will perform on his customers' photocopiers. When we state that problem, we can assume lots of relations of independence between variables and actions. Obviously, every repair or diagnostic operation the service technician performs on a copier does not affect the other machines belonging to the same or another customer. In fact, we can easily divide the problem into several subproblems, one for each machine that needs service. There are many state variables associated with one machine (e.g., current state of different components, results of the tests that have been performed, history of repairs on this machine), but these variables are independent from one machine to another.

The problem is naturally modeled as two-layer architecture.[26] At the highest level, we have the general problem of deciding what customer we will visit and in what order (a problem that contains a strong component of shortest-path planning). The lowest level is constituted by several subprocesses, one for each copier that needs repair. At the lower level, local subproblems have lots of variables and actions that can be considered as private to this subprocess: executing a private action affects only the private variables of this process.

The subprocesses are bound together at high level by a small set of shared variables representing shared resources: the total time the technician can spend working on copiers on this day, the (limited) set of spare parts that is available to him, and the location of the agent (which can be seen as a particular shared resource). As a consequence, as long as we are concerned only with describing the problem, we can easily add, remove, or modify a copier/subproblem. The modification of one subprocess does not affect in any way the other processes. New copiers can be plugged to the general architecture like Lego pieces, the shared variables playing the role of the studs that keep the construction together.

The problem has a natural structure that makes its description compact and its modification easy and incremental. Unfortunately, this structure vanishes when we move from problem description to the solution space. If there were such a structure at the level of solutions—that is, optimal behaviors—we could expect that the addition or removal of a copier does not affect our plan when we are working on another copier. But this is not true.

To see this, imagine that we are currently solving a particular customer's problem and we plan to put the customer's machine fully back to order before moving to our next customer. This is our current local policy for this customer: finish all of the work here before leaving. Now, we suddenly add a new copier that competes with our current task for some particular spare parts. If we add that this new copier belongs to our top-priority customer and that we are committed to solve that customer's problems first, we might decide to drop our current work, save the spare part for the most important customer, and move to the top-priority customer immediately. The addition of a new process has changed the local policy of the other processes, which contradicts the principle of incrementality. This example shows that, even when a problem domain exhibits a convenient structure that helps describing it (and a very large majority of real problems do), the optimal behavior to solve this problem can have no structure at all. Therefore, in principle, there is a certain degree of complexity beyond which we are better off working in the problem space rather than working on the behavior space.

As we saw, several of these limits have possible solutions that would be worth researching in the domain of video games and XR.

As we said, every planner has its limits in terms of the complexity of the problems it can handle within its budget or even within any reasonable time. In academic research, the power of deliberative AI has been pushed to its current limits by merging it with ideas from machine learning. Therefore, the last main section of this chapter discusses this third and last paradigm.

Machine Learning

We have thus far been discussing behavior in the context of algorithms and methods that produce fixed policies for action. These approaches rely on human authoring of behavior, either directly by providing explicit rules for behavior (in the previous section), or indirectly by providing a model of the dynamics of the simulation and a mechanism for planning using this model. In contrast to those methods, we now turn to approaches based on learning behaviors from data. Learning from data can be appealing because it greatly reduces the amount of knowledge required to build the AI. We can possibly build an AI for a problem that we do not understand very well or at which we are not very good. It does so by trading-off computational time and large datasets. It is also appealing in situations in which we would like the learned behavior to generalize to unseen circumstances.

These approaches fall under the broad umbrella of machine learning, which comes in three different flavors:

Supervised learning

> This is concerned with learning a mapping from a set X to a set Y by example. In the case of a common machine learning application, we want to map images to labels describing their contents; for example, (cat photo → "cat"). For this purpose, we create a learning model that accepts pictures as input and outputs labels such as "cat," "dog," "bird," and so on. Next, we define a loss function that assigns a numerical value for the difference between the desired outcome and an observed output from the model. In short, we measure how well we are doing by a numerical value. Using a large dataset of examples in the form of pairs (picture, label), we can now improve the model to reduce the loss in the future, therefore increasing the likelihood of a correct mapping.

Unsupervised learning

> This approach is about learning structure in data without a clear mapping from one set to another as an objective. This is useful, for instance, to understand or compress data.

Reinforcement learning

> This is about learning behaviors by interacting with a real-world process or a simulation. The agent is guided to the desired behavior through the use of a reward function. Unlike a loss function, a reward function does not directly describe how well a model is doing, but rather is provided when the agent enters certain states, and corresponds to the desirability of those states. In other words, the goal is not to learn the reward function (which would be a case for supervised learning), but to find a behavior that leads to visiting the most desired states the most often. It is strongly related to automated in that we are concerned with producing action sequences instead of single-shot decisions. Indeed, the model

underpinning most reinforcement learning algorithms is a planning model whose parameters are initially unknown and must be learned by interacting with the simulation.

The relevance of reinforcement learning for the problems discussed in this chapter is straightforward. Not surprisingly, the links between this discipline and video games has grown to be very strong. The research community has recognized the relevance of video games as test beds for reinforcement learning algorithms. Simple arcade video games are now the community favorite test bench to evaluate the performances of new reinforcement learning algorithms.

There are two main components to an application of machine learning: the data and the algorithm. We can consider both of these within the specific context of authored behavior within simulated environments (video games and XR). Reinforcement learning gets its data from interacting with the simulation itself. Another type of application learns from human demonstrations; that is, (expert) user data. This approach is called *imitation learning* and is discussed later in the chapter.

Reinforcement Learning

Reinforcement learning is an approach in machine learning to arrive at desired behavior, which we call a *policy*. The mapping we are interested in machine learning is between states s and actions a. In some cases, this mapping is probabilistic and takes the form $p(a \mid s)$. In many circumstances, an agent might not have access to the complete definition of the state of a simulation. In such cases, we say that the agent has access only to observations, which are limited and derived from the true state. A simple example of this is to consider a simulation of a large city. In this simulation, the state consists of the entire position and trajectory of all the cars on the virtual street. We can imagine that an agent within one of these virtual cars might have access to a first-person view from that vehicle of the other cars in front of it. This limited set of information then corresponds to an observation. The problem of reinforcement learning is then to learn a mapping $(o \mapsto a)$, or a probability $p(a \mid o)$, which maximizes the reward function over time.

Compared to the planner-based approaches discussed in the previous section, reinforcement learning can take place in the absence of a forward model of the dynamics of the simulation. These methods are referred to as *model-free*. Although they require significantly more interaction with the environment, they are very general in that they make no assumptions or requirements on the specifics of the environment.

There are two broad categories of methods which are designed to solve reinforcement learning problems. These are the *value-based* and *policy-based* methods. In the value-based methods, the agent attempts to learn an estimate of the value of each state $V(s)$, or the value of each state–action pair $Q(s, a)$. This value represents the discounted sum of future rewards expected, as demonstrated in Equation 10-1.

Equation 10-1.

$$V(s) = E\left[\sum_{t=0}^{\infty} \gamma^t r(t) \mid s(0) = s\right],$$

$$Q(s, a) = E\left[\sum_{t=0}^{\infty} \gamma^t r(t) \mid s(0) = s \wedge a(0) = a\right],$$

where $s(t)$ is the state of the system at time t, $a(t)$ is the action performed at time t, $r(t)$ is the reward received by the agent at time t, and $\gamma \in [0,1)$ is the discount factor. The discounted sum of rewards is typically utilized in order to constrain the agent to policies over finite sets of time. It is also convenient for allowing a trade-off between short-term gain (smaller discount term) and long-term gain (larger discount term). In this approach, the value function is learned via interaction with the environment itself. After a good value estimate is learned, the agent can simply use the argmax over Q-values in a given state as the policy, as shown in Equation 10-2.

Equation 10-2.

$$a^*(s) = \arg\max[Q(s, a)]$$

This is the optimal action in state s. Examples of algorithms that fall under this class are Q-learning, SARSA, and TD-learning, and these methods are typically applied in tabular settings in which states or state–action pairs can be explicitly enumerated.[43, 44]

In addition to value-based methods, there is the class of policy-based methods. Here, instead of learning a set of value estimates, we directly learn a policy for acting. This policy is referred to as $\pi(a \mid s)$ and provides a set of probabilities over action a conditioned on a state s. This policy can be improved using the policy gradient algorithm. The intuition behind this approach is to use the observed discounted reward obtained by a policy during evaluation as a means of improving the policy directly. For cases in which the outcome was better than expected, we increase the probability of the action associated with that outcome. For cases in which the outcome is worse than expected, we decrease the probability. The policy gradient algorithm was developed for use in the case of linear function approximation.

Deep Reinforcement Learning

The methods we've just discussed work well for small state spaces, for which the probabilities for actions or value estimates can be enumerated for all states and represented in memory as simple arrays and matrices of floating-point values. In most simulations of interest, however, this is not an assumption that can be made. If we return to our previous example of a simulated city, the possible combinations of vehicles and pedestrians far exceeds what is possible to enumerate. Furthermore, if we use the raw pixels available to the agent from within the virtual car, even this observation space is intractable. Here, we need methods that allow for complex function approximation to represent the value function $V(s)$ or $Q(s, a)$, or the action probabilities $\pi(a \mid s)$. In many cases, the function approximator of choice is a neural network with multiple hidden layers, leading to the technique known as *deep reinforcement learning*. The "deep" refers to the multiple layers of inference performed by these neural networks. These multiple layers are often necessary when there cannot be a simple linear mapping between the observations and actions. In the case of raw images as input, this is almost always the case, except for the simplest of images.

The approach of applying function approximation to reinforcement learning has had great success in recent years. Starting in 2013 with DeepMind demonstrating that its Deep Q-Network—a deep neural network used to approximate Q-values from raw images—could learn policies for playing Atari games better than humans,[28] there have been successes every year pushing the state of the field further. It is now possible to learn policies using deep reinforcement learning to do everything from locomotion,[31] to playing real-time strategy games,[45] to solving dozens of tasks using a single network.[8] The key algorithmic elements to enabling these successes in deep reinforcement learning have focused on getting the advantages of using a neural network as a function approximator while mitigating the disadvantages of such an approach. This means taking advantage of their ability to model complex nonlinear functions without falling into their inherent instability and difficulty to interpret. In the value estimation domain, this instability has been overcome by using something called a *target network*, which is an old copy of a model that is used for bootstrapping, rather than the most current one. This was the approach taken in the Deep Q-Network,[28] and has been adopted to most subsequent value-based deep learning approaches.[24] In the case of policy-based methods, this means constraining the divergence of the new policy from the old one using a variety of methods, often based around the KL-divergence in the action-space of the policy. The two most popular of these approaches are *Trust Region Policy*, which enforces a hard KL constraint,[38] and *Proximal Policy Optimization*,[39] which enforces a soft constraint.

Imitation Learning

So far, we have discussed learning behaviors from scratch using only interactions with the simulation/game/XR. In most cases, however, this can be sample and time inefficient because learning takes place via trial and error. It is also the case that the desired behavior must be specified via a reward function. Unfortunately, these reward functions are often difficult to specify in a way that completely aligns with the desired behavior. For example, if the desired behavior is for an agent to perform a backflip, what rewards should be provided in order to encourage that behavior in a trial-and-error fashion? In many cases, it becomes much more intuitive to simply provide a set of demonstrations of the desired behavior. These demonstrations can then be used to learn a model of behavior.

There are a few ways in which this can take place. The first is that the demonstrations can serve as dataset inputs and outputs to be used to directly learn a mapping function in a supervised fashion. This approach is referred to as behavioral cloning; this is the most straightforward but not necessarily the most efficient. Consider again the example of a virtual agent driving the streets of a simulated city. There might be some particular point at which there is a fork in the road. If the demonstration data contained equal examples of going left at the fork as well as going right, the model learning with behavioral cloning would likely learn to go through the middle! It is also the case that behavioral cloning suffers from compounding errors over time because an agent's behavior leads it to drift away from the state space of demonstrations provided during the learning process.

There are a number of approaches that attempt to overcome these difficulties. They mainly fall under the domain of *inverse reinforcement learning*.[1] In this approach, the algorithm attempts to uncover the reward function that the demonstrator was following and use that reward function to guide the learned model. Approaches such as this allow for the best of both worlds in that the agent learns via a dense reward function that covers the entire state space as well as a properly specified reward function, which will encourage the desired behavior. One contemporary approach in particular is *generative adversarial imitation learning*, which uses a learned discriminator to provide the reward signal to the learning agent.[14]

Combining Automated Planning and Machine Learning

The previous section focused on methods that use models of the world/problem faced by the AI and take advantage of these models for behavioral planning. In contrast, we are now focusing on model-free reinforcement learning, which produces optimal behavior without an explicit model of the problem, but by instead interacting with a simulation. These two approaches need not be opposed and separate. Indeed, (arguably) the most impressive results in the field of decision making have arisen from intelligently combining the two. The most well-known recent example is DeepMind's success at Go playing using its AlphaGo system.[42] AlphaGo is based on a deliberative model of the game of Go that can be used to predict the outcome of various sequences of decisions following the state–space search mechanism outlined earlier. However, AlphaGo augments this planning system using deep neural networks trained to both act as a value estimator and a policy. The value estimator associates values to states. It is used to prune the depth of the planning search tree, limiting how far into the future the search process must go. The policy network associates probabilities to state–action pairs: it estimates the probability of an action being optimal in a given state. It is utilized to prune the width of the search tree, enabling the search process to focus only on nodes that are seen as more probably under an optimal policy.

The algorithm adheres to the following protocol: the results of the planning process are used as training data for the neural networks, providing them value and policy mappings from which to learn. In return, the machine learning systems are used to accelerate the planning process, pruning both the depth and the width of the search space. It enables a deeper search and better policies to be found. These improved policies are fed back to machine learning to increase the accuracy of the learned values and action distributions. The process is repeated many times, with the planning and learning system feeding each other with increasingly accurate data. In this way, both systems are able to iteratively improve and improve each other in the process. This approach enabled AlphaGo to defeat the world champion in the game.

Aside from playing board games at super-human capacity, combining the two methods can enable developers to trade off in real time between accuracy (provided by traditional planning) and speed (provided by a neural network function approximator) in decision making. The increased speed during evaluation is gained at the price of increased training time beforehand. In many cases, however, this is an acceptable trade-off, and one similar to the trade-off made when considering prerelease development time on any behavioral within a simulation. Combining these methods can also be crucial for situations in which a large number of decisions must be made in a simulation, some with greater fidelity than others.

Applications

Reinforcement learning and imitation learning carry lots of promises of great AIs for games and XR. Reinforcement learning opens the road to creating agents that can solve problems that we do not understand completely. It contrasts strongly with previous approaches that require either being able to describe problems perfectly (deliberative AI and automated planning) or to solve problems sufficiently well (reactive AI). Machine learning can also enhance the power of planners through combined approaches such as AlphaGo, which represent the state of the art in problem solving and decision making. Remarkably, the reinforcement learning research community has grown strong links with the video-game culture by adopting games as their favorite benchmark. It contrasts with the practical fact that only a very tiny minority of commercial games use concepts of machine learning nowadays. However, there is little doubt that the infatuation of the reinforcement learning research community for games will very shortly provide a return to the industry. Indeed, machine learning does bring solutions to practical problems faced when designing game AI. So, let's now examine what is currently doable, and what we think the close future will most probably bring.

Returning to the discussion in the section "Behaviors" in the introduction to Figure 10-1, we stress that the strongest impact of machine learning has been in the perception layer of autonomous systems: understanding complex numerical data coming from sensors (of which data mining can be seen as an instance). The first successes of deep learning were in domains such as computer vision, motion recognition, and NLP. When we get to decision making and behavior generation, machine learning has proven particularly valuable for solving tasks in the lowest levels of the architecture in Figure 10-1. Deep reinforcement learning excels at solving Atari arcade games, which are more based on reflexes and a good coordination than difficult problem modeling and solving. Racing, fighting, and sports simulation are great domains of applications of reinforcement learning. This is not very surprising. Earlier, we stressed that lower-level sensory motor tasks are mostly multidimensional continuous optimization problems (as opposed to discrete, combinatorial optimization). At the same time, perception problems also have a continuous, multidimensional nature. It also resonates with the impressive results of machine learning in animation generation, another (very) continuous domain.[15, 16, 17] In practice, reinforcement learning is a great candidate for controlling agents at the lowest sensory motors level.

What we learn from academic study is also the difficulty of reinforcement learning techniques, in their current state, to tackle the highest levels of the hierarchy of Figure 10-1. One of the most difficult arcade games for deep reinforcement learning is *Montezuma's Revenge*. It involves solving puzzles by sequencing long series of actions such as picking up a key in one room to open a door in another. Executing these plans can last up to several minutes of real time, which is a strong contrast to the few seconds of planning—at most—that are required to solve *Space Invaders* or *Breakout*.

Conclusion

AI is a rich field proposing different approaches to the problem of behavior generation. Rather than seeing them as competing, we prefer to stress the complementary nature of these approaches. We believe that the design of a behavioral AI system for a video game or an application of XR must begin with a clear decomposition of the general problem into several subtasks and understanding the constraints bearing on each subtask. Then, the most appropriate approach must be chosen for each module. Although there is no absolute rule that can applied in all cases, some general principles can be outlined:

- If we know exactly what behavior we want to generate and this behavior does not involve solving a difficult problem such as shortest path, resource management, or intelligent exploration, reactive AI is a great candidate. It must be expected, though, that the development of the AI will be a tedious process requiring many trial-and-errors to fix all the particular cases the behavior needs to cover.

- If the behavior we want to generate includes solving difficult problems and we know perfectly how to describe these problems, or if we do not have the resources to fix a reactive AI case by case, deliberative AI should be preferred. However, it requires technical skills to implement the planning engine.

- If the problems we have to solve are too difficult or we do not know exactly how to describe them, we can give a try at machine learning. This is particularly true for behaviors at a small scale in term of space and time. Machine learning is still a fast paced research area, and applications in the domain of digital entertainment and XR are very limited at this time. Therefore, some research efforts must be expected.

Putting together the strengths of the three main paradigms in behavioral AI is key to addressing the new challenges of XR.

References

1. Abbeel, Pieter, Pieter Abbeel, and Andrew Y. Ng. "Apprenticeship Learning via Inverse Reinforcement Learning." *Proceedings of the Twenty-first International Conference on Machine Learning (ICML 04)*, New York (2004): 1–8. *https://stanford.io/2C858vK*.

2. Blum, Avrim L., and Merrick L. Furst. "Fast Planning Through Planning Graph Analysis." *Artificial Intelligence*, 90 (1997): 281–300. *https://www.cs.cmu.edu/~avrim/Papers/graphplan.pdf*.

3. Buckland, Matt. *Programming Game AI by Example*. Wordware Game Developers Library. Burlington, MA: Jones & Bartlett Learning, 2005.

4. Buttner, Michael. "Motion Matching - The Road to Next Gen Animation." In *Nucl.ai Conference 2015*, Vienna (2015). *http://bit.ly/2Hl6Rl7*.

5. Champandard, Alex J. "Planning in Games: An Overview and Lessons Learned." AiGameDev.com. 2013. *http://bit.ly/2HhffCa*.

6. Dawe, Michael, Steve Gargolinski, Luke Dicken, Troy Humphreys, and Dave Mark. "Behavior Selection Algorithms: An Overview." *Game AI Pro* (2013): 47–60. *http://bit.ly/2EyJqSi*.

7. Dill, Kevin. "What Is Game AI?" In *Game AI Pro*, edited by Steve Rabin, 3–9. Boca Raton, FL: CRC Press, 2013. *http://bit.ly/2Hh7Qm1*.

8. Espeholt, Lasse, Hubert Soyer, Rémi Munos, Karen Simonyan, Volodymyr Mnih, Tom Ward, Yotam Doron, Vlad Firoiu, Tim Harley, Iain Dunning, Shane Legg, and Koray Kavukcuoglu. "IMPALA: Scalable Distributed Deep-RL with Impor-

tance Weighted Actor-Learner Architectures." arXiv preprint arXiv:1802.01561, 2018. *https://arxiv.org/pdf/1802.01561.pdf*.

9. Ghallab, Malik, Dana Nau, and Paolo Traverso. *Automated Planning: Theory and Practice*. Burlington, MA: Morgan Kaufmann, 2004. *http://bit.ly/2IPYvUD*.

10. Ghallab, Malik, Dana Nau, and Paolo Traverso. *Automated Planning and Acting*. Cambridge (England): Cambridge University Press, 2016. *http://bit.ly/2tQst0w*.

11. Goodfellow, Ian, Yoshua Bengio, and Aaron Courville. *Deep Learning*. Cambridge, MA: MIT Press, 2016. *http://www.deeplearningbook.org*.

12. Graham, David "Rez". "An Introduction to Utility Theory." In *Game AI Pro*, edited by Steve Rabin, 113–128. Boca Raton, FL: CRC Press, 2013. *http://bit.ly/2SNIGxu*.

13. Hilburn, Daniel. "Simulating Behavior Trees: A Behavior Tree/Planner Hybrid Approach." In *Game AI Pro*, edited by Steve Rabin, 99–111. Boca Raton, FL: CRC Press, 2013. *http://bit.ly/2TmmWhH*.

14. Ho, Jonathan and Stefano Ermon. "Generative Adversarial Imitation Learning". In *Advances in Neural Information Processing Systems 29*, edited by D. D. Lee, M. Sugiyama, U. V. Luxburg, I. Guyon, and R. Garnett, 4565–4573. Curran Associates, Inc., 2016. *http://bit.ly/2C6YEgL*.

15. Holden, Daniel, Taku Komura, and Jun Saito. "Phase-Functioned Neural Networks for Character Control." *ACM Transactions on Graphics*, 36, no. 4 (2017): 42:1– 42:13. *http://bit.ly/2NHc5sx*.

16. Holden, Daniel, Jun Saito, and Taku Komura. "A Deep Learning Framework for Character Motion Synthesis and Editing." *ACM Transactions on Graphics*, 35, no. 4 (2016): 138:1–138:11. *http://www.ipab.inf.ed.ac.uk/cgvu/motionsynthesis.pdf*.

17. Holden, Daniel, Jun Saito, Taku Komura, and Thomas Joyce. "Learning Motion Manifolds with Convolutional Autoencoders." In *SIGGRAPH Asia Technical Briefs*, ACM (2015): 18:1–18:4. *http://www.ipab.inf.ed.ac.uk/cgvu/motioncnn.pdf*.

18. Horti, Samuel. "Why F.E.A.R.'s AI is still the best in first-person shooters." *Rock, Paper, Shotgun*, 2017. *http://bit.ly/2UkcTWx/*.

19. Humphreys, Troy. "Exploring HTN Planners through Example." In *Game AI Pro*, edited by Steve Rabin, 149–167. Boca Raton, FL: CRC Press, 2013. *http://bit.ly/2VFWSuC*.

20. Kapadia, Mubbasir, Seth Frey, Alexander Shoulson, Robert W. Sumner, and Markus Gross. "CANVAS: Computer-Assisted Narrative Animation Synthesis." In *Eurographics/ACM SIGGRAPH Symposium on Computer Animation*, The Eurographics Association (2016). *http://bit.ly/2XGYtSn*.

21. Kelly, John Paul, Adi Botea, and Sven Koenig. "Offline Planning with Hierarchical Task Networks in Video Games." In *Proceedings of the Fourth Artificial Intelli-*

gence and Interactive Digital Entertainment Conference (2008). *http://bit.ly/2SK09qT*.

22. Lau, Manfred and James Kuffner. "Behavior Planning for Character Animation." In *ACM SIGGRAPH/Eurographics Symposium on Computer Animation (SCA)* (2005): 271–280. *http://bit.ly/2TBSf7u*.

23. LeCun, Yann, Yoshua Bengio, and Geoffrey Hinton. "Deep learning." *Nature* 521 (2015): 436–444. *https://www.nature.com/articles/nature14539*.

24. Lillicrap, Timothy P., Jonathan J. Hunt, Alexander Pritzel, Nicolas Heess, Tom Erez, Yuval Tassa, David Silver, and Daan Wierstra. "Continuous Control with Deep Reinforcement Learning." arXiv preprint arXiv:1509.02971, 2015. *https://arxiv.org/pdf/1509.02971.pdf*.

25. Metz, Cade. "A New Way for Therapists to Get Inside Heads: Virtual Reality." *The New York Times*, July 30, 2017. *https://nyti.ms/2HmNLer*.

26. Meuleau, Nicolas, Ronen Brafman, and Emmanuel Benazera. "Stochastic Over-subscription Planning using Hierarchies of MDPs" In *Proceedings of the Sixteenth International Conference on Automated Planning and Scheduling (ICAPS-06)* (2006). *http://bit.ly/2VDdWRM*.

27. Millington, Ian and John Funge. *Artificial Intelligence for Games*. 2nd ed. Burlington, MA: Morgan Kaufmann, 2009.

28. Mnih, Volodymyr, et al. "Human-level control through deep reinforcement learning." *Nature* 518 (2015): 529.

29. Nau, Dana S., Tsz-Chiu Au, Okhtay Ilghami, Ugur Kuter, J. William Murdock, Dan Wu, and Fusun Yaman. "SHOP2: An HTN Planning System." *Journal of Artificial Intelligence Research (JAIR)* 20 (2003): 379–404. *https://arxiv.org/pdf/1106.4869.pdf*.

30. Orkin, Jeff. "Three States and a Plan: The A.I. of F.E.A.R." *Proceedings of the Game Developers Conference (GDC)* (2006). *http://bit.ly/2Ui4BhP*.

31. Peng, Xue Bin, Glen Berseth, KangKang Yin, and Michiel Van De Panne. "Deeploco: Dynamic locomotion skills using hierarchical deep reinforcement learning." *ACM Transactions on Graphics (TOG)*, 36, no. 4 (2017): 41.

32. Rabin, Steve (editor). *Game AI Pro*. Boca Raton, FL: CRC Press, 2013. *http://www.gameaipro.com/*.

33. Rabin, Steve (editor). *Game AI Pro 2*. Boca Raton, FL: CRC Press, 2015. *http://www.gameaipro.com/*.

34. Rabin, Steve (editor). *Game AI Pro 3*. Boca Raton, FL: CRC Press, 2017. *http://www.gameaipro.com/*.

35. Ramirez, Alejandro Jose and Vadim Bulitko. "Automated Planning and Player Modeling for Interactive Storytelling." *IEEE Transactions on Computational Intelligence and AI in Games* 7 (2015): 375–386. *http://bit.ly/2Tw9Hdm*.

36. Russell, Stuart and Peter Norvig. *Artificial Intelligence: A Modern Approach*. 3rd ed. Upper Saddle River, NJ: Prentice Hall Press; 2009. *http://aima.cs.berkeley.edu/*.

37. Schmidhuber, Jürgen. "Deep learning in neural networks: An overview." *Neural Networks* 61 (2015): 85–117. *http://bit.ly/2TnMZ8c*.

38. Schulman, John, Sergey Levine, Pieter Abbeel, Michael Jordan, and Philipp Moritz. "Trust region policy optimization." In *International Conference on Machine Learning* (2015): 1889–1897.

39. Schulman, John, Filip Wolski, Prafulla Dhariwal, Alec Radford, and Oleg Klimov. "Proximal Policy Optimization Algorithms." arXiv preprint arXiv:1707.06347 (2017). *https://arxiv.org/pdf/1707.06347.pdf*

40. Senson, Alex. "Virtual Reality Therapy: Treating the Global Mental Health Crisis." *TechCrunch* (January 2016). *https://tcrn.ch/2HgM9CK*.

41. Shaker, Noor, Julian Togelius, and Mark J. Nelson. *Procedural Content Generation in Games: A Textbook and an Overview of Current Research*. New York: Springer, 2016. *http://pcgbook.com/*.

42. Silver, David, et al. "Mastering the game of Go with deep neural networks and tree search." *Nature* 529 (2016): 484.

43. Sutton, Richard S. and Andrew G. Barto. *Reinforcement Learning: An Introduction*. MIT Press, 1998. *http://bit.ly/2EzyDXX*.

44. Szepesvari, Csaba. *Algorithms for Reinforcement Learning*. San Rafael, CA: Morgan and Claypool Publishers, 2010. *http://bit.ly/2tTtXay*.

45. Vinyals, Oriol et al. "StarCraft II: A New Challenge for Reinforcement Learning." arXiv preprint arXiv:1708.04782, 2017. *https://arxiv.org/pdf/1708.04782.pdf*.

46. Young, R. Michael, Stephen Ware, Brad Cassell, and Justus Robertson. "Plans and Planning in Narrative Generation: A Review of Plan-Based Approaches to the Generation of Story, Discourse and Interactivity in Narratives." *Sprache und Datenverarbeitung, Special Issue on Formal and Computational Models of Narrative* 37 (2013): 41–64. *http://bit.ly/2IRWaJa*.

PART VI

Use Cases in Embodied Reality

Technology is only as good as its applications. In the following chapters, we look at how immersive technology is being used in the real world.

Readers are likely familiar with "The Hype Cycle," a hypothetical graph (see Figure VI-1) that describes the growing pains of new technologies. Since the first head-mounted display (HMD) was created in 1968, eXtended reality (XR) has seemed trapped in the trough of disillusionment. Since XR's return to public consciousness here in the twenty-first century, we've seen many false starts, from Meta's collapse to the privacy backlash against the Google Glass.

Although some might take these failures to indicate that XR is yet another overhyped technology, the applications presented in this chapter beg to differ. Slowly but surely, XR technology is finding its niche, climbing toward the plateau of productivity, application by application.

In Chapter 11, Dilan Shah, cofounder of YUR, Inc. examines how we can tailor immersive technology to people with different health conditions. The health-care industry is a space in which processes and procedures must be strictly adhered to in order to ensure optimal care. How can virtual reality (VR) be adapted to this space and what benefits can it provide? In this chapter, we provide a deep-dive practical example of how hand tracking can stabilize tremors in Parkinson's patients in a virtual environment.

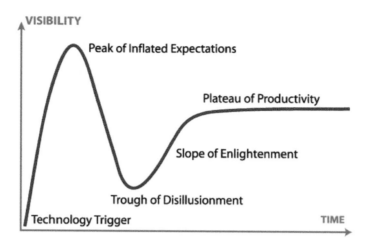

Figure VI-1. The Hype Cycle

In Chapter 12, Marc Rowley takes a look at XR's role in the delivery of sports entertainment to fans. Marc recently closed out 18 years at ESPN to found a startup that generates live CGI images of sporting events. Each field has its own demands, and nowhere is latency and immersiveness a more hyped part of the entertainment medium than in sports.

Finally, in Chapter 13, VR engineer Rosstin Murphy of STRIVR takes us through four real-life use cases of enterprise VR training, including flood houses, factory floors, store robberies, and the delivery of some very bad news.

XR technologies are no longer just technology demonstrations. With Walmart's investment in 17,000 Oculus Go's, XR is turning the corner and climbing the slope of enlightenment. There will still be speedbumps and false starts, but in the examples you see in this section, we see the first real examples of XR applications that will stand the test of time.

I hope that these chapters can inspire you to build your own practical applications. The next big immersive application might come from you; get out there and build!

CHAPTER 11

The Virtual and Augmented Reality Health Technology Ecosystem

Dilan Shah

This chapter covers issues related to design of virtual reality (VR) and augmented reality (AR) experiences deployed in a health-care context, and provides a tutorial for using motion data from controllers to reduce the visible tremor of a Parkinson's patient in a virtual environment. At current, the global health-care outlook is defined by an ever-growing set of policies, public-health measures, delivery methods, community-based clinical research, therapies, and technological innovations. No single technology is addressing all of the problems of health care alone, and now from deep learning applied to protein folding to precision health to population health, there are many different approaches being taken to solve difficult health challenges.

In health care, everything from the sophisticated (i.e., fMRI) to the simple (i.e., the efficient scheduling of appointments) all have a role to play in the delivery of care. VR and AR technology are relatively new and aren't yet considered a convention, let alone standard of care, within any domain of health. Problem spaces include pain reduction, post-traumatic stress disorder (PTSD) treatment with exposure therapy, and amblyopia treatment. These spaces have proven ripe for VR as a therapy delivery technology, while surgical training and planning has found use cases for AR. To avoid systemic bias and facilitate more of a worldview of the subject of how VR and AR apply to health, substantial details about formal organizations, oversight bodies, and approval processes are omitted. Instead, this chapter discusses more about high-level efforts that can be made to better design health technology using VR and AR. It's important to know that patients must consent before they can try any application or experiment, and there are review boards expressly for such purposes. Finally, this chapter covers commercial and academic approaches to addressing problems in planning and guidance, wellness and preventative care, as well as therapies implemented in clinical settings.

VR/AR Health Technology Application Design

Creating VR and AR applications requires developers to take into consideration the physical milieu the user will be in when using the technology. Whether, for example, the user is the patient in the pre-op room, alone before a procedure, or the user is a family member who is in the patient's room.

The design process should include spending time to understand these environments and what happens during typical scenarios. We might adequately interview physicians, nurse practitioners (NPs), staff, and other involved personnel to answer questions like the following:

- If a patient is a user, will the family be interested in spending quality time with the patient in X environment or is the patient alone?
- To what degree will the setting require interruptions to the virtual experience?
- What is the user's mobility?
- What should the duration of the experience be?
- Can the user wear headphones?

Some second-order considerations might be:

- Will the VR and/or AR device be sanitary and how?
- Following the experience, what is the process for keeping it that way?
- Who will facilitate the experience and how much time will that take?
- Does the user feel safe?

Again, the scope of the chapter doesn't include US Food and Drug Administration (FDA) or other regulatory requirements, but by taking a look at the patient value assessment approach, as shown in Figure 11-1, you can see how constrained this space becomes. Adding proper stakeholder research and forethought about the physical interfaces at the heart of a successful health technology application. There are a few examples of FDA-approved VR use cases, namely VRPhysio by VRHealth and Mindmaze. VR for those who aren't developing apps for the patient, there are also preventative health use case evaluation frameworks and physical spaces to consider for those applications, as well.

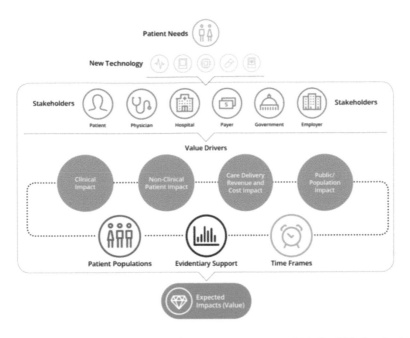

Figure 11-1. "A Framework for Comprehensive Assessment of Medical Technologies: Defining Value in the New Health Care Ecosystem," codeveloped with Deloitte Consulting LLP

Standard UX Isn't Intuitive

The design of VR and AR applications has evolved significantly in the past few years alone, stabilizing the way that many different systems are made and tasks are done. Look no further than the Virtual Reality Toolkit (VRTK) (see Chapter 7). However, looking at "locomotion" as an example—often found in VR applications, locomotion is the way a user can move through a virtual environment—there are many forms, from Bézier curves to "choose an orientation" to waypoint-based teleportation in the canon of VR user experience (UX).

And yet, even so, when used outside of the context of gaming or those who are in the immersive technology industry, it's clear that things that might seem commonplace and easy to understand actually aren't. This extends to even the basic input gestures for AR hardware because many haven't used these systems before. Therefore, cleverly work without user interfaces when possible; for example, by opening up directly to the main virtual environment in which the core activities take place.

Another common type of input seen in certain applications is *hand tracking*, which allows users to see virtual hands that reflect the movement of their own via technology like Leap Motion. We can see this in one of Embodied Labs' new cancer patient–

focused embodied learning experiences, which is both a form of keeping the user engaged but also a form of combatting the disconnect users feel when they don't see their hands in VR. Of particular note, Embodied Labs (*https://embodiedlabs.com*) also focuses on building out a desktop UI dashboard from which to launch experiences. Consider employing a desktop interface as well as one for VR or AR. This is to take advantage of the not-so-unfamiliar keyboard and mouse inputs. Virtual environments that need to be "reset" or "expire based on time" should loop or be organized in a manner that isn't dependent on clicks to restart.

In the upcoming example project, Insight, to minimize accidental clicks, a user must hold a controller for a minimal time in place for an action to be accepted. This component, known as *adding friction* for a better UX, is used to slow the user down to keep actions deliberate. Sometimes, there is a trade-off with this kind of design choice, and if it is a point of frustration don't let it linger for users—change it rapidly.

Pick a Calm Environment

With the Insight project, measures were taken to create an environment that contrasted with that of a typical patient or study environment. Placement by the water and audio in the form of a subtle wind chime invite a sense of relaxation.

The use of VR within palliative care improves quality of life via scenic environments. This is no doubt in part because of the willingness on behalf of developers to think in terms of "worldspace" not "screenspace" and storyboard scenes from a bird's-eye view in order to make sure the viewer is drawn in. Using spatial audio plug-ins for relaxation cues (examples might include gentle rustling, wind blowing through some chimes, or the sound of waves) will help draw a user into the environment and increase believability.

Convenience

Another way that VR and AR are being deployed into health organizations is to create economies of efficiency. To save doctors and nurses time in the clinic, for example, Augmedix offers a documentation automation platform powered by human experts and software. Although its platform of choice is Google Glass (and therefore isn't quite AR), its delivery requires a head-worn device, which frees physicians from computer work and allows them to focus on what matters most: patient care. Augmedix serves 12 of the nation's leading health systems, across most clinic-based specialties, with an average physician productivity increase of 30%.

In the next section, we discuss how to automate finger–nose touch assessments of visuomotor tremor, which is also the aim of the paper submitted to Arxiv (*https://arxiv.org/abs/1809.05970*) in 2018 by the team behind Insight. Because a finger–nose touch test is administered largely via the game logic built in to the Unity-based application, it allows a physician to proceed with other tasks and provides convenience.

Tutorial: Insight Parkinson's Experiment

Parkinson's disease is a slow-progressing neurodegenerative disorder with symptoms including tremor, limb rigidity, slowness of movements, and problems with balance. Advancement of the disease can severely affect quality of life from physical disability to depression. Insight, is a VR patient-centric platform for Parkinson's-disease patients and their family. Insight was built on the foundational observation that normal VR controllers can transmit high-frequency position and orientation data.

What Insight Does

Insight works as a VR assessment tool, management, and health education application. Patients typically see a physician to monitor disease progression and adjust medication and rehabilitation therapy at set interval clinic visits based on symptoms. Insight stays with the patient throughout their life, continuously assessing the user between visits and aiding their providers at the clinic.

The platform draws upon current care via third-party health information such as medical records and movement data collected in VR to create an assessment of the patient's health status, provide personalized rehabilitation exercises, and guide the physician team in data-driven decision making. Before the patient begins rehabilitation exercises, they touch a set of wind chimes in a virtual house, shown in Figure 11-2, which then transfers symptoms over to the virtual world. For the remainder of the experience, the movement and sounds of the wind chimes signify the symptoms of the patient while the patient's movements will now be tremor free. The patient is then guided through evidence-based personalized rehabilitation exercises that while improving physical function also collect data for disease progression assessment. At the end of the assessment, the patient receives an overview of their current health status, including medications, Insight's health score derived from symptom measurements, and an option to contact a physician through telemedicine. This physician will have a report generated by Insight that includes the collected symptom information.

Figure 11-2. The Insight environment is a tranquil waterfront room with views of the sky and a gentle wind chime to allow a patient to relax a bit more when doing the reaching assessment

Insight provides a platform for voluntary data collection.

How It Was Built

The Insight Patient Data platform was built by using a combination of Unity 2017.3.0f3 game engine and MATLAB and Python data analysis tools.

Low-pass filter for hand tremor

The most crucial part of this project involved a transformation of the way someone with tremors actually moves versus how it appears they are moving when viewing their own hand through a VR device. Built by using a low-pass filter, or moving average, the Smoothed Hand C# Script attached to the user's hand model captures transform position and rotation data from the VR-tracked input object as input and outputs smoothed data for the transform of the hand model.

Environment

The inspiration for the environment was heavily influenced by one mentor, Hannah Luxenberg, who explained that rather than an art direction similar to a clinic, the aim was to create a soothing ambiance. A majority of the models were created in Maya by Serhan Ulkumen. Using Unity's terrain system, the terrain was generated by using a heightmap and then trees were placed.

Data analysis and reporting

Essentially, the team collected X,Y,Z tremor values from the position of the VR controller, and thereafter data analysis provides details pertinent to the patient and caregiver about the tremor.

Here's the pseudocode:

Imports to support data analysis and functions

```
import numpy as np
import pandas as pd
import matplotlib.pyplot as plt
import matplotlib.gridspec as gridspec
import os.path
```

Loading the patient data file

```
while True:
    try:
        file = 'patientData.csv'
        data=pd.read_csv(file)
        print(data.head())
        print()
        y=[]
        z=[]
        x=data.iloc[:,0].values
        y=data.iloc[:,1].values
        z=data.iloc[:,2].values
        print(type(x))
        nbins=30
        Xr=np.fft.fft(x,nbins)
        X=abs(Xr[1:round(len(Xr)/2)])
        Yr=np.fft.fft(y,nbins)
        Y=abs(Yr[1:round(len(Yr)/2)])
        Zr=np.fft.fft(z,nbins)
        Z=abs(Zr[1:round(len(Zr)/2)])
        x2=x-x.mean()
        y2=y-y.mean()
        z2=z-z.mean()
        fig1 = plt.figure()
        #print(type(fig))
        tt=np.linspace(0,np.pi,len(X))
        plt.plot(tt,X,tt,Y,tt,Z,alpha=0.6)
        plt.xlabel('Frequency (Normalized)')
        plt.ylabel('Amplitude')
        plt.title('Frequency Response')
        plt.legend(('X-axis', 'Y-axis', 'Z-axis'),loc='upper right')
        #plt.show()
        fig1.savefig('plotF.png')
        fig1.savefig('plotF.pdf')
        fig2 = plt.figure()
        score=int((1-(1.07*(x2.std()+y2.std()+z2.std())))*100)
```

```
gs = gridspec.GridSpec(1, 2, width_ratios=[4,1])
print(gs)
ax1 = plt.subplot(gs[0])
tt2=np.linspace(0,len(x2)/50,len(x2))
plt.plot(tt2,x2,tt2,y2,tt2,z2,alpha=0.6)
plt.xlabel('Time (s)')
plt.ylabel('Movement')
plt.title('Movement Insight')
plt.legend(('X-axis', 'Y-axis', 'Z-axis'),loc='upper right')
ax2 = plt.subplot(gs[1])
plt.bar(['Higher is better'],score,alpha=0.6,color=['C3'])
plt.ylim((0,100))
plt.title('Insight Score: '+str(score))
#plt.show()
fig2.savefig('plotT.png')
fig2.savefig('plotT.pdf')
```

Computing statistics around tremor values

```
stats2show=[x2.std(), y2.std(), z2.std()]
fig3 = plt.figure()
```

```
plt.bar(['X','Y','Z'],
Stats2show,
alpha=0.6,
color=['C0','C1','C2'])
plt.xlabel('Axis')
plt.ylabel('Tremor')
plt.title('Tremor values')
fig3.savefig('plotS.png')
fig3.savefig('plotS.pdf')
print('Analysis Completed!')
```

Imports to support creating a PDF read-out of the tremor values and initializing important variables

```
import time
from reportlab.lib.enums import TA_JUSTIFY
from reportlab.lib.pagesizes import letter
from reportlab.platypus import SimpleDocTemplate, Paragraph, Spacer, Image
from reportlab.lib.styles import getSampleStyleSheet, ParagraphStyle
from reportlab.lib.units import inch
doc = SimpleDocTemplate("form_letter.pdf",pagesize=letter,
                        rightMargin=72,leftMargin=72,
                        topMargin=72,bottomMargin=18)
Story=[]
```

Let's take a closer look at what's going on:

- The accelerometer data is loaded (`data=pd.read_csv(file)`).

- The x, y, and z components are extracted into x, y, and z variables, respectively, in these lines:

```
x=data.iloc[:,0].values
y=data.iloc[:,1].values
z=data.iloc[:,2].values
```

- Fast Fourier Transform (FFT) of each component is calculated and the first halves (0 to pi in normalized frequency domain) are distributed into Xr, Yr, and Zr variables, respectively.

- The frequency response of each component (as a function of the normalized frequency: 0 to pi) is plotted (see Figure 11-1).

- A score reflecting the standard deviation (shaking) of the signals recorded is calculated—more shaking will yield lower scores (score=int((1-(1.07*(x2.std() +y2.std()+z2.std()))))*100).

- Standard deviation of each axis (x, y, z) are calculated and plotted in the following lines:

```
Xr=np.fft.fft(x,nbins)
        X=abs(Xr[1:round(len(Xr)/2)])
        Yr=np.fft.fft(y,nbins)
        Y=abs(Yr[1:round(len(Yr)/2)])
        Zr=np.fft.fft(z,nbins)
        Z=abs(Zr[1:round(len(Zr)/2)])
```

- Note that lines 36, 38 and 47 have slightly changed (revised).

For brevity, the remaining code for putting together the PDF report of the patient's movement is omitted; to see that code, go to the GitHub repository for this book. It requires nesting strings and filenames for media within formatting code blocks provided by the ReportLab library. The Devpost post (*http://bit.ly/2Two1TS*) contains a video showcasing the resulting application in action, and the code is linked to within the GitHub repository (*http://bit.ly/2F6VnQm*).

Hardware used:

- HTC Vive

External assets used:

- SteamVR (*http://bit.ly/2VVRa7E*)
- Frames Pack (*http://bit.ly/2HfEZj5*)
- Post-Processing Stack (*http://bit.ly/2T1LUOf*)

Tools used:

- For analysis, packages used included NumPy and Pandas
- For visualization, MatPlotLib

Textures for models:

- CGTextures

Companies

The following section covers companies that are using VR and AR to help people in a variety of ways within health care. To begin, Stanford University Professor of Radiology and Electrical Engineering and Bioengineering, and IMMERS co-director, Brian Hargreaves, PhD, has articulated a nice breakdown of where value lies along the immersive technology spectrum in the clinic. For background, IMMERS is an incubator for medical mixed reality (MR) and eXtended reality (XR) at Stanford University.

MR or AR is useful in areas that require information overlay on patients, such as planning, guidance, and assessment. Although VR is used for its immersive component, that might make it easier on a physician in training to grasp a medical topic or explain that topic to a patient.

Planning and Guidance

Planning and guidance have been characteristically surgery related in VR and AR health technology use cases, but some, including Archform's orthodontic aligner software, based in Unity, are seeing the potential for immersive technology within workflows that are different.

Surgical Theater

Precision VR allows neurosurgeons, patients, and their family to "walk" through the patient's own anatomical structure. For example, the surgeon, patient, and family can stand with an artery to their right, bony skull base structures at their feet, and, with a look over their shoulder, they can observe the tumor or vascular pathology. This immersive experience enables them to understand their pathology and their surgical plan.

Osso VR

Osso VR is the leading validated VR surgical training platform designed for surgeons, sales teams, and hospital staff of all skill levels. The company's product offers highly realistic hand-based interactions in immersive training environments that contain the latest, cutting-edge procedures and technology.

Archform

Archform, a software company providing orthodontists with intuitive dental correction tools, points out that for its users the charm of using a VR interface is being able to see *.stl* files in 3D—thereby speeding up the workflow. For its users, the process of manipulating a tooth and checking dental alignment from a multitude of angles is enhanced by being able to control the orientation of the model quickly and view it in VR.

Experiences Designed for Medical Education

The following experiences are all comparable, though some like the Stanford Virtual Heart Project or Embodied Labs' experiences might stand to benefit a particular type of caregiver.

Embodied Labs

Storytelling within VR requires a tremendous attention to detail, and, particularly if the goal is around embodied learning, the experience must capture many of the details of real life. Embodied Labs uses 360-degree video along with various interactive elements to convey patient experiences to caregivers. Recent experiences use voice and hand tracking, allowing users to take on the role of the patient in the presence of family members during particularly important milestone events during critical stages of various diseases.

Lighthaus

Lighthaus, a San Francisco Bay Area technology company, and its own David Axelrod, MD at Stanford Lucille Packard Children's Hospital, a pediatric cardiologist, collaborated on a project called the Stanford Virtual Heart Project (SVHP). Used by students and practitioners, SVHP was built to break down various pediatric heart abnormalities and the procedures needed to remedy each in an interactive VR experience. The project opens up to a library of hearts, and as the user, you can pull each into the main area for interactivity. The viewer can spin the heart around, as depicted in Figure 11-3, and view the procedure required to fix the malady.

Figure 11-3. A user wearing an Oculus Rift turns a virtual heart around in-place as it beats

MVI Health

MVI Health, a joint venture between Penumbra and Sixense, is VR hardware geared to be wipeable with controllers equipped for use in medical training scenarios. As such, its main demonstration at GDC 2018 was a thrombectomy for which MVI Health's technology was used to train someone virtually how to suck a clot (thrombus) from a blood vessel.

The affordances of being able to reset all appliances at the click of a button, avoid mess, and enable performance review make this a clear example of why medical education would need MVI Health's product offering over other training methods for this procedure.

The Better Lab

The Better Lab, based at the University of California, San Francisco, applies design thinking to patient-centric problems. Currently, the company's VR project covering trauma patients and funded by the HEARTS grant is close to wrapping for standalone headsets in the coming year. Zuckerberg San Francisco General (ZSFG) is the only Level One trauma center in San Francisco. Of the 255 trauma cases admitted each month, 90 are high-level "900 activations" that require speed and intense coordination across multiple departments. Each trauma team configuration is new as providers and staff rotate by shift and month. To account for the variation in team composition, practitioners must have a standard language and process informed by a sense of empathy for one another's roles, concerns, and priorities. This experience captures real 360-degree patient-consent footage to show the orchestra-like coordination of care provided at a Level One trauma facility.

Experiences Designed for Use by Patients

The following companies are deploying AR and VR in ways that afford direct benefit to a patient. VRPhysio, by VR Health, is an FDA-approved product.

Vivid Vision

Vivid Vision treats people with Amblyopia. The process is to start with a VR world and split the scene into two images: one for the strong eye and one for the weak eye. Next, decrease the signal strength of objects in the strong eye and increase it for the weak eye to make it easier for them to work together. As the patient progresses, the goal is to no longer need any modification of images to combine them and see in depth all the time. Each week, the patient needs a little less help, so the difference between the eyes becomes smaller and smaller. With practice, the two eyes learn how to team up and work together.

VRHealth

VRHealth specializes in developing medical tools and content while delivering real-time analytics. Its product, VRPhysio, is FDA registered (*http://bit.ly/2Hh7Fbl*) as an exerciser and range of motion assessment tool. To start, VRPhysio opens with a Range of Motion (ROM) assessment, as demonstrated in Figure 11-4. A virtual physical therapist demonstrates the movements and the application affords customization of patients' sessions according to their ROM assessment and treatment plan.

Figure 11-4. The inside of the virtual environment and an avatar to help with the administration of the ROM test

Then, they choose a short video from a wide range of content—music clips, TED Talks, short movies, and more. Finally, detailed summary reports are generated for each training session.

USC ICT Bravemind (Courtesy of USC Institute of Creative Technologies)

Bravemind is an application for clinicians specializing in treating PTSD. It provides an alternative to conducting exposure in a war zone and/or retraumatizing individuals with combat-related PTSD. Two main virtual environments included Iraq and Afghanistan. Patients can engage in foot patrols, convoys, medical evacuations via helicopters in numerous scenarios. Each scenario allows the clinician to customize the environment to include explosions, firefights, insurgent attacks, and roadside bombs. The extent of coalition forces and civilian injuries, damage to the vehicle (if convoy scenario is used) and directional explosions can be changed. Sound effects include the typical sounds of a combat zone (i.e., weapon discharge), ambient city noises (e.g., call to prayer, insects buzzing), radio chatter, aircraft overhead, and more. Vibrotactile feedback delivers sensations normally associated with engine rumbling, explosions, firefights, and corresponding ambient noises. A scent machine can be used to deliver situation-relevant scents (e.g., cordite, diesel fuel, garbage, gunpowder).

Firsthand Technology, SnowWorld

More than a decade of research and clinical studies have shown that immersive VR can significantly reduce pain, relieve stress, and build resilience. Firsthand Technology has been a part of the pioneering research teams that have established the field of VR pain control and helped build the first VR pain relief application, SnowWorld.

VR pain control research dates back to Ramachandran and Rogers-Ramachandran (1996) who discovered the link between synthetic visual images and physical pain when they used a low-tech "virtual reality box" made with mirrors to relieve amputees' phantom limb pain. In 2000, a team at the Human Interface Technology Lab (HITL) led by Director Tom Furness and psychologist Hunter Hoffman published its first results, showing that computer-generated VR can significantly reduce a patient's pain. Numerous subsequent studies using the SnowWorld found VR is significantly more effective than other diversions such as movies and screen-based computer games.

Firsthand Technology has compiled a list of key references and journal articles on VR pain relief research in its VR Pain Relief Bibliography (*http://bit.ly/2TCOYor*).

Proactive Health

When thinking about health care in the United States, it's often with a reactive connotation. One falls sick and then seeks antibiotics, one has a heart attack and then needs statins and cholesterol medicine, and so on. Proactive or preventative health is defined as an optimization for personal health when your health is in relative stasis. For example, the notion of going to exercise falls into proactive health because it can help reduce risk factors for numerous diseases when done consistently. The following companies play a role in proactive health using VR or AR.

Black Box VR

Black Box VR takes VR and mixes it with decades of exercise science and behavior-change research to reinvent the concept of a brick-and-mortar gym. Founded by the previous CEO of Bodybuilding.com among others, Black Box VR combines VR game concepts with resistance machines with some examples including cable machines that can automatically adjust to meet player weight and height criterion.

YUR, Inc.

YUR uses spatial computing (both AR and VR) to get individuals more active, engaged, and informed. From data collected from multiple individuals using renowned active titles such as Beat Saber, YUR has found that calorie burn from using VR games can be significant. YUR's role is to show users health data predicated on VR inputs alone.

VR as an effective weight-loss tool is generally speaking unintentional. VR captivates the senses and body enough to cause users to move enough that weight loss can come as an ancillary benefit. This is a historic paradigm shift because fitness has been notorious in its failure to stimulate the mind. YUR sees a combination of the entertaining nature of gaming with the physical benefits of exercise as a true movement toward disruption of the stereotypical formats of fitness.

Case Studies from Leading Academic Institutions

Though academic institutions covered herein included only the University of California, San Francisco, Stanford, and Case Western Reserve University, many other academic institutions are working to enable and enact solutions to real challenges in health care via AR and VR group collaboration.

Some of the applications produced by Stanford and Case Western Reserve University are breast surgery, medical education using AR overlay on patients, needle guidance, orthopedic surgery, brain procedures, and other surgery.

At Stanford, one pilot study used the Microsoft Hololens to create a patient-specific app that aligned MRI imagery revealing where a lesion lay to a patient's breast in order to overlay the lesion on the actual site, as illustrated in Figure 11-5.

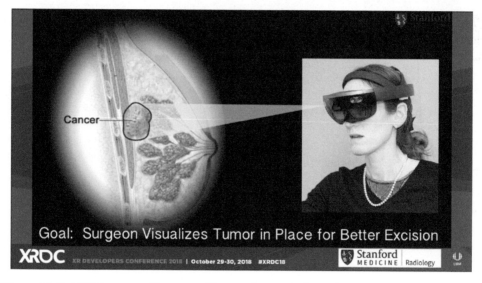

Figure 11-5. MRI images of breast and legion (supine) aligned to a patient and viewed using the Microsoft HoloLens

The summary of the results of that study include an initial improvement in all measures; however, aligning an AR rendering with a patient is still a challenge. Future improvements in alignment come from areas like computer vision and markerless tracking. Stanford Medicine Department of Radiology has illustrated this possibility with Intel's RealSense camera. Figure 11-6 shows a comparison of the HoloLens app against standard procedure for estimating location of palpable tumors.

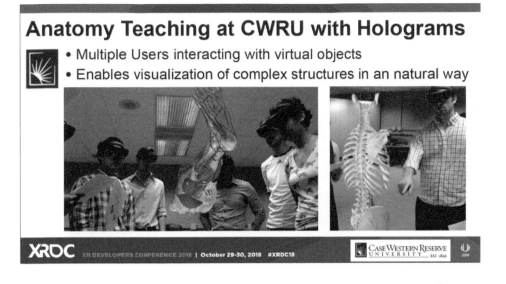

Figure 11-6. In this image, students use the HoloLens with their hands to interact with models

Work done at Case Western Reserve University uses AR in an educational context to teach anatomy by enabling multiple students to interact with virtual models. For complex structures, this paradigm of multiple people viewing a model might help students quickly resolve misunderstandings together.

Taking MRI image mapping using AR a step further is Case Western University's pipeline for real-time MRI and HoloLens rendering (Figure 11-7). This allows for the use of intuitive HoloLens display of volumetric MRI data as it's acquired with substantially little waiting involved.

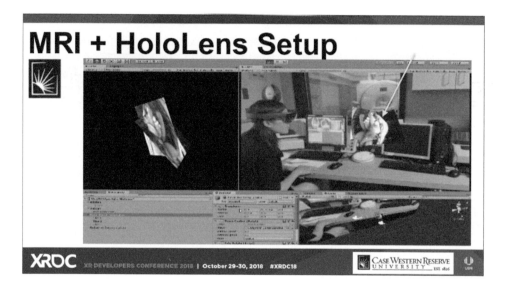

Figure 11-7. The MRI reconstruction pipeline based in Unity (the conductor of the MRI wears the Microsoft HoloLens and from their point of view, it's possible to view a patient's MRI data in real time)

Stanford also has a few more applications using the HoloLens to take advantage of AR overlay on a patient for improved care, wherein an object used in the routine standard of care is tracked positionally. Two examples of these objects are an ultrasound wand and a needle, as illustrated in Figure 11-8. In both cases, a practitioner is able to use the tracked data to more precisely see an area of a body or place a line, respectively.

Figure 11-8. A practitioner getting a real-time overlay of ultrasound image data on top of a patient's arm (normally, the practitioner would need to look over at a separate screen without MR)

The repercussion of in-place augmentation has yet to really be expounded on, but it is interesting to imagine how this might affect, for example, the speed in the delivery of care or other factors. Will this format of viewing improve diagnostic abilities and reduce error?

There are also MR applications for planning from (see Figure 11-9) Stanford in sur-gery domains including kidney transplants, lung resection due to lung cancer, and orthopedic surgery. These are typically areas for which a nick dealt to a blood vessel or certain "lobes" can be problematic, and the use of MR might afford physicians a new, more modern, more helpful UI for respective planning tasks where the patient is in fact augmented.

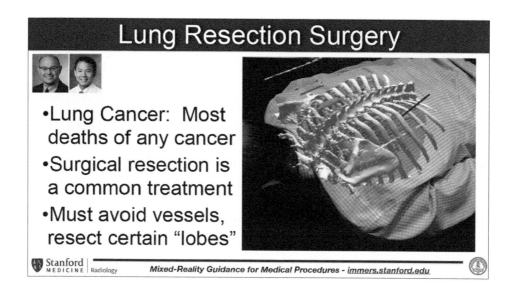

Figure 11-9. Here, a patient is augmented with a virtual lung as physicians prepare for a lung resection treatment

The ongoing efforts at Case Western Reserve University and Stanford might be leading medical higher-education institutions in equipping faculty and students with VR and AR technology. The final example, shown in Figure 11-10, given by Stanford involves MR usage in various orthopedic contexts.

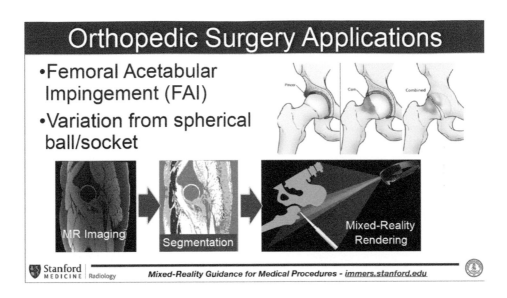

Figure 11-10. Orthopedic surgery application facets include surface representations and 3D models, tools (within the body), resection, motion, and virtual impingement simulation

In closing, VR and AR health technology applications and problem spaces span planning and guidance, medical education, therapies used in a clinical setting, and proactive health, among others. These applications bring together teams of researchers, game programmers, artists, and physicians—and enable potentially meaningful breakthroughs for people with motor disabilities, as shown in the Parkinson's Insight code tutorial in this chapter. For the Parkinson's Insight project, VR provides a means to quantify an otherwise analog finger–nose touch test. In review, the use of VR and AR in health technology will change as the technology evolves and the affordances and maturity of the hardware improves.

CHAPTER 12

The Fan Experience: SportsXR

Marc Rowley

Introduction

This is truly an amazing time to be a sports fan, and thanks to technology, the future of sports is unlimited. This chapter focuses on augmented reality (AR), virtual reality (VR), and sports. The connections that we as fans have with sports have driven developments in media and technology over the past few years at a ferocious pace. Sports has been one of the most consumed content categories in the global digital media marketplace and is moving technology forward for more sports AR and VR experiences.

Here are the ground rules that developers need to know:

- Sports are events in which rules are set, contestants compete, and there is a result.
- AR and VR use technology to create and enhance content. The best example of this is the "First-and-Ten line" from Sportvision in 1998.
- Live action matters, it creates a sense of wonder, an anticipation, a wanting to not miss out.

To explore this juggernaut more thoroughly, this chapter is separated into three parts:

- Five key principles of AR and VR for sports
- The next evolution of sports experiences
- Making the future

First, proper introductions. I'm Marc Rowley, and I consider myself an AR/VR pioneer, having worked on live AR in sports for more than 20 years. I have five Emmy awards, multiple global innovation awards, and I have founded several AR companies. As I see it, the best moment for a storyteller is to see the audience's reaction when you show them something they have never seen.

The goal when you are creating a product for sports fans is to make something magical. If you do this, people will come back for more. The First-and-Ten line for American football and the offsides line in futbol/football/soccer are the best magical moments in sports. They show you something you know is there, but you can't see it without technology.

I spent 18 years at ESPN creating new technology like the rundown graphic, the virtual play book, and the first-ever multiview camera pylon. I left this post at ESPN in 2017 to work on the next wave of AR and VR. Currently, I am the CEO of Live CGI. My team has created the full digital broadcast live AR player of a live event in CGI (computer generated images) with simultaneous streaming capabilities to all devices.

Now, before we crack on, we need to get to a baseline. Research matters.

Yes, we know you have heard that before—when you are dealing with sports products, double it. The reality is this, it is highly likely that someone has already thought of your idea. They might have already worked on it or started it before you. Yet, if you believe and can prove the problem exists and your solution is special, there is an amazing rush awaiting you. When you create and deliver a product that changes how people see their game you will be riding a high like none other. Luckily, the best ideas in sports are public. All you need to do is start with a patent search.

Figures 12-1 and 12-2 present two quick examples from two patents that mold how we watch live sports right now. Figure 12-1 is a patent for a system for enhancing the television presentation of an object in a sporting event, and Figure 12-2 is a patent for presenting content and augmenting a broadcast. Patents might not seem interesting to read at first but if you take the time, you will find they create a clear path to problem and solution. You don't need to spend weeks, but you should spend at least 40 hours making sure you have a good foundation of what has come before you. This will help increase your chances of succeeding.

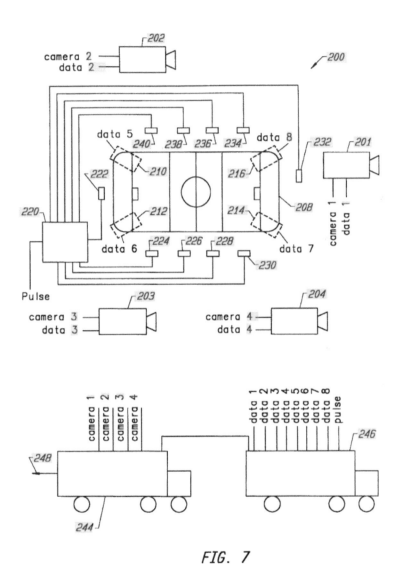

FIG. 7

Figure 12-1. The path of how cameras are used to locate position relative to a field of play

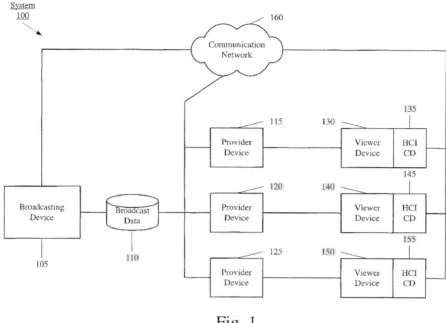

Fig. 1

Figure 12-2. A workflow for how data can process to recreate play output, which is key to understanding how an AR element is created

Now, let's get into what you need to know when creating products for sports.

Part 1: Five Key Principles of AR and VR for Sports

OK, the stage is set for the five principles of AR/VR in sports:

- The moment is everything
- Nothing is live
- Flat images/sense of presence
- 20/80 rule
- Time matters

Let's begin by asking two questions.

Why are sports special? What would sports be like without AR and VR?

The answer to the first question is easy—it is the moments; *the moment is everything.* Sports have three phases: pre-event, the event itself, and post event. And yet every contest, every event, can be defined by critical moments. It is these moment above all that people crave. They want to be there live, to be in that moment, to be wrapped in all the glory, the pain and the triumph. Sports is one of the greatest escapes from reality ever provided. For a few hours you can leave your world behind and live in this one created for you to experience amazing moments.

Now, let's address the second question.

Consider tennis, in which officials let an algorithm and virtual cameras decide whether a ball is in or out of bounds (Hawkeye). You might think about a broadcast of American football during which there is a yellow line—the first-down line—superimposed on the screen that is not actually there in real life. All good choices, but not where we need to go. We need to deconstruct the essence of sports.

Let's begin by taking away replays. No more replays. That changes it a bit, right?

Then, take away the live score and clock graphic. Now all you have is a video feed of a contest and you have no idea who the teams that are playing and what the score is.

Now take away the broadcast video, the audio, and the live text updates.

What remains are arenas where people go to compete, and people come to watch. That is the baseline we need to start from and where we were about a hundred years ago. All of the layers we just peeled away are AR. In fact, a broadcast itself is a VR representation.

This is worth repeating, what you are seeing is not real. It is all a presentation that is created for you.

You might be thinking, wait a minute. I can see sports on my TV without using a VR headset. Yes, you can, and what you are watching is not live. It is a representation of an event. A director shows you camera angles, and in your brain, you create a map of the arena and your brain computes the changes and fills in the gaps. That's right; the camera shows you only about 90% of the action and then the director makes your brain create the rest with fast cuts and high-paced graphics and music.

This is a critical point: if we get lost here, the rest of this chapter fails.

Nothing Is Live

Live is a belief we have in that what we are processing in our brain is happening at the moment we are viewing it. In fact, if you are on the court watching a match, your brain is processing images at 13 milliseconds. This means that what you are seeing happened actually .0013 seconds ago. But to you it feels like it just happened. To you it is absolutely live. But if we tried to explain this to the average consumer, they would have a very confused look on their face. In sports, "live" is generally accepted to have three different stages: Live, Live Live, and Live to record or live to tape (LTT).

To many, live content can be anything within a minute of the action happening. For example, you might be watching content at home on a Chromecast, but you are talking with a friend at the game and you find out there is a 40-second delay in getting to you. It is still called live, but the rules are bent a bit.

Live Live is for content that is under a four- to five-second window

Taken a bit farther, if you are in an apartment in New York City and watching a baseball game in the Bronx, you are likely watching it on a delay of 5 to 60 seconds depending on your service. This happens because video signals have data. That data needs to be transmitted from the camera to the production switcher and then to a transmission hub, which then sends it to a broadcast central area where is it routed to a TV signal or to an internet signal and broken into packets, and then sent over the vast array of network switches to be assembled on the device you are on. This is why different people can see the same video at different times.

Live is something we have convinced ourselves exists in sports, news media, and in many other areas. Just know that this is all a virtual construct that we are choosing to agree is live—and even that might change in a bit.

One story that we like to tell from the late 1990s happened when automated data began being displayed on TV screens and accessible via the internet. Consumers began noticing that a score would change before they saw the video. In one instance, an angry gambler called a major broadcaster to find out how they were able to predict the score so accurately. The funny thing is it all came down to math. Video files are larger and take longer to send. Data files such as a clock and score are smaller and take less time. Thus, you might see a digital scoreboard update before the video. Most major broadcasters now have code to handle this, but at the time it was a big surprise. This has mostly gone away as latency in video has been reduced, but in some places, you can still see it. Live is how you perceive it.

Let's continue with the live sports example.

All around the world, broadcasters put cameras in locations to capture *flat images* of an event that is played in a three-dimensional space. They then take multiple cameras and intercut them to give people the perception of depth, time, and space—broadcasters create a virtual reality that the majority of the world accepts as the real event. Yet, in the business we know that this method has limitations.

A camera is only as good as the location at which it is placed, the focal point, the iris, the shading, the lighting, the signal strength, the pixels back to the production head end, and, most important, the team assembling this representation. But make no mistake, you are watching a flat representation of the real world.

Producing a flat sporting event requires several components. Camera operators, switchers, audio, operations, cables, and many more. They are all working to create a virtual representation of a game with multiple dimensions on your flat screen. For the past 80 years, this is how people watch sports. And as with any industry as it matures, people find ways to add elements and improve. As with any media category, there are usually two different levels of critical moments in the evolution of the category. Sports are no exception.

Here is a list of the top five sports AR and VR storytelling features in the first 50 to 60 years of live sports:

1. Live transmission
2. Announcer audio
3. Video
4. Replays
5. Score graphics

And here is the list of the next five sports AR and VR features in the past 20 to 30 years:

6. Live on-screen storytelling graphics
7. The highlight
8. Augmented rule graphics
9. Live streaming media to internet devices
10. Social media interaction

Each of these elements have helped craft how users see and experience sports. All with one single goal: providing the consumer with a *sense of presence* in order to manifest a sense of wonder, amazement, and anticipation all for that one moment in sports that matters, the critical point at which the outcome is in doubt and the consumer leans forward wanting more.

Think about it, what if there were no highlights, how would you be able to watch a play, to get a quick recap. What if you could not see a graphic on the screen and what if umpires had to make all the decisions in tennis? What if you could not see a First-and-Ten line in a football game? What if you could not see an instant social message from your coach or favorite player? Each of these elements augments our sports experience.

But it is what is coming next that is going to be truly revolutionary. In the late 2000s, I worked on a team at ESPN that looked to take the First-and-Ten AR technology and use this to better enhance storytelling to get viewers to watch longer. That is what the broadcasting business is all about. You are in business to make as much money as you can for as long as you can. In sports, you make that money by having transactions with the customer. Either directly from their wallet to you or indirectly by selling their attention to a partner (advertisers). We can do this via impressions, viewers, and other means. What rose to prominence over the years has been one metric: time spent.

Time spent is the factor that motivates many partners. It means that the consumer is interested in the product and interested enough to give significant time. It encapsulates clicks, eyeballs, movement, and everything. One of my old executives had a saying that has become rather true. Content consumption comes down to a *20/80 rule*.

The 20/80 rule goes like this. If you took your total audience of users who consume and spent time with your product (content/platform), 20% of the users will be your heaviest. They will make up 80% of your action. The other 80% of your users will make up 20% of your consumption. This happens after your audience matures. In the first months of your product, it might go crazy or it might be a slow burn, whatever way you go in sports the 20/80 rule has been proven to be a good metric.

My goal was always to keep that 20% interested and see whether I could move it to 21% or 22%. The rationale is that you are not going to get the casual consumer to make big life changes. It just does not happen, but if you can get the hardcore consumer to change, you will see a lift in the casual consumers. This does not mean that you are always capturing the full audience, though. Just look at the rise of Esports. The consumers were there and they were underserved, now as their consumption grows, we are seeing similar patterns. Only, the Esports patterns are evolving at a much faster pace as consumers go from game title to game title looking for the next best thing.

What does this have to do with AR and VR? Everything. It is a baseline for you when you are testing, when you are building, and when you deliver your first initially viable product. Everyone has the same amount of time in a day. How people use their time is the only currency that matters. It does not matter whether you are building an app for kids in a hospital or putting on the Super Bowl, time is your goal. If you get users to spend time you can make a social, financial, or educational impact—or even all of them. *Time matters*.

Now we have a set of ground rules, so let's recap the five key principle points:

1. The moment is everything
2. Nothing is live
3. Flat images/sense of presence
4. 20/80 rule
5. Time matters

Part 2: The Next Evolution of Sports Experiences

In the next few years, we are going to see products that attack each of these five points; they will be the guide posts as the sports experience is redefined. These changes will happen at a global scale previously thought impossible simply due to the proliferation of internet devices and the minimization of the learning curve for new consumers.

The changes will be swift and will focus in three key areas:

- Connection
- Display
- Interaction

Connection rates in the world have been changing rapidly as have the compression systems for delivering the data. Once, 3G was the hallmark, now it is being replaced with 4G, 5G, LTE, and every other upgrade coming out. What this means at a basic level is that the amount of data you can drive is becoming larger and faster, and this will likely continue to grow at exponential rates, which will fuel the growth in AR and VR experiences. Data is directly related to latency. Latency is the delay a consumer experiences in the live action to the actual world. That is what creates the live effect. As a developer, producer or distributor, you need to follow and understand the relationship between those two factors. *Latency matters.*

For example, the first test of a large-scale single-unit VR camera at a sporting event hanging over the field was traveling at speeds from 20 to 30 miles per hour on wires suspended in the air. The camera was sending 9,000,000,000 bits of data per second going over a fiber line into a converter that sent 20,000,000 bits of data to a switcher that changed that data into 10,000,000 bits of data. Finally, it is mixed back to the 20,000,000 bits and sent on to the consumer. That is 9 gigs, to 20 megs, to 10 megs and back up to 20 megs per second of data. The reason it is written with all the zeros is to impart the full scope. 9,000,000,000 bits of data every second is crazy insane, no mobile device could handle that today—but tomorrow it might.

This leads us to the innovators at small and large companies alike who are working to solve the problems of compression and signal speed to create AR and VR experiences that run on new displays. Full VR headsets, AR goggles, and other devices all need a feed of data going to them. And as we previously went over, we all need a fast-live connection for content to work with sports. *Live is all that matters.*

When it comes to displays, the future will be mapped by graphics processors and then optical hardware. Some might think it is the visual hardware first; however, Apple and Google changed that by launching ARKit and ARCore. Unity, Unreal, and others have created the framework to make amazing experiences. These factors have flooded the market with VR and AR devices. Now, as a developer, you don't need to wait for hardware to proliferate: there are already one billion devices ready. Consumers already have the hardware.

Graphics processors are commonly referred to as GPUs. They are the engine that will unlock live AR and VR in the next few years as the connection rates improve. GPUs take the graphical data and make images. GPU speeds and capabilities are your second market for growth.

GPUs have grown exponentially due to a variety of factors consistent in display technology, with one major exception: the Bitcoin boom. The rise in Bitcoin "mining" has driven processor speeds to very high levels as miners compete to earn more Bitcoins. This gave an unexpected boost to VR and AR work. It enhanced the power to create really immersive experiences by driving processor speeds. Another recent change is the advancements in *ray tracing*.

All of these technology factors are great, but they are nothing without the story. The story is everything. People don't buy technology, they buy stories, they buy things, and use things that tell them stories. The oldest lesson in mass experiences is tell me a story.

The third evolution of the sport experience will be changing how the content is created. Right now, kids grow up with custom controls in gaming, they get feeds from social media personalized to them. Yet when they watch a broadcast, they have one producer, one director and a few cameras fed to them. This will change when rights holders push the creators and distributors to give users more control. The day is coming when an artificial intelligence–driven director auto cuts sequences to tell the live story in a produced package to each individual consumer from the same game.

The first big change for this has been Esports, where users can comment, interact, and control their experience. The walls between fan and athlete are coming down. Although traditional broadcasters balked at this at first, they slowly came around when the revenue numbers showed the reality that we all know too well: consumers always win.

This is an important set of data to consider when you are creating a product. It has been proven time and time again that if you try to stop the pace of content consumption, a vacuum can and likely will be created. In this case, when the old media companies stalled on Esports interactivity, they allowed Twitch.tv to capture huge audiences.

Think about it. There was nothing stopping Sky Sports in the United Kingdom, ESPN in the United States, or FOX Sports, or any other entity from creating Twitch; they just missed it, and now Twitch.tv is part of Amazon and capturing huge global audiences.

Even though Twitch.tv has multiple types of content, the two that stand out here are streamers playing games and Esports property's streaming on their platform. According to the Esports Observer in 2018, the top four Twitch streaming entities accounted for almost 500 million hours. Streamers Ninja and Shroud paired with Riot Games and The Overwatch League set the bar high. When consumer watch on these platforms, they can interact with other consumers via chat bars and they can also support their teams and players.

Please don't ever forget this rule: the consumer always wins, and from here on out, know that *all consumers want control*.

Part 3: Making the Future

The future is built on the innovations of the past. The future of sports AR and VR is coming at an ultra-fast rate. Thanks to the proliferation of devices, the focus on latency, and changing consumer behaviors, it will not take 80 years for the next quantum shifts.

The time to redefine sports is now, the time to change AR and VR is now. The developers who build products that are fast, tell stories, and provide audience control will create products that succeed.

When you sit down to build this future, you must think about your workflow. How is the content entered, where does it go? What is the overall macro view and what is the micro view? To do this, you need to create two documents for your team. One that simply outlines what you are going to do. In sports terms, this is the game plan. Each coach has a game plan. In football, you decide whether you are running an I-formation or a shotgun; in baseball, it is a shift; in Esports, it is how long do you jungle or who is your support.

Then, you need to create a micro view. This is the script of the play: where each asset is going to go; who is going to block whom; who is going to take on which role? After you have done this, you can look into how your product is going to work.

Let's take a look at a recent patent filed for a system of transmitting a live event through computer-generated images. Figure 12-3 presents the overview, a simpler approach. Figure 12-4 offers more details. In most cases, you don't want to share these, because they are part of your special sauce for how your product is made; however, after you have filed the patent, and the information is public, it is fair game for anyone. Thus, as with everything, it all comes down to execution. The best thing about sports is that the playing field is public, it is not that way with all products. In sports, as the saying goes, "You are what your record says you are."

Workflow systems for capturing and live streaming to multiple devices.

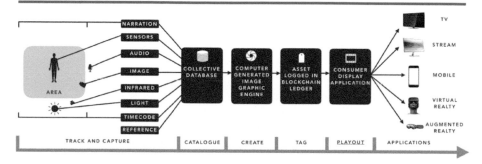

Figure 12-3. The workflow for capturing seven live datasets, adding a recorded dataset, and streamlining all of them into a visual presentation process—by pushing all data points into a CGI engine, the narrative is changed to being native to each platform's individual rendering capabilities

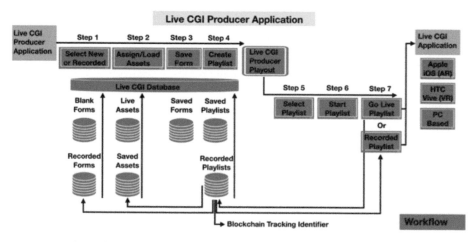

Figure 12-4. The individual steps a producer undertakes to create a live stream (when you are creating your product, this step is one of the most important; How does each click happen? What does each touch trigger? Thinking through your process is key)

Now into the details. The first and foremost factor in sports is to focus on latency; speed is the ultimate feature. Friction hurts latency, complicated hardware hurts latency, and convoluted systems hurt latency—focus on being fast. This also means that you must be accurate. It does not do anyone any good to be fast and wrong.

Next up, tell a story. All users want to be entertained. Tell a story of the event and tell a story that people care about. Even if the story is just about the user, just about their team. That is the story they want, and by giving it to them, they will come back for more. As a developer, you don't need to be a great storyteller, but you need to talk to one. You need to find a storyteller, a writer, someone with the gift of gab, and make sure that your product tells a story.

The final guide is giving consumers control. Give consumers what they want and let their preferences, their likes, and their dislikes create the experience.

So, let's recap these guideposts:

- Latency matters
- Tell me a story
- Consumers want control

You might be asking, "OK, but how do you test for this?" Well, you can test for latency with simple math. How long does it take to get from A to B? You can test for story continuity by asking consumers what they got out of your product. And you can measure how much they like the control you give them by checking their movements. You can measure all of these things, but where do you start? For my teams it has always been the *rule of 10*. We don't put anything in a product that the user wants to use or see less than 10 times. Once or twice is a novelty; three to four times, you might show a friend. Five to nine times, and you like it but don't need it. 10 or more times and you have to have it.

A good example of this happened in a football game in 2008. The New Orleans Saints had an electric player named Reggie Bush, and the new product rolled out for the game showed his speed. They captured him at 22 miles per hour (mph). Although this is amazingly impressive, the audience members computed it against a car and 22 mph did not sound impressive. Yet, if you think about it, 22 mph converts to 32 feet per second, or 10 yards per second. It did not matter; the number did not resonate with the audience. Think about this when you are building your product, will it resonate, do people care, does it make an impact?

Ownership

Before we end this chapter, we need to talk about the money in sports. There is a squishy area in sports where people think the big leagues are selling the game or the event to the ticket holders. Even though there is some revenue that is derived from that individual point of sale, the majority of the revenue over the past 50-plus years has been through media rights, licensing, and content bundles. This means that leagues are less about sports and more about intellectual property and content. However, on the face of it, many folks might debate this point. Yet, when you look at league contracts, look at what media companies are buying, and look at the value it is, the answer is clear. Sports is all about content. This change has affected how products are made and created huge influxes of cash into the market.

For example, if you make an interactive viewer for rugby, you need to keep track of the minutes, the hours, and how the content was used. This is key to how leagues and players monetize their performance. This is true in Esports as well as billiards. The overarching business driver for many billion-dollar deals is time.

Yes, you need to think about latency, you need to tell a story, and you need to give up control. And, you need to keep track of it all to be able to deliver an accounting of the experience. The reason why this is listed last in this section is to reinforce how important it is. If you build everything awesome but miss out on the basic accounting of the experience, you limit your likelihood of success as well as your growth potential. You need to be sure to build in a tracker.

Figures 12-5 and 12-6 show two workflow snapshots from a public patent for footage reporting (US20110008018A1). In it, you can see how the team outlined a simple tracking mechanism for capturing footage when it is being created and then cataloging it before it was sent via stream for consumers. This simple system redefined how footage rights deals were negotiated in the late 2000s. It does not need to be complicated, it just needs to keep track of what is being consumed and how.

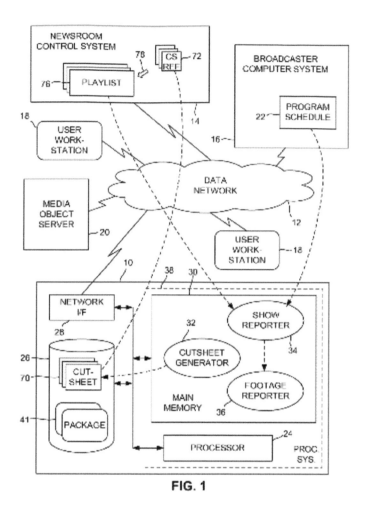

FIG. 1

Figure 12-5. The workflow for how a broadcast system uses tagged data and a cutsheet to associate the data with the video

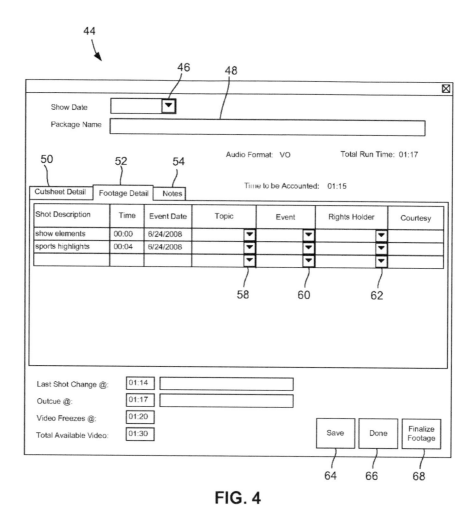

Figure 12-6. Data entry for the cut sheet, which is where individual producers assign preset data to the new video they created (The beauty of this system is all the deal points, restrictions, and individual business processes are hidden from the user, who is just asked to input the topic, event, locator, and courtesy. Those four items create an intricate catalogue that helps the business monetize content)

Final Thought

You might not like this, but here goes: no one cares about your struggle until you are part of an amazing moment.

This might come across as harsh, but the faster you accept it, the faster you can get to succeeding. In sports, we learn that no one cares about the athlete's struggle until they have succeeded. I had a number on my office wall for a few years, and only a few people ever guessed what it meant. The number was 1,184. That is the number of players who are tremendous athletes who were going to be released at the end of the NFL preseason when the 32 teams cut their rosters down from 90 players to 53. Some of those thousands of young players will get jobs, but for a lot of them, it is over. They all put in 15-hour workouts to get ready for professional football, just for a shot at training camp. Then, in one moment, they are cut.

Think of this when you start your product. When you build, when you create for sports, focus on bringing the fan into that journey of that athlete who rises to meet the moment. It can be a fantasy baseball game, a training application or a live stream —no matter what you do, create something that people will want to keep coming back to again and again.

Also, don't share your business. The biggest mistake you can do at the minute the fan is hooked on your product—the minute the consumer is ready for the moment—is to show them your business model or wait for something to break.

Conclusion

This is the most amazing time in history to be working on sports products. The speed of technology is able to catch up and enhance the speed of live sports. With so many recorded content experiences it is the truly live ones that affect large swaths of people's lives. When you build your product focus on the moments, focus on latency, focus on the story and give the consumers control.

Focus on the fan: they make the game interesting, they follow the stories, and they are all that ultimately matters.

CHAPTER 13

Virtual Reality Enterprise Training Use Cases

Rosstin Murphy

This chapter is about virtual reality (VR) enterprise training, focusing on the usage of *spherical video*. In writing this chapter, my goal was to put down what would have been most useful to us, when we were getting started. I hope it can be useful to you.

Introduction: The Importance of Enterprise Training

Enterprise training will be the first major success story for VR because of how well VR's strengths and limitations match to the enterprise training environment. Training is a bigger market than people think; in 2017, $121.7 billion was spent on gaming, but $362.2 billion was spent on training.[10, 13]

In 2018, STRIVR shipped 17,000 Oculus Go head-mounted displays (HMDs) to Walmart. That's multiple HMDs in every single Walmart store in the United States, with more than a million Walmart employees having access to enterprise training in VR every day. That's impact. Figure 13-1 depicts STRIVR's makeshift warehouse, where everyone is pitching in to perform quality control on each headset.

Figure 13-1. 17,000 HMDs being prepared for shipping (© STRIVR 2018)

For VR to be successful, it needs to solve one specific problem at scale and do it better than any other technology. Enterprise training is an industry ready to be transformed. Enterprise training is that problem.

This chapter lays out use cases, challenges, and approaches to building content and scaling customers of VR training, with a focus on spherical video as a training medium.

Does VR Training Work?

The best way to learn something is to do it. For tasks like learning to fly an airplane or performing open heart surgery, this isn't always safe or possible. People have invented various methods of conveying information about a task without actually putting scalpel to skin. Reading a manual about a task is one of the least immersive ways to learn, whereas being led through a task by an expert is one of the most immersive.

Being trained in VR can't currently match having a human instructor walk you through a task one on one, but it can get close while being much cheaper and more scalable.

Figure 13-2 shows a scatter plot with one axis representing cost and scalability, and the other axis representing effectiveness. On one end, consider the training manual. You can send it anywhere, print it on demand, or read it on a screen, but it's not a very effective teaching tool, especially when you consider teaching a physical task like tying a knot. A training manual is highly scalable, but not very effective.

On the other end of the spectrum is one-on-one expert mentorship, the most effective form of training. A human instructor knows everything about their subject and can walk you through it step by step, engaging you, guiding you, challenging you, and responding to your progress. However, this requires the valuable time of a highly paid expert. This form of training is highly effective but costly and difficult to scale.

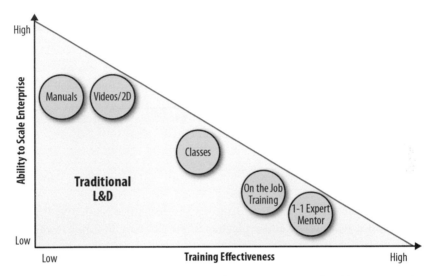

Figure 13-2. Scalability versus effectiveness of training options (© STRIVR 2018)

The promise of VR is to build something as cheap to distribute as digital text, but as effective as one-on-one expert mentorship.

With that in mind, can VR training be that effective? No study has conclusively proven it, but there is more and more evidence pointing in that direction.

VR creates a physiological response closer to reality than any other medium. The classic example of this is "the plank," in which a user wearing an HMD with room-scale tracking is placed into a 3D computer graphics environment where they're suspended at a great height above a city. In reality, the user is standing on a beam of wood resting on the floor, but from the user's perspective they're teetering on the brink of death. Few users who try this experience can deny the visceral physical effect it has on you: your balance teeters, your legs buckle, and every step forward makes your heart race.

You learn best when you are doing something real, and VR feels real.

When training adult learners, creating an experience that feels real is a key to motivating them and helping them absorb new knowledge.[6] VR brings learners closer to reality than any other training medium, with less risk and expense.

VR training is a particularly good fit for the needs of adult learners. In *The Adult Learner*, Malcolm S. Knowles posits that adults have different learning needs than children. When an adult learns, they are motivated by practical concerns. Why am I learning this? How can it be useful? In what real-life situation will I be able to apply this knowledge? Training in VR provides many benefits over non-experiential learning:

Engagement

VR is an interaction-rich environment in which learners are constantly called upon to engage. Just putting on the headset and looking around means you're already interacting. In the "Store Robbery Training" interaction scenario, for instance, the robbers first approach the learner from behind, and the learner must physically turn their head around to see what is happening. VR forces the user to be an active participant in the experience.

Context

Good VR training puts the learner in a realistic environment in which the skills they are learning will be useful. In the "Flood House Training" scenario, the difference between Category 1 and Category 3 water is not academic; it's the difference between tearing out and replacing all the flooring in a house versus simply drying it out.

Motivation

The learner can see consequences of their actions. Applying the new skills effectively will demonstrate a good outcome, and failing to apply the learning will result in harm. For example, in the "Wire Down Training" scenario, failing to communicate the danger of a downed wire results in a pet dog being electrocuted.

At STRIVR, there have been opportunities to perform small studies on the efficacy of VR training. In the next section, we look at a use case in which the efficacy of a VR training method was tested against one-on-one expert mentorship.

Use Case: Flood House Training

A flood house is a real house that is intentionally flooded several times a year, so that insurance professionals can train. There are roughly 30 or so of these houses throughout the United States. An expert instructor works with a small class, and together they dry out the house and repair or replace what has been damaged. This is one of the most effective training methods because of how closely it matches reality.

Building a house, flooding it, and then repairing it is, unsurprisingly, expensive. The damage done to the house is real and costly. Plus, because there are only a few flood houses in each state, trainees must be flown to the location.

However, this outlay of expense is worth it, because of the huge amounts of money at play. For example, Hurricane Florence in 2018 caused insurance losses of three to five billion dollars. Not all insurance claims are made with honest intent, and fraud accounts for about 10% of claims. Having well-trained insurance professionals who can reduce that number is crucial to insurance companies. But what if they could get the same results with less expense?

STRIVR set out to create a VR version of a flood house training course, working closely with expert instructors. Camera crews recorded spherical video at the house from the perspective of a student being taught one on one, and then designers built a VR training module using those videos. In this case, the VR training module was made to comprehensively cover everything that would be taught during the class, regardless of whether every aspect of the training was a "good fit" for VR.

After the VR training module was built, STRIVR took a class of 60 students and ran half of them through the real flood house, and the other half through the VR training module. STRIVR's data team then assessed the difference in effectiveness between the real flood house training and the VR experience.

In STRIVR's VR training module, a narrator guides the trainee through an insurance claim scenario in which they must assess water damage done to Lisa's house. The trainee is kept engaged by being asked to interact with locations in the video (Figure 13-3) or answer multiple-choice questions about what they've learned (Figure 13-4).

Figure 13-3. A marker question is used to keep the learner engaged and interacting during the lesson

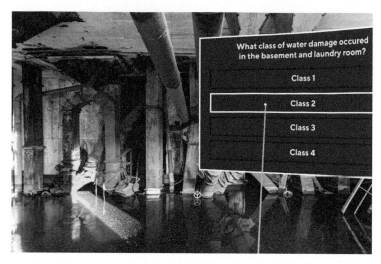

Figure 13-4. A multiple-choice question about categories of water damage

STRIVR tested each group of trainees on their knowledge both before and after each training, to see how much they improved. They found that both groups improved by roughly the same amount in both the Water Mitigation training and the Framing training. This shows comparability; the experience in VR was roughly equivalent to being flown out to the actual flood house but at much less expense. Both groups improved, as illustrated in Figure 13-5, and there was no statistically significant difference between their results.

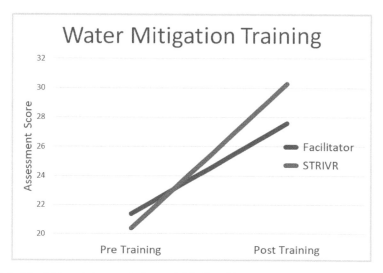

Figure 13-5. The VR training and the real-life flood house training yielded comparable improvements (© STRIVR 2018)

Data collection is also a benefit of VR training. STRIVR kept track of users' movement data by logging their head and hand movements. One question in particular was very difficult for trainees, with more than half getting the wrong answer. The data analysis team saw that the group of trainees who answered incorrectly had more movement than the trainees who answered the question correctly. The data team speculated that this could mean trainees were fidgeting, scanning the environment, or not paying close attention. Because it was a small sample size, no hard conclusions could be drawn, but as tools improve, insights like these could be used to create more adaptive content.

STRIVR learned a couple important lessons from this use case:

Content should be bite-sized

Content designers tend to overestimate the amount of time users want to spend in VR. It's important to break up content so that users can take breaks. 20 minutes is a good benchmark for a training session, so an individual lesson should be well under this amount of time.

Not all content is a "good fit" for VR

Because STRIVR wanted to include all of the content from the on-site training, it made the mistake of including content that was not a good fit for VR. For instance, in one section the trainees must use mathematical equations to calculate the amount of necessary air movers (see Figure 13-6). Under normal circumstances, trainees would have access to a calculator, but this was not provided in the VR scenario. This is a good example of the kind of learning that is better done in a classroom: it requires an outside tool, and doesn't play to the strengths of the VR medium.

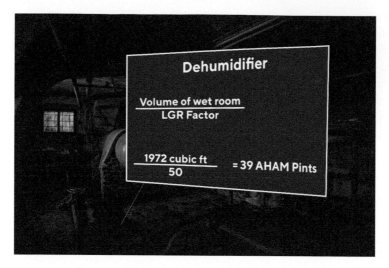

Figure 13-6. Asking the learner to do calculations without context is not a "good fit" for VR

What Is VR Training Good for? R.I.D.E.

VR isn't for every use case. STRIVR uses the acronym "RIDE" for determining the best places in which to use VR:

- Rare
- Impossible
- Dangerous
- Expensive

Here are some examples of situations fitting these criteria:

Rare

Black Friday is rare, occurring only once each year, and yet it's a critical financial moment for retailers. High turnover means that not enough employees carry over knowledge and experience from year to year.

Impossible

Store robberies are impossible to predict, but failure to react appropriately in this situation can result in loss of life. It's difficult to know how you'd react in this type of situation until you experience it yourself.

Dangerous

A factory floor with improperly observed safety procedures is dangerous to stage, but it's critical for employees to be able to recognize and correct errors quickly.

Expensive

As we saw in the use case earlier in this chapter, insurance professionals are trained in "flood houses," which use real houses and water to realistically portray flood conditions. Although this training is realistic, it is also expensive.

Right now, spatially oriented VR training is best for tasks that involve a human body interacting in an environment or with another human. Tasks that involve interfacing with a computer screen are particularly ill suited to VR, because these tasks could be more easily done through a common computer interface. Because of the nature of modern work and office jobs, this does eliminate a number of possible use cases.

What Makes Good VR Training?

Good VR training should be the following:

- Spatial
- Simple and accessible
- Short
- Goal-oriented
- Scalable

Let's take a closer look at each characteristic:

Spatial

VR training should be spatial in order to take advantage of the 3D nature of VR, calling out locations above, behind, and below the user. This emphasizes the user's embodiment and helps improve recall.

Simple and accessible

A big advantage of VR is accessibility, and your control scheme needs to reflect that. Modern video games use complex and unintuitive control methods that rely on gamers' experience and familiarity with the genre; you know this if you've ever watched someone unfamiliar with first-person shooter games attempt to move, shoot, and look around at the same time. Most VR hardware supports simple point-and-click hand controllers. Point-and-click is great because it's conceptually similar to using a computer mouse or a laser pointer. Avoid making the user learn a variety of buttons and interfaces. You're trying to teach real-life skills, and the more you bring forward the nature of the controllers, the less your experience will map comfortably to reality.

Short

Sessions should be bite-sized. VR training sessions should be no longer than about 20 minutes. This helps to prevent headsets from becoming uncomfortable as well as making it easier for users to absorb content at their own pace. If your content is divided well, users will feel comfortable jumping in and doing a piece of training, knowing that they'll soon be able to decide whether to continue or get back to another task in real life. Having a low barrier for entering and training means users will log in more often.

Goal-oriented

Because session times must be short, and learners' time is at a premium, VR is best used for learning tasks that have clear rules and procedures rather than for experimenting in a sandbox-like environment. (However, as technology improves and VR becomes more natural and comfortable, sandbox training might find more uses.)

Scalable

VR's advantage over other training mediums is that it is both high quality and scalable. Keep this in mind as you build your platform and content. It should either be easy to create new content or the content created should be highly reusable by a large number of users.

Spherical Video

A spherical video is a recording in which every direction of view is captured at once, allowing the viewer to physically turn their head to see different aspects of the video. The overall effect is as if the viewer were physically present at the location the video was shot, with the notable difference that the viewer cannot move or affect the environment in any way.

Spherical video is rarely thought of as a "first choice" for VR training content. When enterprise customers describe the kind of training experience they'd like to build, what comes to mind is a fully interactive, completely realistic 3D computer graphics environment.

But, for a training framework to be scalable and efficient, it needs to be quick and easy to build content. You need a tool. If you tried to build a system for creating 3D training content that could do anything a client might want (e.g., laparoscopic surgery, vehicle simulations, customer interactions), by the time you were done adding features, you'd probably be left with something that looks like a fully featured game engine.

Remember, a major advantage of VR for training is scalability. It should be cheap and fast to create trainings for large numbers of people. The more labor intensive creating a training is, the less often you'll be able to update it, and the less content you'll be able to produce. Although video games have existed for decades, the current state of the art for enterprise training is still 2D video, because video is easy to create, maintain, update, and replace.

Spherical video is about as easy to shoot as conventional 2D video, while offering a number of benefits in regard to interactivity.

The Benefits of Spherical Video

Here are some of the benefits of using spherical video:

- Scalable
- Easy to generate content
- Inexpensive
- More interactive than 2D video

When building VR training, it's necessary to re-create the training environment. With spherical video, this is simply a matter of filming that environment *in situ*. This guarantees that your filmed result is perfectly realistic and matches the real environment exactly.

When humans are a necessary part of the training, real instructors and employees can be helpful. These people will already have the right uniforms, know the procedures being taught, and have experience demonstrating them. (Caveat: as we discuss later, it is always worth hiring real actors when filming roles that require a portrayal of emotion or on-camera poise.)

With our current level of technology and computer graphics, right now there are no VR-capable graphics that can approach video's level of realism.

The Challenges of Spherical Video

However, there are also challenges in using spherical video to create content.

Some situations are difficult to stage, even once for a camera. For these, we can use video editing to create the necessary effect, but this can create an unrealistic result.

Another challenge is that employees and instructors at the site might not be natural actors who perform well on film. If the training is for something like a store robbery, real actors might be necessary, creating additional expenditure. It's critical to get the content right the first time because returning to the site to reshoot or digitally cleaning up the video are both expensive and time consuming.

But the biggest challenge of spherical video is interactivity within the experience.

Interactions with Spherical Video

When considering what can be accomplished with spherical video, one of the first places to look for inspiration is 2D video. What forms of interaction are possible with 2D video, and what advantages does spherical video bring in comparison?

Reaction

As with any media, a portion of the user's interactions take place within the user's own head, as they watch and listen to the information being conveyed, and then process it. Even without asking for direct interaction, the user interacts with the media with their internal expectations, thoughts, and questions. In this way, 2D and spherical video share a requirement that the content be engaging, interesting, well produced, and relevant. When producing spherical video for training, a background in the techniques used to make 2D video entertaining is essential.

Gaze

Gaze is a significantly richer form of interaction in spherical video than it is in 2D video. In a 2D video, the viewer is watching a bounded screen. The camera movement and shot transitions are deliberate choices by the editor to focus the viewer on certain places and times. But in spherical video, editing must be kept to a minimum to avoid disorienting the user. This means that a greater demand is placed on the viewer; the viewer is the camera, and they must take an active part in looking around and absorbing the information. In STRIVR's "Store Robbery Training" experience, for example, the learner is first approached by the robbers from behind and must turn their head in order to see them. In this way, gaze can be a powerful interactive tool in spherical video.

Multiple-choice questions

In contemporary elearning environments, video is often bookended with multiple-choice questions. In spherical video, multiple-choice questions can be presented from within the experience, rather than outside of it, adding context to the user's decisions. For example, in Figure 13-7, one of the robbers points a gun at you and demands that you give him access to the safe. Seeing time freeze and hearing a heartbeat sound as you frantically try to decide what to do is a much more emotionally engaging experience in a spherical video than it would be on a computer screen. Spherical video also gives you the opportunity to use locations or objects in the video as "answers" to a question. In Figure 13-8, a football quarterback is prompted to select the location of his "runfit" after watching the first few seconds of a down.

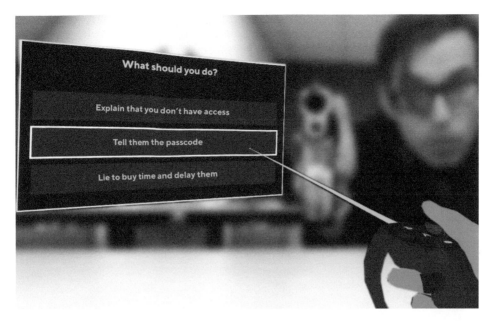

Figure 13-7. Multiple-choice questions have added context in a VR environment where you can see the consequences of your choices

Figure 13-8. A football player must identify his "run fit" by selecting the correct location in the video

Points of Interest

Spherical video has a powerful interaction tool that was rarely used with 2D videos: pointing and selecting locations within the video. This is possibly the best form of interaction with spherical video because it gives the learner an opportunity to interact directly with the medium. Points of Interest (PoIs) can be used informationally, to draw attention to key objects in the video, as in Figure 13-9.

Figure 13-9. Points of Interest can be used informationally to highlight key interest areas in the video

PoIs can also be used in the context of a "hidden object game," in which the user is presented with only the video and asked to identify a class of item or mistake. Nothing is visible on the video other than the prompt, and the user must click in various places, searching for items or locations that match their target. This is great training because the learner is forced to look closely at their surroundings, consider them, and interact with them in a context similar to reality. This technique was used frequently in "Factory Floor Training," in which the user is asked to identify trip hazards and other dangers in their environment. Pictured in Figure 13-10 is a scenario in which the user has found five PoIs and has about a minute left to identify the remaining 16.

Figure 13-10. A "scene hunt" is an exercise involving finding mistakes or other hidden items in the environment

Choose your own adventure

Finally, there is a way to "cheat" and interact more directly with videos. The 1983 laserdisc arcade game *Dragon's Lair* was one of the earliest examples. In this game, the player inputs simple commands in response to an animated cartoon. If they input the correct directional input at the correct time, the video continues. If they fail, the character is shown dying. Although video can't interact directly with the user the way an interactive computer graphics experience can, it's possible to film multiple videos portraying different results, which can show the trainee consequences of wrong actions they could take. In STRIVR's "Wire Down Training" experience, for example, if the learner fails to inform a caller about the danger a downed wire can hold for pets, the learner will hear the caller's dog being electrocuted.

To avoid a combinatorial explosion, it's best to follow a "string of pearls" approach to designing branching content; only allow learners a limited amount of deviation from the scenario you're teaching before guiding them back to the right path.

Use Case: Factory Floor Training

Factory floors are huge, loud, chaotic, and full of hidden dangers. In one study, safety errors in 10 factories cost a major food manufacturer five digits in the month of April 2015. Five digits. Not money, fingers.

A common thread for factory training is *mistake identification*. Given a spherical video of a factory floor, can employees identify safety violations around them?

The factory floor provides clear examples of the benefits of spherical video over 2D video. It's easy to look at a PowerPoint slide with a picture of a loading vehicle on it, and understand that the loading vehicle is dangerous. But the loading vehicle that hits you isn't the one you see coming. The vehicle that hits you is the one you *didn't* see, the one that came from behind. Spherical video, like reality, comes at you from all angles.

To satisfy the client's needs, STRIVR built a feature called *scene hunt*, in which trainees must identify hidden points of interest in the video. All around the scene are hidden "hitboxes," which the trainee has a limited time to find, as shown in Figure 13-11.

Figure 13-11. In a "scene hunt," the learner must find mistakes within a time limit and select an area containing a mistake, for the mistake to be revealed

If the user doesn't find all the hotspots in time, they are notified of what they missed, as demonstrated in Figure 13-12.

Figure 13-12. After the time expires, mistakes the learner didn't find are revealed and must be interacted with

One of the great things about this kind of training is the ease in capturing footage and building the training. Factories usually have records of past accidents, knowledgeable veteran employees, and manuals that categorize potential errors. STRIVR found that it was easy to either identify real mistakes on the factory floor or to safely generate them with the help of instructors.

The Role of Narrative

You're going to have a tough time getting learners to train if the training experience is boring. One of STRIVR's major reasons for being is that the current state of the art for training…well, sucks. And a big reason for this is that it's boring. *Gamification* has been a buzz word in the industry for years, but the focus has been on points, daily bonuses, and dopamine rushes. Why do people play games? Because they're entertaining. They're fun, they're slick, they're polished, and, usually, they give you a reason to care.

When you're playing a game, you're not just learning to fly a space fighter for kicks. You're learning to fly a space fighter so you can defeat the evil emperor who killed your father. Especially for an adult learner, giving their learning a goal and a context goes a long way toward making it more immersive and engaging.[8] Giving a task a goal adds an extra dimension to it and unlocks a little extra from the learner's brain.

If you want to build VR training experiences that trainees will actually complete, you need to have narrative. You need *task-oriented learning*.

It can be difficult to embody the user in spherical video. The camera doesn't have a physical presence, which can make the user feel like a ghost. Rather than letting the user focus on their lack of a body, you should film your video with characters who speak with the user, engage with them, and guide them. Humans are social animals, and our brains are keyed up for analyzing faces and reading social cues. Training the user by having them interact with a human instructor is a huge upgrade over using a disembodied voice. One-on-one expert mentorship is the ideal training scenario, and filming an instructor is the closest we can get to that in the context of spherical video.

This means that filming spherical video for training is a lot more like filming a movie than you might think. You need to have an interesting and engaging script, with characters and a story arc. If you want to make the best VR training you can, it also means that you need to hire actors.

Use Case: Store Robbery Training

A store robbery is a great example of a scenario that is nearly impossible to train on normally. Without any way to predict a robbery, the nearest training scenario would be a deeply involved workshop or roleplay.

In "Store Robbery Training," STRIVR built a narrative-driven experience to test trainees on what they had learned about appropriate responses to a store robbery. Rather than build this VR training to teach all of the necessary skills, Store Robbery Training was built as an introduction and exit exam to supplement a class or online training.[8] As a result, STRIVR's instructional designers were able to focus more narrowly on things that work well in VR.

Store Robbery Training puts the learner in the position of a store manager opening up for a day of work with their coworker. While the learner is paying attention to the door, the robbers come up from behind, startling the learner's coworker and forcing the learner to physically turn around to see what's happening. The learner is then forced to cope with the situation and interact by answering multiple-choice questions, the theme of which is cooperating with and not antagonizing the robbers. The store has insurance and contingencies, and the role of the store manager is to prevent any harm in coming to their employees or anyone in the store. In this experience, if the learner chooses the wrong answer, a voice prompt will advise them on what the correct course of action is and why. Although STRIVR had used multiple-choice questions in many previous experiences, this was one of the first times they were utilized in such an immersive fashion. When the robber questions you, time slows down, the screen blurs and turns black and white, and a heartbeat sound gives a feeling of intensity. Figure 13-13 shows the stopped-time effect, which anchors the multiple-choice question in an immersive context.

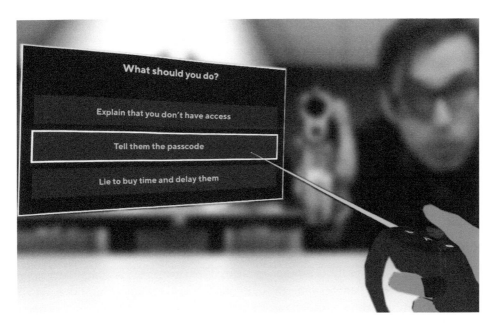

Figure 13-13. When the robber questions you, time slows down, the surroundings blur, and a heartbeat sound adds a feeling of intensity

Store Robbery Training is a good example of a training experience that would not be possible without actors and a script. A robbery is a frightening and emotional experience; if the human characters don't convey those emotions, the learner won't be appropriately primed to react, and the experience will be comedic rather than scary.

The value of this training is its ability to prepare the learner mentally. The training forces the learner to visualize how to react and what to do. If the situation occurs in reality, the learner can fall back on a model of behavior that they've already rehearsed virtually.

While building this training, STRIVR's designers noticed how strongly the learner's gaze is drawn to human characters, and they began to utilize embodied human instructors for future trainings, rather than disembodied voices. Having actors interacting with the learner offered many advantages. The learners were more engaged, but also more embodied themselves. For a situation in which a participant in VR doesn't have a visible body, having a human whose height you can relate to helps you feel more present in the scene. Another benefit was in gaze direction. Rather than put arrows or signs around the scene, it feels very natural for human characters to walk or point to direct the learner's gaze.

One last thing to mention: when building an experience that has the potential to be traumatic or triggering, it's crucial to let the learner know that they can abort at any time. For this training, we made sure that the learners were aware that they could pause, press the Oculus Home button, or physically remove the headset at any time if they felt uncomfortable.

The Future of XR Training: Beyond Spherical Video

In this chapter, the focus has been on VR, and especially spherical video, as a training medium. Spherical video hits a sweet spot because it's easy to capture and provides a realistic result. However, we've also discussed that spherical video can be limited in its interactivity and fidelity.

What about other technologies? Where will XR training go in the future? In the rest of this chapter, we look at improvements and alternatives to spherical video.

Computer Graphics

The other major option for portraying a training environment is computer graphics (CG). CG gives great benefits in terms of interactivity. 3D models can move dynamically within an environment without needing to be filmed in an infinite variety of positions.

However, 3D graphics need to be modeled, animated, and lit. Building 3D assets and an interactive scenario is time consuming. It took Rockstar Studios more than three years to develop *Red Dead Redemption 2*; these kinds of timelines are typical for game companies. Because of these considerations, when building a CG training experience, it's critical that the training be essential and evergreen.

Use Case: Soft Skills Training

This use case highlights a VR training framework that was built with CG. Soft Skills uses virtual humans to simulate difficult conversations, such as giving an employee a negative performance review. The trainee first chooses an avatar to represent themselves. They're introduced to the scenario and then prompted with what to say. Figure 13-14 shows an example of a prompt. The virtual human reacts, and the conversation moves on. Despite the prescribed nature of the experience, most users believe that the virtual human is reacting to and adapting to what they've said.

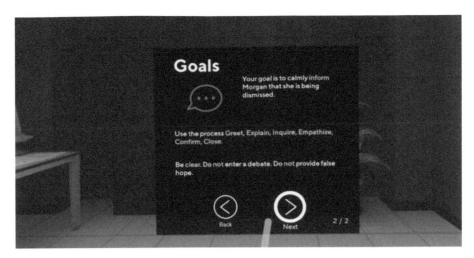

Figure 13-14. The learner is guided through the broad strokes of what they should convey at each step (© STRIVR 2018)

The real impact of Soft Skills training happens after the conversation. The whole time you are following the prompts and speaking to the virtual employee, your voice and movements are being recorded. At the end of the experience, everything is played back with the roles reversed. In Figure 13-15, the learner is about to swap places with Morgan, the troubled employee. Sitting across from yourself and watching your words come out of another person's mouth is a powerful experience. When I went through this training the first time, I said many things that I later realized came off as rude. For instance, early in the conversation, I said that the meeting was "no big deal." Hearing it back on the other side of the table, I had a visceral reaction to how insincere that sounded.

Figure 13-15. After the conversation, the learner watches a playback of their own words from the perspective of their conversation partner (© STRIVR 2018)

Soft Skills is a good example of reusable application that can benefit from an investment in CG.

Soft Skills training is a reusable framework for an essential skill: communication. The majority of corporate jobs require communication skills, from assisting customers over the phone to managing teams of diverse employees. Because the same CG framework can be used for many different kinds of communications trainings, the investment of effort in building the 3D environments and avatars can have a chance to pay off over time.

CG in this context has many benefits over spherical video. For instance, one voice can be used with many different customized avatars to control for the appearance of the virtual human. Animations can be reused across avatars. The environment and avatar can be mixed and matched. Branching scenarios are easier to build with CG, as well, because the virtual humans can react dynamically to the user like video game characters can.

The Future: Photogrammetry

Photogrammetry is an attractive technology for capturing real-life environments, objects, or people and making them into 3D models. Thousands of photographs are taken of a subject from every angle, and then these images are combined into 3D models.

However, it's difficult to build perfect 3D models from photogrammetry techniques alone. A lot of cleanup work has to be done to plug tiny gaps in the models and to fix other blemishes.[9] At STRIVR, we used this technique to build a virtual grocery store wet wall, and our 3D artist Tyrone had to spend more time than we anticipated cleaning up both the captured environment and interactable elements. Figure 13-16 shows a particularly troublesome piece of broccoli.

Figure 13-16. Using photogrammetry to create models of real-life objects is still labor intensive (© STRIVR 2018)

Photogrammetry is a technology to consider, but keep in mind the challenges. This is a technology to keep an eye on as techniques improve.

The Future: Light Fields

Light fields are an exciting new technology that use a rotating ring of cameras to capture all the light entering a spherical area. This results in a captured area in which the viewer has full parallax. Whereas with mono spherical video, a viewer is confined to a single perspective, light fields allow the user to translate their head to see different angles of a scene,[5] as demonstrated in Figure 13-17.

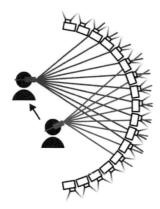

Figure 13-17. Light fields allow head translations to provide different perspectives

Full parallax greatly improves the viewer's sense of presence, a key to creating higher-quality training experiences. If you haven't had a chance to try it, do try Google's "Welcome To Light Fields" demonstration. The result is striking.

As of 2018, there are still too many limitations on this technology to widely adopt it. The recorded area is about two feet in diameter, which is still small enough that the user's head can easily exit the space. The rotation speed of the camera rig also means that only still images can be captured; appropriate for some training experiences focused on a static environment but less useful for anything involving actors or dynamic movement. However, light fields are a capture technology to watch.

The Future: AR Training

VR is a technology that, wherever you are, takes you someplace else and lets you experience it. AR is a technology that changes your perception of your existing world; it takes reality and then augments it.

VR is transportational; AR is transformational.

AR's natural place is on-the-job assistance, but there are a couple key technologies that are not quite mature enough. For AR to provide useful on-the-job assistance, it must be able to do something that a human brain couldn't, with enough accuracy to be safe and useful. We're getting close. We have software that can translate text and replace it on the fly, and image recognition that can swap faces. But 99% accurate isn't good enough for many use cases; we need to be 100% accurate. Hardware is also an issue. AR headsets need to be more comfortable and lightweight before people are interested in wearing them for eight hours each day.

Despite all that, there is potential for AR in dedicated location-based training. Take the flood house, and then imagine a training environment in which AR teaches you and trains you in a real environment. This would provide the benefit of exploring a real physical training space with the ability to give individualized feedback and assistance.

Similar technology is already in use. Museums and tourist destinations use audio tour devices that sense your location. Another great technology to look at is The VOID,[12] which uses a mix of wearable VR, location tracking, and physical space to create an immersive entertainment experience.

The Future: Voice Recognition

Voice interfaces will be a huge addition to the training toolkit when we can cross that final accuracy threshold. A significant aspect of the training we do is interpersonal: training on customer service or interpersonal conflict resolution. Voice recognition could provide the perfect medium and control scheme as soon as it becomes integrated into an HMD's toolkit, but first it needs to become reliable enough to work under all conditions, including a noisy retail backroom.

The Future: The Ideal Training Scenario

Imagine for a moment the future. A world with no limits, with AR contact lenses and strong AI. What would training look like?

Mary Poppins. Don't laugh!

Mary Poppins comes out of the sky on a magic umbrella and transforms a mob of horrible children into model citizens. The children don't even realize that they're being trained, because the training is fun. Mary Poppins strikes a perfect balance between guiding, challenging, and nurturing her charges.

This is what it would take to have the perfect training experience. Strong AI that can understand who the learner is and train them based on their needs.

This kind of scenario is far out. In 2018, AR contact lenses and strong AI don't exist. But considering an ideal world and thinking about where training could go in the future can be a great tool for figuring out how to get there, especially when considering what technologies to invest in and how to prepare.

References

1. Bailenson, Jeremy N., K. Patel, A. Nielsen, R. Bajcsy, S. Jung, and G. Kurillo. "The Effect of Interactivity on Learning Physical Actions in Virtual Reality." *Media Psychology*, 2008. 11: 354–376. *https://stanford.io/2C9Hdw5.*

2. Belch, Derek, interview, 2018.

3. Bowie, Fraser G. "Experiencing Danger Safely is My Virtual Reality–Experience Matters." Experience Matters, 2018. *http://bit.ly/2XFrKwY.*

4. Cordar, Andrew, Michael Borish, Adriana Foster, and Benjamin Lok. "Building Virtual Humans with Back Stories: Training Interpersonal Communication Skills in Medical Students." *Intelligent Virtual Agents (IVA)* 8637 (2014): 144–153. *http://bit.ly/2HdB4SU.*

5. Debevec, Paul. "Experimenting With Light Fields." Google, 2018. *http://bit.ly/2VDENNK.*

6. Knowles, Malcolm S., Elwood F. Holton III, and Richard A. Swanson. *The Adult Learner.* 5th ed. Houston, TX: Gulf Publishing Company, 1998.

7. Kraemer, Shannon, Sharon Hoosein, and Tyrone Schieszler, interview, 2018.

8. Mir, Haider, interview, 2018.

9. Schieszler, Tyrone, and Masaki Miyanohara, interview, 2018.

10. "Size of the Training Industry." Training Industry, 2017. *http://bit.ly/2TwPqV0.*

11. Spinner, Amanda, Joe Willage, and Michael Casale. STRIVR internal presentation, 2018.

12. "Step Beyond Reality." The VOID. *https://www.thevoid.com/.*

13. Wijman, Tom. "Mobile Revenues Account for More Than 50% of the Global Games Market as It Reaches $137.9 Billion in 2018." Newzoo, 2018. *http://bit.ly/2C3e9X6.*

Afterword

Tony Parisi

Building the Mirrorworld

VR. AR. MR. XR. AI. CV. ML. AR cloud… the list goes on.

This isn't just a grab-bag of trendy tech buzzwords; it comprises the foundation of a spatial computing future that is right around the corner.

We are moving to a new paradigm for accessing information, consuming entertainment, learning, doing our jobs, and communicating with each other. It's a shift from 2D graphical representations viewed on flat screens—pinhole cameras into today's incomprehensibly vast digital world—to immersive 3D visualizations of objects and spaces laid out all around us. This will not only imbue us with brand-new superpowers that allow us to transcend space and time; it will, generally, make these computer thingies that are inextricably enmeshed in our daily lives so much easier to use. We live in a 3D world: people move, think, and experience in three dimensions. Isn't it time our computer interfaces got out of the way and let us do the same with digital information? It's about the digital, made physical.

Perhaps more significantly, this step change is also about making the physical digital. Every mobile phone is already a camera; add another camera or two, and with a little help from computer vision algorithms powered by machine learning data, we have digital x-ray vision capable of recognizing images and objects and laying bare their contents for all to see. Every real-world object becomes its own display surface that can be enhanced with animated fun or useful knowledge about its capabilities, price, provenance or other interesting information.

This technology is on the market today, in the crude form of VR and MR headsets and AR-capable smartphones. Someday soon, these amazing new capabilities will be presented via sleek wearable devices like smart glasses that will have us looking at the world with our heads up again, and free up the hand that holds the phone. Further down the line, wearables will be supplanted by contact lenses, retinal projection, direct neural interfaces and/or holographic projection, so that we won't even have to put a device on our heads at all. Someday.

Think Princess Leia on the tabletop, or the Holodeck. Or the holographic display for Jarvis, Tony Stark's virtual assistant. Or, pick your favorite envisioning from the science fiction canon. However we imagine it, it will probably not look quite like that. But I can say with conviction that spatial computing will be the interface to everything, from a future version of Wikipedia to the entertainment center in the cabin of your self-driving car. Kevin Kelly recently revived the term *mirrorworld*, as apt a term as any to describe this blend of the physical and the virtual. It starts with an overlay of digital information on physical stuff, then moves to a full "digital twin" of the physical world around us that contains everything, reflects it, and enhances it—a 3D skin on the Internet of Things.

The infrastructure powering this transformation is rooted in real-time 3D graphics, computer vision and machine learning, and low-latency networking. The computer industry is taking its first steps toward building a global system comprised of devices, software, and communication protocols to support this dream, but again, everything today is in crude form. There's no ubiquitous device, or even one or two go-to products. And mirrorworld today consists of silos: purpose-built applications to solve a business problem; online stores for delivering entertainment content; walled-garden social communities with face-filter and animoji-based customization. Content creation is an arduous, coding-centric exercise of integrating myriad tools and SDKs, and managing fragmentation between devices and operating systems. The mirrorworld of tomorrow will be more integrated and fluid, a new spatial world-wide web, hyperlinked and with instant access to 3D information. Content creation will be just that: make some 3D stuff, tag it, drop it onto the digital twin of the physical world and, permissions depending, anyone can access it, annotate it, and share it using any spatial computing device.

To paraphrase William Gibson: the mirrorworld is already here, but it's not evenly distributed. The good news is, we can start designing and building for it with today's systems in anticipation of tomorrow's reality. The broad collection of techniques and technologies you read about in this book are here to stay, though over time, the alphabet soup of acronyms will likely be absorbed into a set of core system capabilities that we all take for granted, much the way we do today with developing for web or mobile. At that point, the vexing VR/AR/MR distinction will be a thing of the past, and we'll all have a common, colloquial term for it. (Who knows? Maybe we'll be calling it mirrorworld.)

Till then, this book was a great place to start. Hopefully it can serve as a guidebook for years to come as you embark on your journey. See you in the mirrorworld.

Index

Allegorithmic Substance Painter, 70

AlphaGo, 245

ambient audio, 179

amblyopia treatment, 267

anatomical structures in XR, 212-213

anatomy teaching at CRWU using Hololens, 271

anchors, 93

Android, 76, 82, 86, 110-111

animation, 35
    clips representing a gait, 233
    generation using machine learning, 247
    in data and machine learning visualizations, 202-204
    making simpler with spatial computing tools, 34
    using virtual reality for, 55-57
    Weird Type app, 41

Apple
    AR cloud data and, 127
    AR platform, efforts to solve relocalization problem, 101
    ARKit, xx, 107
        (see also ARKit)
    debut of ARKit at WWDC, 121
    Human Interface Guidelines, 204
    iPhone, release of, 13
    The Machines game, using multiplayer system, 115

AR cloud, 76, 119-128
    challenges faced by features, 123
    cloud-hosted shared SLAM maps, 101
    dawn of, 123
    description of, 121
    difference from mobile cloud of today, 122
    envisioning, nice-to-have and must-have features, 119
    importance of, 120
    privacy and AR cloud data, 125-127
    usefulness of ARKit and ARCloud without, 122

Archform applications for orthodontists, 265

ARCore
    AR before, 123
    as Tango-Lite, 110
    building with, 111
    lighting, 113
    limitations of, 121
    maps, 92

    usefulness without AR cloud, 122

ARKit, 76, 107-109
    AR before, 123
    comparison to other AR platforms, 112
    lighting, 113
    limitations of, 121
    maps, 92
    mysteries explained, 109
    plane detection, 109
    SLAM and, 76
    usefulness without AR cloud, 122
    visual inertial odometry (VIO), 79

art, 59
    (see also optimization of 3D art)
    making 3D digital art using virtual reality, 47-55

artificial intelligence (AI), 223
    (see also character AI and behaviors)
    artificially intelligent machines, 32
    deliberative AI, 233-240
    future design, women's role in, 36
    reactive AI, 229-233
    sensory data from sensory machines powered by, 31
    spatial computing powered by, designing for the future, 35
    strong AI in future enterprise training, 319

ARVR Academy, xx

audio, 178-183
    in AR, 182
    in VR, 179-182

audio modalities (HCI), 14
    best uses in HMD-specific interactions, 17
    cons, 17
    current state of, for spatial computing devices, 20
    example use case, surgery room, 17
    in cycle of typical HCI loop for console video game with controller, 18
    pros, 17

Audio Source settings (Unity), 181

Augmedix, documentation automation platform, 258

Augmentation Research Center (ARC), 9

augmented reality (AR), xvii, 223
    6DOF AR platforms, 142
    Adobe AR Residency program, 41
    Adobe's AR story, 42
    before ARKit and ARCore, 123

brain visualizations, 212
Bravemind application for PTSD treatment, 268
browsers
    support for WebXR specification, 198
    supporting ARCore, 110
    VR headset within, 208
button/touch inputs, 148

C

C#, xx, 196
    porting data visualizations to Microsoft
        Hololens, 217
C++, xx, 196
    VR application development in, 138
CameraRig (Unity), setting up in VRTK, 165
cameras
    creating 3D model of a camera, 60
    depth cameras aiding VIO systems, 87
    photometric calibration, 84
    pinhole model, use in geometric calibration,
        83
    relocation, state of research in, 99
    stereo cameras on phones or HMDs, 87
    tight integration with IMU, 82
    use to locate position relative to field of play,
        278
    virtual, 139
capsule collider, 171
Cardboard (see Google)
Case Western Reserve University, VR/AR appli-
    cations, 270
    taking MRI image mappings using AR, 272
cathode-ray tubes (CRTs), 7
CG (computer graphics), use in training, 314
    soft skills training, 314-316
CGI (computer generated images), 278
CGTrader, 73
character AI and behaviors, 223-251
    behaviors, 226-229
    deliberative AI, 233-240
    introduction to, 223-226
    machine learning, 241-247
    reactive AI, 229-233
        adaptability, 231
        complexity and universality, 231
        feasibility, 232
cities, smart (see smart cities)
Clancy, Timothy, 213
climbing, 169

cloud, 119
    (see also AR cloud)
code examples from this book, xxiv
cold start, 102
colliders, Unity built-in capsule collider, 171
colors, PBR textures defining colors repre-
    sented on a model, 69
combinatorial explosion, 229
    example in reactive AI, 232
companies using VR and AR in healthcare,
    264-269
    experiences designed for medical education,
        265
    experiences designed for use by patients,
        267
    for proactive health, 269
    planning and guidance applications, 264
complexity
    in reactive AI, 231
    run-time complexity in deliberative AI, 238
compression and signal speed to create AR/VR,
    285
computer graphics, using in training, 314
    soft skills training, 314-316
computer vision, 31, 224
    combined with hand gestures and biometric
        data, 39
    in augmented reality, how it works, 75-129
        future of AR computer vision, 88
computers
    human interactions with (see human-
        computer interactions)
    miniaturization of, 12-14
connection speeds, 285
consumers, giving control in sports XR, 289
content creation, 322
    evolution in sports XR, 286
    in AR and VR, 277
content for VR training, 301
context, effective data visualizations in XR, 200
control input scheme, 149
controllability
    in deliberative AI, 238
    in reactive AI, 231
    trade-off between autonomy and controlla-
        bility in game AI, 233
controllers
    2D and 3D controls, using in VRTK, 160

for spatial computing, 14-19
    audio modalities, 17
    cycle of typical HCI modality loop, 18
    physical modalities, 16
    types of common HCI modalities, 14
    visual modalities, 14
history of
    computer miniaturization, 12, 14
    modalities through World War II, 7
    post-World War II modalities, 8-10
    pre-twentieth century modalities, 4-6
    reasons for covering, 14
    rise of personal computing, 10-12
how hand tracking and hand pose recognition change HCI, 23
    voice, hands, and hardware inputs over next generation, 24-27
new modalities, 20
spatial computing and new HCI design paradigms, 202
terminology, 3

I

image data viewable by humans, protecting, 125
imitation learning, 244
immersive computing systems, current controllers for, 21-23
immersive content, developing, 135
"Immersive Data Visualization: AR in the Workplace", 211
IMU (inertial measurement unit), 82
    calibration and modeling, 85
    defined, 128
    different IMUs for different devices, 86
    in ARKit, 107
    really good IMU error removal in ARKit, 109
    requirement for tightly integrated hardware and software, 82
infographics, 205
    interactive big data visualization vs., 194
Input Scene (VRTK), 163
inputs, 3
    asymmetric freeform computer input, 9
    controlling software with senses in 3D, 40
    gestures for AR, 257
    in typical HCI modality loop, 18
        video game example, 19
    rules of computer input, 8

types used post-World War II, 8
Insight project, 258
    Parkinson's disease experiment, 259-264
integrated development environments (IDEs), 138, 196
intelligent exploration, 234
interaction features, examples in VRTKv4, 162
    Interactable Objects, 163
interactions
    common paradigms, 183-188
        inventory for VR, 184-187
    in categories of data visualization in 2D and 3D, 205
    in sports XR, 286
    with spherical video, 305-309
Internet of Things (IoT), 322
inventory system for VR, 184-187
inverse reinforcement learning, 245
iPhone, 107, 111, 142
    as turning point for small computer industry, 13
    reaction to ARKit at launch, 121
    running ARKit, 167

J

Jacquard, Joseph, 4
JavaScript, 196
    frameworks for data visualizations for the web, 208
jitter/judder, 103
joysticks, 8
    rollerball as alternative to, 8
    XR HMD packaged cotrollers tracing back to, 21
JSON (JavaScript Object Notation), 208

K

Kalman filter, 129
    in ARKit, 107, 108
keyboards, 5
    for miniaturized computers, 12
keyframes, 92
    use in building SLAM maps, 98
Korsakov, Semyon, 4

L

latency, 285
Laws of Simplicity (Maeda), 205

About the Authors

Lead Coeditor

Erin Pangilinan is a Diversity Fellow at USF Data Institute's Deep Learning Program. She is also a proud Silicon Valley native, UC Berkeley alumnus, computational designer, software engineer hybrid, and startup consultant. As lead coeditor and contributor to this anthology, she initially conceptualized this project and contributed a chapter on data and machine learning visualization design and development. In 2017, she was selected as a Diversity Fellow at the University of San Francisco (USF) Data Institute Deep Learning Program. In 2018, she was selected as a fellow in Oculus Launch Pad. Since 2015, she cofounded and scaled two diversity and inclusion nonprofit organizations focused on education and professional development, ARVR Academy serving women and underrepresented communities, and Filipino Americans in STEAM (Science Technology Engineering Arts in Math) FASTER. In her prior career in civic engagement, she last worked as official campaign staff to former Deputy US Secretary of Commerce, Congressman Ro Khanna, and founder of Tech For Obama, Steve Spinner. Find her on Twitter at @erinjerri and online at erinjerri.com.

Coeditors

Steve Lukas is the CEO of Across Realities and an account manager in developer relations at Magic Leap. He has served in various capacities throughout the XR industry, from product management and venture capital at Qualcomm Ventures to forming his own AR/VR company, Across Realities. He is on Twitter as @slukas.

Vasanth Mohan is the founder of FusedVR. Vasanth (AKA Fuseman) started the FusedVR YouTube channel in April 2016 in an effort to increase the number of people excited about creating VR content, specifically with the HTC Vive and Unity. Since then, he has worked at Udacity to develop the VR and ARKit Nanodegree as well as worked with the SVVR community to teach development workshops in and around the Bay Area.

Contributors

Harvey Ball is the creator of VRTK. He has been a developer for almost 20 years, mostly building enterprise systems in the web space (and non-web applications). He started developing for VR in 2016 as a hobby, and started working on VRTK soon after because he believes the platform can benefit from getting as many people developing for VR as possible.

Jazmin Cano is the User Engagement Manager at High Fidelity. She has been developing 3D content for virtual reality since 2013 with a focus on designing experiences to onboard users who are new to social VR. At High Fidelity, she leads the team responsible for exploring safety and comfort in social spaces for VR, as well as helping design environments, events, and policies for multi-user experiences. In her free time, Jazmin creates 3D environment art for VR by modeling and texture painting and enjoys gaming. If she's not in front of a computer, she's probably exploring the wilderness for inspiration. Find her on Twitter at @JC_3D.

Tipatat Chennavasin is a general partner of the Venture Reality Fund investing in early stage VR and AR companies. He has experience creating VR/AR content and became convinced of the power of VR when he accidentally cured himself of his real-life fear of heights while developing in VR. He has established himself as a VR/AR industry spokesperson and thought leader, and has contributed to many publications and presented at various industry events worldwide. He has looked at over 4,500 companies in the space and has invested in 30. He is also a prolific VR artist and Google artist-in-residence.

Clorama Dorvilias is a developer advocate of VRTK. Clorama discovered VR in 2015 researching methods for counteracting harmful social biases for her MA Thesis at University of the Arts London. She has since created VR experiences spanning across various clinics and institutions, including University College of London and Hyphen-Labs, LLC, that utilize proven research methods to increase empathy and combat social biases. Her work expands institutions in healthcare, education, public sector, and the workplace. She credits VRTK for her success to be able to submit a concept prototype at Oculus Launch Pad in a short time, winning seed funding to launch the Teacher's Lens app on the Oculus store and starting her company Debias VR. Debias VR works with Fortune 500 companies to create implicit bias testing and trainings, utilizing the unique capabilities of VR to track progress and measure behavioral data.

Arthur Juliani is a senior software and machine learning engineer at Unity Technologies, as well as a lead developer of Unity ML-Agents. A researcher at the intersection of Cognitive Neuroscience and Deep Learning, Arthur is also currently working toward a PhD at the University of Oregon in Psychology. He is on Twitter as @awjuliani.

Nicolas Meuleau is the Director of AI Research at Unity Technologies. Nicolas is a researcher in AI with expertise in decision making, automated planning, and machine learning. During his 25-year career, he developed and deployed autonomous decision systems in a variety of application domains, including space, aeronautics, automotive, and finance. He joined Unity in 2016 as Director of AI Research to promote the development of AI tools in the Unity game engine. There he supervises several research projects around game AI and intelligent decision making in games.

Matt Miesnieks is the CEO and Cofounder of 6D.ai, the leading AR cloud platform and his third AR startup. Matt is renowned as one of the AR industry's thought leaders through his influential blog posts. He cofounded SuperVentures (investing in AR), built AR prototypes at Samsung, and had a long executive and technical career in mobile software infrastructure before jumping into AR back in 2009. He is on twitter as @mattmiesnieks.

Silka Miesnieks is Head of Emerging Design at Adobe. Silka is behind many spatial design and AI-related features found in Adobe products and services today. Silka identifies the untapped potential of design tools and services and reimagining the tools of the future with teams throughout Adobe. She comes from a land down-under, with her husband, two sons, and a bottle of whiskey to lower her blood pressure. Previously she cofounded Dekko with a goal of humanizing technology using AR. Always one with an entrepreneurial spirit, Silka also mentors startups and women in tech. Find her on Twitter at @silkamiesnieks and online at Silka.co.

Rosstin Murphy is an Iranian-American VR engineer at STRIVR. His greatest pleasure in life is to put joy on the faces of the people who use his software. Rosstin started creating XR experiences in IBM R&D, where he spearheaded the development of Immersive Insights. He currently works at STRIVR as a VR Engineer, contributing to the development of STRIVR Creator and STRIVR Player. You can find him on Twitter as @RosstinMurphy.

Victor Prisacariu is cofounder and Chief Scientific Officer of 6D.ai, a San Francisco startup making semantic 3D maps of the world on commodity mobile hardware. He received a graduate computer engineering degree from Gheorghe Asachi Technical University, Iasi, Romania, in 2008, and a DPhil degree in Engineering Science from the Department of Engineering Science, University of Oxford, UK, in 2012. He continued there, first as an EPSRC prize postdoctoral researcher, and then as a Dyson Senior Research Fellow before being appointed an Associate Professor in 2017. His research interests include semantic visual tracking, 3D reconstruction, and SLAM.

Marc Rowley CEO and cofounder of Live CGI and a five-time Emmy winner. While at ESPN, he invented the Pylon Camera and SportsCenter Rundown and was awarded multiple patents for Augmented Reality. At Live CGI, Marc has invented the first one to all live CGI broadcast system. Marc is an avid gamer and reader.

Dilan Shah grew up in Laguna Niguel, CA, and is cofounder and Chief Product Officer of YUR Inc., a Boost VC company where he works on mobile. He is a long-time developer and helped build Unity's new industrial XR applications training resources featuring projects across ARCore and ARKit, Hololens, Oculus Go, Oculus Rift, and HTC Vive. Dilan is an early adopter of spatial computing (VR and AR), evangelist, and product professional. He is an autodidact and earned degrees in Business Administration and Computer Science from USC. His blog is thelatentelement.com and he is on Twitter as @dilan_shah.

Timoni West is the Director of XR Research at Unity, where she leads a team of cross-disciplinary artists and engineers exploring new interfaces for human–computer interaction. Currently, her team focuses on spatial computing: how we will live, work, and create in a world where digital objects and the real world live side by side. Timoni serves on the OVA board and is an advisor to Tvori and Spatial Studios, among others. In 2017, Timoni was listed in Next Reality News' Top 50 to Watch. Additionally, she serves on XRDC's advisory board, is a Sequoia Scout, and was a jury member for ADC's 2018 Awards in Experiential Design.

Colophon

The animal on the cover of *Creating Augmented and Virtual Realities* is a cape pangolin (*Manis temminckii* or *Smutsia temminckii*). This species of pangolin has two recognized binomial names and several more among laypeople, such as ground pangolin, South African pangolin, Temminck's ground pangolin, and even "scaly anteater." The cape pangolin is native to southern and eastern Africa and gets the name "temminck" from a Dutch zoologist who directed the National Museum of Natural History of the Netherlands in the nineteenth century, Coenraad Jacob Temminck.

Africa has four of the eight species of pangolin. The cape pangolin lives on land, while other African pangolins are arboreal. Cape pangolins populate forests, brush, grasslands, and savannah, deterred neither by high nor low rainfall, but even this expansive habitat is facing dramatic reduction and threatening the species.

Cape pangolins have brown, olive, or sometimes purplish scales made of keratin. Their scales protect them from predators and have sharp back edges. When in danger, these creatures roll up into a tight ball, exposing the sharp ends of their scales. Five long claws on each paw and a gripping, or prehensile, tail help cape pangolins defend themselves. They will also hide in the burrows of aardvarks and aardwolves.

An adult cape pangolin can weigh anywhere from 15 to 39 pounds with a length of 32 to 55 inches from head to tail. The lifespan of a cape pangolin tops out around 10 years. Several states protect pangolins from hunting, but the World Wildlife Foundation designates all eight species as Vulnerable to Critically Endangered.

With their long, sticky, narrow tongues that stretch nearly 10 inches, cape pangolins slurp up insects like ants and termites. They don't need any teeth to keep their diet balanced, and they don't have any.

Many of the animals on O'Reilly covers are endangered; all of them are important to the world. To learn more about how you can help, go to *animals.oreilly.com*.

The cover illustration is by Karen Montgomery, based on a black and white engraving from *Myers Kleines Lexicon*. The cover fonts are Gilroy Semibold and Guardian Sans. The text font is Adobe Minion Pro; the heading font is Adobe Myriad Condensed; and the code font is Dalton Maag's Ubuntu Mono.